ANNIE MILLER spent... of Economics at Heriot-Watt University in ... business economics, econometrics, mathema... mists. In 1991, with her colleague Douglas ... comparing different schools of economic thought in the late 20th century (Mair *et al*, 1991).

In 1984, Annie was a co-founder of the Basic Income Research Group (BIRG), which changed its name in 1993 to the Citizen's Income Trust (CIT). She has been a trustee since 1989 and is currently its Chair. She contributes regularly to its *Citizen's Income Newsletter*. She gives talks to groups around the UK, and has presented papers on BI at conferences here in the UK on the continent and in North America.

In January 2014, her local MSP, Jim Eadie, hosted a seminar and round-table discussion on 'Beyond Welfare Reform to a Citizen's Income' at the Scottish Parliament, at which Annie and the late Professor Ailsa McKay were keynote speakers. In her personal capacity, she presented written evidence to the Scottish Parliament's Expert Working Group on Welfare (2013) and to the Smith Commission (2014). Since politics in Scotland is now different from elsewhere in the UK, her fellow trustees at CIT encouraged her to set up a sister organisation in Scotland, the Citizen's Basic Income Network Scotland.

Annie became a member of the Religious Society of Friends (Quakers) in 1978. Her faith, her belief in 'that of God in everyone', and her commitment to the Quaker testimonies (values) of peace, equality, integrity and simplicity inspire all her work.

In this vital contribution to the debate about how we ground our welfare system more squarely on social justice, Annie Miller has done Scotland and the UK a service. It combines personal reflections with passion and technical adeptness, making the case for a Universal Basic Income powerfully in the process. Amongst many other achievements, this work presents the under-articulated feminist case for change – a vital component of the debate that should be more central. To be highly recommended.

ANTHONY PAINTER, Director of the Action and Research Centre, Royal Society for the Encouragement of Arts, Manufactures and Commerce

A Basic Income Handbook

ANNIE MILLER

Luath Press Limited
EDINBURGH
www.luath.co.uk

First published 2017

All royalties to be shared between
Citizen's Basic Income Network Scotland, SCIO no. SC046356, www.cbin.scot and
Citizen's Basic Income Trust, charity no 1171533, www.citizensincome.org

ISBN: 978-1-910745-78-6

The paper used in this book is recyclable. It is made from low chlorine pulps
produced in a low energy, low emissions manner from renewable forests.

Printed and bound by
Bell & Bain Ltd., Glasgow

Typeset in 11 point Sabon by
3btype.com

This book is dedicated to the memory
of the late
Professor Ailsa McKay
1963–2014

Contents

8

List of Figures

List of Tables

List of Abbreviations

AIDS	Acquired immune deficiency syndrome
AHC	After Housing Costs have been deducted
BHC	Before Housing Costs have been deducted
BI	Basic Income
BIEN	Basic Income European/Earth Network
BIRG	Basic Income Research Group
Blue Book	UK *National Accounts, the Blue Book*, published each year.
CB	Child Benefit
CBI	Citizen's Basic Income/Child Basic Income
CBINS	Citizen's Basic Income Network Scotland
CI	Citizen's Income
CIA	Central Intelligence Agency (USA)
CIT	Citizen's Income Trust/Citizen's Basic Income Trust
CTB/CTR	Council Tax Benefit/Reduction
CTC	Child Tax Credit
DWP	Department of Work and Pensions
EDR	Earnings Disregard
ESA	Employment and Support Allowance
EU	European Union
FBI	Full Basic Income
FES	Family economies of scale
GDP	Gross Domestic Product
HB	Housing Benefit
HBAI	Households Below Average Income
HES	Household economies of scale
HH	Household
HIV	Human immunodeficiency virus (infection)
HMRC	Her Majesty's Revenue and Customs
HMSO	Her Majesty's Stationary Office
HSHLD	Household
IS	Income Support
JSA	Jobseeker's Allowance
KELA	Social Insurance Institution of Finland
LA	Local Authority
LEL	Lower Earnings Level (NI system)
MDR	Marginal Deduction Rate
MIS	Minimum Income Standards

MISUR	Maternity, Invalidity, Sickness, Unemployment, Retirement (NI)
MP	Member of Parliament (Westminster)
MSP	Member of the Scottish Parliament.
MTB	Means-tested benefit
NGO	Non-Governmental Organisation
NHS	National Health Service
NI/NIC	National Insurance/National Insurance Contribution
NIT	Negative Income Tax
NMW/NLW	National Minimum Wage/National Living Wage
NPISH	Non-Profit Institutions Serving Households
OECD	The Organisation for Economic Co-operation and Development
ONS	Office of National Statistics
PAYE	Pay As You Earn
PBI	Partial Basic Income
PI	Participation Income
PT	Primary Threshold, (NI system)
PWC	Parent with care (primary care-giving parent)
S2P	State Second Pension
SCIO	Scottish Charitable Incorporated Organisation
SERPS	State Earnings-Related Pension Scheme
SNAP	Scottish National Accounts Project
STP	Single Tier Pension
TC	Tax Credit
UBI	Universal or Unconditional Basic Income
UC	Universal Credit
UEL	Upper Earnings Level (NI system)
WTC	Working Tax Credit
WWII	World War Two
Y-BAR	Mean gross income per head of man, woman and child

A note about terminology

A BASIC INCOME (BI) is a cash payment where assessment and delivery is based on the individual. It is universal for a defined population, is not means-tested, not selective except by age, and it is unconditional.

The concept has a fairly long history (see the Chronology in Appendix D), and during that time has had several different names, sometimes with extra conditions attached. In 1918, it was introduced as a 'State Bonus'. The Social Credit Movement of the inter-war period called it a 'National Dividend'. Milton Friedman, an American Nobel Prize-winning economist, introduced the concept as a 'Negative Income Tax' (NIT) in 1962. In its original incarnation, it was based on the household and had a 100 per cent withdrawal rate until the cash transfer had been paid off. Thus, originally a NIT was an income available only to poor people, rather than a BI paid to everyone, rich or poor. Its use in today's debates is as a version of BI with an alternative method of administration, based on a fully integrated benefit and income tax system. This is discussed further in chapter 8.

Another Nobel Prize-winning economist, James Meade, used the term 'Social Dividend' from 1935, but implied different things at different times – sometimes as a needs-based system and sometimes as a payment to everyone with no differentiation. 'Social Dividend' was the term commonly used until the early 1980s. Since the 1980s, the term used in the English-speaking world has been 'Basic Income', although in the USA it is often referred to as a 'Basic Income Guarantee' (BIG). Some people dislike the term 'Basic Income', because it sounds too basic, and yet that is really what it is about. The Basic Income Research Group agreed to change its name to the Citizen's Income Trust (CIT) in 1993. It is the only organisation that has consistently used the term 'Citizen's Income' (CI), and this is recognised in the UK. Professor Ailsa McKay always referred to a 'Citizen's Basic Income' (CBI), and the founding group of the new Scottish charity chose to use this term too, with its emphasis on citizenship. The terms CI, CBI and BI can be used interchangeably.

The term 'Unconditional Basic Income' (UBI) was adopted for the European Citizens' Initiative (ECI on UBI) in 2013. Since then the abbreviation, UBI, has frequently been used, but has often been interpreted as 'Universal Basic Income'. These terms are also interchangeable with 'Basic Income'.

My own preferred term is 'Basic Income'. It is shorter, to the point, and avoids the problem of the apostrophe. The presence and position of the apostrophe are crucial, since otherwise it changes the meaning. The apostrophe before the 's' in Citizen's Income emphasises that it must be paid on an individual basis.

Please note that neither a Participation Income, nor a Social Wage, nor a Minimum Income Guarantee (MIG) is a Basic Income. The first is similar to a Basic Income, but it is *conditional* on recipients participating in society (see chapter 7). The latter is a guaranteed minimum income that is *targeted* on people with insufficient income in order to raise them up to a given poverty threshold (Mestrum, 2017). A BI is paid unconditionally to everyone, rich and poor.

Preface

My story – or why it has taken me over 30 years to write this book

I THINK THAT I must have become a feminist at the age of about eight, when I realised that my mother did not have any money of her own, but had to ask my father for every penny – even to buy him a birthday present. He was kind and gentle, but inevitably he controlled the money. My next experience was in the mid 1960s, when, as a young, married, working woman, who believed that marriage was a way of proving how mature and responsible I was, I received my first tax return. This stated that if you were a married woman, you must pass the tax return to your husband for him to fill in on your behalf, (for which you would have to tell him any financial secrets that you may have had, and the reciprocal of which was not required). Of course, any tax rebates would be paid to him, and anyway, I was the one who carried out the financial administration for us both!

I assumed that, as a working married woman, in the period between jobs when I had no earnings, I would be eligible for Unemployment Benefit. However, I was rejected on the grounds that I had made myself unemployed by resigning from my school-teaching post at the end of the school year, which left a month before my next job started. I was told that it was up to my husband to keep me. I was incensed. I had not included the possibility of being a financial dependent into my vision of happy marriage. At that time a married woman could elect to have separate assessment for taxation on her earnings, but not on any other income. This remained the case until married couples became entitled to be taxed separately, starting in the fiscal year 1990–91. I did not think much of either the social security or income tax systems, especially for married women, and started thinking about alternatives. I remember talking about the concept of a 'social dividend' with a friend over breakfast one morning in 1970, who pointed me in the direction of Henry George's *Progress and Poverty* (George, 1879, 2006).

In the mid 1970s, my husband and I separated. People asked why I had got married in the first place, since I knew what I would be letting myself in for? But, obviously, I was ignorant. So I wanted to explore where it said in the Marriage Laws that women have to be treated as second-class citizens.

I bought a copy of the Marriage Act, which turned out to be a leaflet, merely stating who could marry whom, where and by whom. I noticed that it said 'Chapter 15' on the front, so I returned to HMSO and asked for the rest of it. The man laughed and explained that Chapter 15 referred to the fact that it was the 15th piece of legislation going through Parliament that year. So I asked how I could find out about how the Marriage Laws determined the role of women in marriage. He opened a very thick tome, which was an index of all the Acts of Parliament, and looked up 'Marriage'. There followed several pages, each comprising three columns in small print, listing Acts that Marriage affected or was affected by. It seemed that the only way in which people could learn in advance about to what they were committing themselves, was to do a three-year PhD on the subject.

When men and women commit matrimony, they rarely know what the contract says. Not only that, but the small print can change over time, too. The key lies in the fact that the Marriage contract is not a contract between the husband and wife, as many assume. It is between the couple and the State, in which the couple agree to aliment, or maintain, each other, relieving the State from the responsibility of having to support the poorer partner. At the same time, this deprives the poorer partner from any state benefits, unless the other partner agrees to a joint application. In this condition lies the bane of married women. This is the reason why I think that the UK Marriage Laws are unethical, and I would like to see them changed, or at least this aspect of them. When I met my new partner, I declined his invitation to marry him, and we checked that our son would not lose out on his inheritance rights under the current laws. In 1986, *The Scotsman* printed my article, 'The humiliation of an empty purse', about financial dependence in marriage.

I read as much as I could find about Social Dividend and in 1983 I wrote a departmental working paper entitled 'In Praise of Social Dividends', copies of which I sent to people whom I thought might be interested. Later that year, I attended a one-day conference on income maintenance organised by the National Council for Voluntary Organisations (NCVO) in London. During the discussions in the afternoon, I heard other people say, 'You would not have that problem with a Social Dividend'. We managed to identify each other and went off to the pub afterwards to get to know each other and agreed to keep in touch. They included Hermione (Mimi) Parker, Bill Jordan and Philip Vince. We met under the auspices of the NCVO for a few times over the next year and, out of that, the Basic Income Research Group (BIRG) was founded in 1984. I was surprised that, for a group who were in agreement over the concept, we argued fiercely about our individual ideas for Basic Income (BI) schemes. There was a learning process, too, to distinguish between whether we wanted a BI for its own sake, or for what it could achieve. It took quite a time to differentiate between instrument and objective, or means and ends. Also, we discussed whether we wanted a selective, needs-based benefit, or a Social Dividend that would be the same for everyone (of the same age).

The next major event was the conference in Louvain-la-Neuve in Belgium in September 1986, organised by the Collectif Charles Fourier, a small group all of whom had been, were, or were about to become, academics at the Université Catholique Louvain-la-Neuve. They were able to finance the conference from a prize for an essay about a Basic Income, and 60 people from across Europe were invited. The conference was a wonderful experience, had a friendly atmosphere and was extremely stimulating. It concluded by agreeing to set up the Basic Income European Network (BIEN) to keep a network of national organisations in touch with each other and organise a conference every two years. BIEN became the Basic Income *Earth* Network in 2004 because several national networks outwith Europe had become affiliated.

In 1989, BIRG became a charity, (number 328198). My own situation changed dramatically at this time, with a series of close bereavements including the death of my partner/husband after a short illness at the age of 50. Turning 40 with a new baby keeps one feeling young. Becoming the widowed mother of a ten year-old at 50 is quite different. In 1991 BIRG was granted generous funding by the Joseph Rowntree Charitable Trust to employ a part-time director and a part-time administrator. This was on condition that it changed from being BIRG to become the Citizen's Income Trust (CIT), in order to ride on the crest of the wave of a topical debate about citizenship at the time. CIT hosted the fifth BIEN Congress in London in 1994.

CIT touched a low point in 2001, when our then director left, our Chair, Evelyn McEwen, died, and the ten years of generous funding came to an end. The trustees agreed to continue with private donations, volunteer administration and volunteer contributions to the *Citizen's Income Newsletter*. Since then, we have operated on a shoestring, averaging about £3,000pa until recently. The Rev Dr Malcolm Torry volunteered to be the Director, giving an average of half a day per week (with the kind permission of the Bishop of Woolwich), and I agreed to take over as Chair. Since retiring in 2014, Malcolm has given more of his time to CIT. He and I have worked closely together since 2001, and I would like to take this opportunity to acknowledge the enormous contribution that he has made to CIT over these last years. It is probably 90 per cent due to his commitment, hard work, intellect and super efficient administration that CIT has provided such a firm foundation for the BI debate in the UK.

I started writing about BI seriously again in 2005. I had prepared a press release for CIT that ended with the claim that the UK could support a modest BI. It was quickly challenged by Samuel Brittan of the *Financial Times* asking for figures to back it up. An intense weekend followed in which I put all my back-of-envelope figures into context in an article, which Samuel Brittan acknowledged later (Brittan, 2006). Further stimulation came from the publication of the first Minimum Income Standards (MIS) data by the Centre for Research in Social Policy at Loughborough University in 2008 (Hirsch *et al*, 2014), which led to a further article. I explored whether a rule of thumb could be devised for the design of a CI scheme, for those over pension-entitlement age, working-age adults and dependent children that could meet the MIS criteria. I also explored how to cost an earnings/income disregard, where the initial tranche of gross earnings or income is tax-free.

In the meantime, I attended one of the organising meetings for the European Citizens' Initiative on Unconditional Basic Income (ECI on UBI) in Brussels in April 2012, and listened to the discussions about the definition of, and objectives for, Basic Income schemes. Even after all this time, every time I hear such a discussion, I learn something new. Their emphasis on universal, individual, unconditional and high enough for the individual to live a life of dignity with the opportunity to participate in public life is an excellent definition of a full Basic Income. It was disappointing that the ECI on UBI failed to reach the required number of signatures during 2013, but it managed to make 285,000 people around the EU aware of the concept.

An important landmark for me occurred when my local Member of the Scottish Parliament (MSP), Jim Eadie, offered to host a seminar and roundtable discussion entitled *Beyond Welfare Reform to a Citizen's Income: the desirability and feasibility of a CI* in the Scottish Parliament. It took place on 15 January 2014 and was attended by 60 people. Professor Ailsa McKay, of Glasgow Caledonian University, was the principal speaker. Although terminally ill, she presented the case for what she always referred to as a 'Citizen's Basic Income' (CBI) with passion and wit, while I followed on with some relevant facts and figures about its economic viability. Sadly, Ailsa, who had been the voice of CBI in Scotland for many years, died seven weeks later. This book is dedicated to her memory.

The year 2014 continued to be very stimulating in Scotland, as the Scottish people asked themselves fundamental questions during the Independence Referendum debates, such as: 'What sort of society do we wish to create for ourselves and future generations?' The population in Scotland has become politicised like no other part of the UK, and my fellow trustees at CIT encouraged me to set up a sister organisation in Scotland. During the autumn of 2015, a group of us drew up a constitution for a Scottish Charitable Incorporated Organisation, a trust with limited liability, and the Citizen's Basic Income Network Scotland (CBINS) was accepted as a charity (no. SC046356) in February 2016.

Following on from the event in the Scottish Parliament, Willie Sullivan (a friend of Ailsa's) and I approached the Steering Committee of the Scottish Campaign on Welfare Reform proposing that we meet with a dozen or so members to try to devise a set of BI schemes for Scotland. A group of people from voluntary sector organisations in central Scotland met six times between July 2014 and March 2015 to take the idea forward. Faced with a choice of the interchangeable terms, 'Citizen's Income', 'Citizen's Basic Income' or 'Basic Income', the last was preferred. Thus they were, briefly, the Scottish Basic Income Group, with the objective of trying to devise a set of BI schemes that could be implemented by an independent or fully fiscally-devolved Holyrood Parliament.

Three sets of sample schemes were devised:

- minimal entry-level ones with BI levels at least as great as those of the current main means-tested benefits, which thus act as a floor, and demonstrate that even minimal level BIs can offer advantages;
- utopian schemes, where no-one is in poverty at even the highest benchmark, whose reference is the MIS; and thirdly,
- economically viable ones that aim to match up with the official European Union poverty benchmark of '0.6 of median equivalised household income'.

I prepared briefing papers for our meetings, that the group gently but firmly dismantled, which, though painful, was an excellent learning experience. I was given the task of writing up a report of our work together, which I thought would extend to about 10,000 words. After 25,000 words, I realised that it had turned itself into a book. This book is the outcome of those meetings. It attempts to structure the multitudinous facts accumulated during my immersion in the BI debate over more than 30 years, and I could not have written it in its present form without all of those learning experiences right up to the present time.

The structure of the book

THIS BOOK IS intended to fulfil several objectives.

- to demonstrate that a BI would be preferable to the current social security system, although some would be satisfied with a few changes at the margins of the latter;
- to provide the illustrative sample schemes and show that they are economically viable, even if some people do not consider the method of funding proposed here to be politically feasible at the present time;
- to enable those interested to be able to experiment, design and cost their own BI schemes, by demonstrating the process to follow and showing where to access sources of official data;
- to prove useful as a reference work to help to inform the public about BI, and
- to offer some suggestions as to what grassroots advocates could do to share their enthusiasm.

I have tried to write the book so that it can be read on different levels. It is primarily aimed at the general reader, but it must also be accurate and comprehensive enough to satisfy a range of interests including academic economists, social policy experts, civil servants and politicians.

It is ironic that, although the concept is simple, the subject matter relating to a BI is complex. This is for several reasons:

- one is trying to disentangle the unnecessary and avoidable complications of the current social security system when replacing it, to ensure that their current functions are covered by the new system;
- the internal structure of an income maintenance (social security) system and its immediate outcomes are summarised in Tables 3.2 and 3.3 and reveal how interrelated they are. This leads to some repetition in the text;
- the definition of a BI by itself does not provide enough information to enable someone to devise a particular system. An infinite number of schemes is possible. Each is subjective in the sense that it is the outcome of the prioritised objectives, assumptions and constraints of those who devise it. The design and implementation of any one scheme can quickly become complex and technical.

- Although the concept of a BI is fairly simple, it would lead to such a fundamentally different system that its influence would ramify throughout society and affect many aspects of life, which have to be anticipated and assessed.

A further difficulty for the reader arises where the discussion involves some economic analysis. Few of the concepts are difficult. Where some background in economics or social policy would be helpful, this is flagged up and references are given so that those who wish to learn more are able to follow up particular issues.

Some readers have a blind spot where numbers are concerned. Much of Part III of the book is presented in terms of tables of figures, based on data mainly from official sources, so that the case for economic viability is credible. Readers to whom such numbers and tables are anathema should feel entitled to skip chapters 10 to 13, but are encouraged to persevere with chapter 14, where the deliberations in earlier chapters are used to devise and present the illustrative sample schemes.

The book is in four parts. Part I introduces the philosophical and political arguments about why we need change, and poses the question 'what sort of society do we wish to create?' It suggests that the four values (wisdom, justice, compassion, integrity) inscribed on the mace in the Scottish Parliament would be a good starting place.

Part II examines theory and evidence, beginning with the internal structure of income maintenance systems, noting that it comprises four design features that offer choices: the unit for assessment and delivery of a benefit, eligibility, selectivity and contingency. The current system is based on one set of choices and causes problems for benefit recipients. A BI scheme is defined by an alternative set, creating a very different type of society. The relationships between the design features and their outcomes or objectives are summarised in Tables 3.2 and 3.3, which represent the subject matter of Part II. Each design feature is examined in turn in chapters 4 to 7 and its influence on the outcomes is traced. Each of these chapters concludes with a case study of a BI (or a guaranteed minimum income) that has been implemented or piloted. Part II concludes with other evidence from elsewhere in the world, where a scheme has been implemented, piloted or mooted.

Part III demonstrates the economic viability of BI schemes by examining facts and figures. It asks what level of BI would be sufficient, and looks at two different poverty benchmarks against which BI schemes can be matched. It then proposes an alternative benchmark for BI purposes. It shows how to calculate the gross cost of a scheme, and discusses some alternative methods of financing them. I come to the conclusion that a restructured, fairer income tax system would be the best source for the more generous schemes, while recognising that any one scheme could be financed from more than one source. Three sets of increasingly generous, illustrative sample schemes for both Scotland and the UK are presented and costed in chapter 14. A method of costing the schemes is put forward, based on a *flat rate tax* in the proposed restructured income tax system. This is merely to be able to cost and compare the different schemes using a single figure, and in no way suggests that this is the only, or best, way to finance the BI schemes. The information provided in Part III could guide those interested in designing their own schemes, and in this sense Part III may be regarded as a 'do-it-yourself manual'.

Part IV ties up loose ends and addresses practical matters. How would a BI scheme be implemented in practice? What is the political process? How would the actual scheme to be implemented be chosen? How do we get from here to there? Chapter 16 concludes by summarising some of the main points from the book.

Appendix A provides a summary of figures for the UK for 2011–15 and for Scotland 2012–15, for easy reference. They include some population figures, Gross Domestic Product and GDP per capita, total personal income and mean income per capita, for both Scotland and the UK. For the UK only, it continues with expenditure on Social Security transfers, revenue raised by different taxes, the cost of Tax Expenditures, the rates for means-tested and other benefits, income tax and employees' National Insurance thresholds and rates, and numbers of taxpayers by age.

Appendix B provides a hypothetical example of an international BI scheme, and some examples to demonstrate measures of inequality. It also provides other hypothetical examples to demonstrate the redistributive powers of a flat rate income tax that is hypothecated and used only for a BI scheme. It also explores the outcomes of some progressive income tax schedules.

Appendix C lays out the template for an Excel program to work out the cost of your own BI scheme financed by a restructured income tax. Appendix D gives a chronology of BI with respect to the UK. Readers may notice that I like lists.

Acknowledgements

I acknowledge with thanks the dismantling of my misconceptions offered by the members of the Scottish Basic Income Group, their contributions to the debate, and their being instrumental in devising the schemes for Scotland presented here. I am particularly indebted to Jon Shaw for invaluable advice about the current Social Security system. A condensed version of Part II of this book appears as a chapter in a new textbook (Campbell *et al*, 2016), and its excellent editing has also benefited this book, for which I thank Jim Campbell and Morag Gillespie of Glasgow Caledonian University. I am deeply indebted to Morag Gillespie for editing this book very thoroughly on her formal retirement from GCU. I also thank those who have read all or part of the manuscript and offered comments, including my fellow or former trustees in the Citizen's Basic Income Network Scotland, Prof Mike Danson, Maddy Halliday, Jon Shaw, Dr Ben Simmons and Willie Sullivan, together with Gareth Morgan of CIT, Sue Robertson and Jim Pym. Any remaining errors are mine alone.

The Basic Income European/Earth Network (BIEN) has provided many friendships along the way including, among others, Jan Otto Andersson, Jurgen De Wispelaere, Louise Haagh, Seán Healy, Barb Jacobson, Brigid Reynolds, Guy Standing, Philippe Van Parijs, Walter Van Trier, and Karl Widerquist.

I thank the trustees of the Citizen's Income Trust (Citizen's *Basic* Income Trust (CBIT) as from the end of May 2017) for many hours of stimulating discussion and for their permission to quote from the *Citizen's Income Newsletter* and CIT's other publications. The views in this book are not necessarily those of either CIT or the Citizen's Basic Income Network Scotland.

Lastly I thank my family for their forbearance over the years, particularly Jim who has been very patient and helpful while I have been writing this book.

PART I

Philosophical and Political Arguments

CHAPTER 1

Introduction:
How did we get from there to here?

Imagine...

IMAGINE A SOCIETY where every adult receives a regular, unconditional, cash payment on an individual basis that is delivered automatically to one's personal account. This Basic Income (BI) is enough to live on modestly, but with dignity, enabling one to participate in public life. There is no compulsion to work, but most people want to work-for-pay to top up their incomes, to meet other people, for job satisfaction and to be recognised as someone who contributes to society. Some prefer to work long hours on a high salary; others prefer part-time work which fits in better with their work-life balance. Others take time out of paid work in order to care for children and elders, or other family members and friends with disabilities. Although automation has replaced many jobs, there is still demand for highly qualified workers in the new industries, in addition to demand for paid carers, those in the personal services and the creative arts.

Taxes on scarce resources ensure that it is non-material economic activity that continues to grow. There is a buzz in society as many people use their creative abilities to design new products, to make things, and invent new processes. Education is a growth sector, not just for training people for work, but because learning can be enjoyable and satisfying for its own sake. Leisure is another growth industry. Many take up hobbies such as handcrafts, gardening, and rambling. The Arts in many forms take off, both for participant and spectator. Increased financial security has led to a reduction in both the incidence and depth of poverty. The fear, stress and anxiety have lifted and there is a general improvement in health. There is also a reduction in crime. Although one is not protected against the ordinary sorrows of life, optimism is in the air, accompanied by a palpable feeling of good will to and from those around them. People co-operate on local ventures.

Some societies appear to operate on the basis of fear and despair. BI provides a basis of compassion, justice, trust and hope. Let us work together to turn this dream into reality.

Why we need a BI system to replace the current Social Security system

The current social security system was set up immediately after World War II to meet the needs of an economy and society that were very different then.

The economy has changed in many ways over the last seven decades. Manufacturing has declined and given way to services, which is now the largest sector. Full male employment on good wages is no longer the norm. Workers change jobs more frequently than before. Many people are now on low wages, in part-time work, on zero or small hours contracts, in temporary work or insecure jobs. Women comprise a greater proportion of the labour force now. Automation has led to a loss of jobs, initially in middle-income employment, but also among unskilled workers, and eventually it is likely to encroach on the professions (Miller, 2016: 167–8). In the 19th and early 20th centuries, technological change was associated with a change from one type of technology to another, such as from a gas-based to electricity-based technology, or from horse-drawn transport to the steam revolution and to the combustion engine. It led to new jobs replacing the old. However, the scale of the computer revolution with its capacity for information storage, computation, word-processing and communications has led to the automation of many jobs, without the usual replacement by even more employment in the new technology. It is not clear yet whether this trend will continue, or if sufficient jobs to fulfil people's aspirations will transpire. There will always be a role for employment that needs the personal touch, such as care work, personal services, catering, and the creative arts. A reformed social security system should be such that it is able to cope with any outcome of the automation revolution.

Society has also changed markedly since the end of World War II. Beveridge's social security system reflected the needs of the time, but has failed to meet those of a gradually changing society. For example, most lone parents were widows then, but now are single or separated. Although many women had been employed during the war, it was felt that the returning war heroes should have first refusal on post-war employment, and many women were persuaded to return to their former roles as wives and mothers first and foremost. In 1948, 'full employment' was based on male full time work. It was assumed that a man could earn enough to keep himself with his wife at home and at least one child.

Education for both young men and women has been extended, and now there is a higher proportion of women in the workforce than in the immediate post war era. Many women combine paid work with unpaid caring roles and domestic work in the home. The significance and value of women's unpaid work in the home and caring for children and elders that underpins the monetary economy is still unacknowledged. The average age of women at which they have their first child has risen. Marriage breakdown occurs more frequently, more couples cohabit without being married, there are more lone parent families (Donabie *et al*, 2010), and there are complex family arrangements. New Labour set itself the objective of eradicating child poverty by 2020, but failed at their first five-year assessment in 2005. Nevertheless, its Child Tax Credit and increasing support for childcare have contributed to the reduction in child poverty from one-in-three to one-in-four, many of whom live in homes where one or both parents are in work (Belfield *et al*, 2016: 43 T4.2). Poverty and homelessness have increased, and food banks have become far too familiar features, and not just in the city centres of our affluent society. Life expectancy has risen, but there are stark differences between those of the wealthiest and poorest areas in the UK.

Although the idea of a BI is not new, interest in it in the UK has been accelerating in the last four or five years. It has been realised that a BI could help to solve, or at least ameliorate, several growing problems in the UK and indeed in many other countries too. There are at least four drivers that have precipitated this recent interest in BI.

The first is not just a concern about the growing complexity of the current social security system, leading to an increased risk of errors and fraud, but an awareness of the increasingly callous conditionality and sanctions with which the benefits are delivered. The introduction of Universal Credit (UC) was intended to simplify the system by combining six means-tested benefits, which could be accessed via one agency instead of up to four, as previously. If it had ended there, it might have been a welcome small change in the right direction to the system. However, it has been accompanied by harsh conditionality and savage sanctions, often involving the withdrawal of two weeks worth of benefits for the slightest transgression of the system. Also, there can often be delays in the payments of the benefits, especially of Housing Benefit. Delays in payments are a major cause of recourse to food banks, for which claimants must have a referral note and to which they can only apply up to three times in a given period. A BI scheme can significantly simplify the administration of the social security system, end this conditionality and help to give people more control over their lives.

The second driver is that poverty in the UK currently stands at roughly one in five people. This is the highest that it has been for several decades. It is not just one in five adults, but one in five children also, whose future prospects are diminished by this early experience. It is not just unemployed people who experience below-poverty benefits, but many low-paid workers also suffer poverty in spite of in-work benefits such as Child Tax Credit (CTC) and Working Tax Credit (WTC). Poverty undermines health and shortens lives. A BI could help by providing financial security to underpin people's lives.

Thirdly, alongside the increase in poverty is the growing inequality of income and wealth. The result of the EU Referendum is likely to have been a response to the betrayal of the people by the establishment, enriching themselves while ignoring the plight of those whose standard of living had been undermined, by globalisation and automation among other things. A BI can help to redistribute income to some extent, but to do the job properly it would have to be financed by a restructured, fairer income tax system. An individual with gross income less than the mean might expect to be a net beneficiary, and those with more than the mean would be net taxpayers. This is discussed in chapter 12.

The fourth driver is the most compelling, since it could affect more people, and include middle classes who are worried that their offspring will not be guaranteed the privileged jobs that they have enjoyed in the past. It concerns the pace of technological change and the perceived threat of increasing 'robotisation' in the economy. Automation has already led to decreases in many traditional types of employment, and at this stage it is not certain whether the heralded increases in new jobs will manifest.

Clearly the current social security system is not meeting the needs of the most vulnerable people in society. This will be exacerbated if the traditional one-to-one relationship between employment and income is no longer reliable. A BI can be seen as the new method of providing incomes for everyone, however the labour market develops in the future.

The post World War II consensus welfare reforms – how did we get from there to here?

William Beveridge's report on *Social Insurance and Allied Services* published in 1942 was a best seller. He identified five giant social evils in society: want, ignorance, squalor, idleness and disease. His solutions were a social security system, the 1944 Education Act, an extensive house-building program, full employment policy and the NHS respectively. Their implementation together became the 'Welfare State', the most significant achievement of the post World War II consensus in the UK. The fact that the war had increased the public debt did not deter the Attlee government from following Keynes' advice to borrow further to invest in a visionary future. In the same way that a private citizen can take on a mortgage of, say, two and a half times their income in those days, the public debt rose to a high of 250 per cent of GDP in 1946 and then started to decline to about 50 per cent by 1975, 30 years later (Debtonation, 2009).

> The first Labour majority government under Clement Attlee was by any measure the most successful the UK has ever experienced judged by the benefits which it has provided to the British people. It was a remarkably successful administration which delivered a phenomenal range of achievements. Moreover, it did so over a very short time, and in the most difficult of circumstances.
>
> ANDERSON *et al*, 2014: 23

Beveridge recommended two benefit systems in parallel. The National Insurance Act of 1946 introduced a contributory National Insurance (NI) scheme with flat-rate NI benefits. The National Assistance Act of 1948, which finally abolished the Poor Law, established a means-tested National Assistance safety net, (also known as Social Assistance), that was less generous than the NI scheme. The contributory NI scheme was designed for a full male employment economy, to provide payments to workers to replace earnings during periods of Maternity, Invalidity, Sickness and Unemployment, together with a Retirement pension (MISUR). Over time, other categorical benefits were developed to address specific situations that were not covered adequately within the NI and Social Assistance schemes, for example, disability benefits (Millar, 2009). Initially it represented an enormous improvement on the previous situation, but now the social security system is in a sorry state and is inadequate to meet the needs of a very different society compared with the 1940s and 50s. So, how did we get from there to here?

The post war consensus in the UK, based on the wishes of the ordinary people, who had fought and sacrificed so much for their country in WWII, to create a better, fairer society, lasted for approximately one generation. Not only did the economy and society change, but so did the political environment. The Thatcher government of 1979–90 heralded a return to an older system (now known as neoliberalism) that swept through Europe more slowly than the UK, but was always more evident in the USA. This phenomenon in the UK has been analysed by among others, Owen Jones (2014: 1–15), Paul Mason (2015: xi–xii, 3–9), Andrew Sayer (2016: 16–18) and in the USA by the Nobel Prize-winning economist, Joseph Stiglitz (2013).

An extreme version of neoliberal ideology can be characterised as the agenda of a trans-global elite of approximately 0.1% of the richest people in the world, whose aim is to protect and increase their power and wealth, through rent-seeking:

> ... getting income not as a reward for creating wealth but by grabbing a larger share of the wealth that would otherwise have been produced without their effort... Those at the top have learned how to suck money from the rest in ways that the rest are hardly aware of – that is their true innovation.
>
> STIGLITZ, 2013: 39–40

Jones argues that the elite in the UK, or the establishment, controls the government through a system of patronage (chap 2), through undemo-cratic lobbying by large corporations (chap 5), and by owning most of the media (chap 3). They employ well-paid professionals and other skilled people who are likely to espouse or fulfil their agenda; they exploit other less skilled workers, and anyone who cannot be exploited is expendable.

Neoliberal ideology includes the following ideas:

- A small state with minimal obligation to its citizens, minimal state intrusion into people's lives and low taxation;

- low inflation;

- privatisation of public assets, which can then be marketed;

- unregulated 'free market' capitalism, which is claimed to be competitive, efficient and self-regulating;

- the deregulation of financial institutions;

- competitive individualism – autonomous, self-reliant individuals, totally responsible for their own well-being only, (but not for anyone else's, in spite of the obvious interdependence between people);

- low taxation leading to the dismantling of the welfare state – individual welfare, private provision of social services, where users pay for services used – sometimes moderated by individual acts of charity.

- the suppression of collective action by the poorest that could challenge the power of the elite.
  JONES, 2014: 6

The expected outcome is a decrease in democracy; increased insecurity, growing poverty and inequality; a decreasing proportion of national income that is created by wages; profits before welfare; the dismantling of the welfare state; more stringent conditions and sanctions introduced in the social security system; the failure of the banking system; followed by austerity leading to recession.

This system has been referred to as 'socialism for the rich and capitalism for the poor'. It was first recognised by Andrew Jackson in the USA in 1832, but the term was probably first popularised by Michael Harrington in 1962, and it has been used consistently by Gore Vidal since 1969 (*World Library*, 2016). Other terms have been used, such as 'corporate welfare', and 'private profits and public losses' especially with respect to the bail out of the banks in the Credit Crisis of 2008.

This somewhat stark depiction of neoliberalism may seem extreme, but evidence of it can be observed in the picture of the UK's post-war economy and society in this chapter.

Guy Standing reviewed the sweep of labour conditions since before the 19th century, starting with Karl Polanyi, who 'depicted the 19th century as an attempt to create a market society in which everything was turned into a commodity, driven by the rising power of financial capital' (Standing, 2009: 3). He charts the phase up to the early 19th century, when the economy was embedded in society in which institutions constrain market forces; its dis-embedded phase lasted into the early 20th century; it was briefly embedded state again for the three decades following WWII, since which time the economy has again been dis-embedded from society. One could even say that society has now become embedded in the economy, rather than the economy being embedded in society.

Over the last seven decades, radical changes have affected society and the economy in the UK, for which the parallel NI and Social Assistance systems were originally designed. In addition, the social security system has been undermined by many marginal changes over the years. The real values of NI benefits have been eroded, so that these are less now than the safety net Social Assistance benefits, which themselves have also become eroded over time (Spicker, 2015). The social security system no longer meets its original purpose of banishing want. It is not just that the benefit levels are low today – few means-tested benefits meet the government's (and the EU's) own official poverty benchmark of 0.6 of median equivalised household income (DWP, 2015). The design of the system causes problems for its recipients (Timmins, 2001). A new system fit for the 21st century is now required.

The post war consensus led to a reduction in income inequalities. However, income inequality grew markedly during the Thatcher years, 1979–90, and has been maintained since then, turning the UK into one of the most unequal countries in the developed world (Murphy, 2011: 100).

The Gini coefficient is a measure of inequality of income or wealth, the values of which lie between 0 and 1, where 0 indicates complete equality, and 1 indicates complete inequality where everything is owned by one person. (See Appendix B for more explanation about the Gini coefficient and other measures of inequality). In 1979 the Gini coefficient measuring income inequality in the UK was 0.24, but it rose to 0.34 by 1991. Since then, it has stayed around 0.35 ± 0.02, including under the New Labour government between 1997 and 2010 (Belfield *et al*, 2015: 32). This was partly due to a steady reduction in real gross wages, as a result of globalisation and automation, but it has been exacerbated by the fiscal policies carried out by all UK governments since 1979 that have failed to stem the tide of redistribution of income and wealth towards the rich compared with the immediate post WWII era (Bell, 2013).

The following observations may be noted:

- Growth benefits the wealthier sections of society, while those in the bottom 10% of the income distribution either have not become better off, or are worse off in real terms (CIA, 2013).

- The light-touch regulation of financial institutions led to the weakening of the Glass-Steagall Act in the USA that separated savers' guaranteed deposits in retail banks from the non-guaranteed ones in investment banks.

- This led directly to the reckless lending by banks in the USA and the UK, followed by further reckless lending on international financial markets, and to their borrowings being greater than their reserves. This was one of the causes of the Credit Crisis of 2007–08, and the perceived need to bail out some large banks out of the public purse, and also provided the opportunity for the austerity response.

- Consecutive governments' housing policy, of encouraging speculative investment in the housing market, coupled with a dearth of new building, has been a method of siphoning off wealth from the aspirant, first-time buyer into the pockets of current owner-occupiers, when they sell up. This has led to soaring house prices in some parts of the country and to higher rents for non-home-owners.

- Average gross wage rates and thus the share of wages in the country's National Income has been allowed to fall over time. The National Minimum Wage (£6.70 per hour for those aged over 25, from 1 October 2015) has not kept up with inflation, and the current government's 'National Living Wage', (the first stage of which was implemented in April 2016 at £7.20 per hour), is nowhere near that recommended by the Living Wage Foundation of £8.25 per hour for the same period.

- High Marginal Deduction Rates, as a result of aggregating the withdrawal tapers of several means-tested benefits (MTBs), have made the effective income tax system very regressive, introducing a disincentive for claimants and low-paid workers to work-for-pay.

- Most MTB levels have been eroded and are below the government's own poverty benchmark.

- The income tax system is full of tax reliefs and allowances, loopholes that benefit those with high incomes, enabling them to avoid paying their fair share of income tax, which reduces the tax base and imposes higher rates of income tax on those who cannot avoid paying them.

The CIA's World Factbook states that 'since 1975, practically all the gains in household income [in the USA] have gone to the top 20% of households', (CIA, 2017: para 4). In 2007, the CIA made a similar statement about growth in the UK over the previous three decades having gone to the top 40% of households. In rich societies growth tends to benefit wealthier people, but during a recession, suddenly we all are in this together, and the poor must shoulder their share of grief. The cycles of growth – recession – growth leads to a ratchet effect of increasing inequality. The UK government opted out of the Social Protection for Workers clauses in the Maastricht Treaty of 1992, preferring a 'flexible labour market', which encouraged growth at the expense of the wages of the workers. Globalisation has had a drastic effect on the labour market, depressing wages of unskilled and low-skilled workers, from which UK governments could have taken steps to protect workers, but chose not to do so.

The imperatives of global finance have further increased inequality.

The financial regulators in the UK and USA must have been ignorant of, or rejected, the observation attributed to Thomas Jefferson, 1802:

> I believe that banking institutions are more dangerous to our liberties than standing armies. If the American people ever allow private banks to control the issue of their currency, first by inflation, then by deflation, the banks and the corporations that will grow up around [the banks] will deprive the people of all property until their children wake-up homeless on the continent their fathers conquered. The issuing power should be taken from the banks and restored to the people to whom it properly belongs.

Light-touch regulation of the banks and other financial institutions started in the UK in 1986 with the Big Bang deregulation of the stock market and the privatisation of the London Stock Exchange. Later, the weakening of the 1933 Glass-Steagall Act in the USA led directly to various corporate scandals. Greed and recklessness led to the rise of the sub-prime mortgage market in the USA, accompanied by similar irresponsible lending to many home-owners in the UK. Financiers invented new financial instruments that were so complicated that few understood them or their implications. The failure of the unofficial, but formerly widely-respected, Credit Rating Agencies, in labelling toxic bundles of debt with a triple 'AAA' rating, was one of the many factors that led to the Credit Crisis of 2007–08, and the subsequent bail-out of the banks, who were too big to fail and would otherwise have brought down sterling as a currency (Jones, 2014: 256–7).

The misguided policy response of 'austerity' by the UK coalition government in 2010 contravened all of Keynes' policy recommendations for dealing with a recession, which he had developed during the recession of the 1930s. Few current academic economists support the austerity policy. Wren Lewis (2015) makes a convincing case for claiming that the 2010–15 UK coalition government used the reduction of the deficit, (and thence the accumulated public debt, that was not high by historical or international standards), as an excuse for imposing its austerity policy for ideological reasons, causing an avoidable delay in the UK's economic recovery. This begs the question: when there is a big hole in the economy, why keep digging? Similarly, the public was presented with the choice of increasing the public deficit by further borrowing or reducing welfare payments, omitting other options, such as increasing taxation on wealthier people. One consequence of austerity is that, although the absolute poverty rate in the UK was already substantial at 21.6 per cent in 2013–14 (13.6 million people),

Looking further ahead, planned benefit cuts over this parliament will hit low-income working-age households hardest, and will therefore tend to put upwards pressure on absolute income poverty – including in-work poverty.

BELFIELD *et al*, 2015: 63

In this way, low-income groups are paying the price for the government's protection of the banks.

Successive governments' housing policy has included selling off Council Housing, while preventing councils from using the proceeds to replace the housing stock. The 'right-to-buy' policy is a real disincentive for councils to build new homes, which they would probably soon have to sell off at a discount. This right ended on 1 August 2016 in Scotland. The de-mutualisation of Building Societies to become banks, endorsed by government in the 1980s, has not been a success. Government housing policy over the last four decades, of encouraging speculative investment in housing, has led to inflationary property booms in the UK, where realised capital gains were spent on consumption and helped to fuel demand. The subsequent house-price slumps have led to bad debts and negative equity. The lack of new house-building over the decades has added to the upward pressure both on house prices and on rents in the private-rental sector. This particularly affects poor people adversely and helps to put higher Housing Benefits into the pockets of private landlords.

Why not just improve the current social security system?

It is not just the below-poverty levels of the benefits that cause problems. The whole structure of the social security system is flawed.

It has been suggested that a reformed NI system could be re-introduced. However, the NI system really works best in a full employment economy. It works well in some Nordic countries where most of the population is highly educated and trained in skills for the economy, and who have a strong work ethic. There, it is supported by highly-trained nursery nurses in publicly-provided nurseries, which enable women to take a full part in the economy. It is also supported by high rates of income tax.

The definition of 'unemployment' for a contributory unemployment benefit introduces rigidities that discourage part-time employment. It is difficult to see how a contribution-based system could cope with the current employment situation, characterised by insecure, low-waged, zero-hour and small hours contracts, and the UK's flexible labour market.

Self-employed people in the UK do not get much protection from the contributory NI system. Also, a contributory system is necessarily a conditional system, which does not give people so much choice over how they live their lives as a BI system would. Both the NI and Social Assistance systems are designed to take account of men's employment patterns, and fail to take account of the unpaid work carried out mostly by women that underpins the monetary economy.

The current social security system is not addressing society's problems satisfactorily. Higher levels of benefits are necessary to prevent poverty, but also, the Social Assistance system is too complex and is beset by structural faults that affect most claimants adversely, but specifically women. These faults are explored in more detail in chapters four to seven. One obvious fault is the inherent disincentive to work-for-pay that is caused directly by the means-testing aspect. The withdrawal of aggregated means-tested benefits, together with the deductions of income tax and NI contributions from incomes, creates a high Marginal Deduction Rate (MDR) facing claimants and low-waged workers (Miller, 2016: 170), (DWP, 2010: 8, para. 14). Together with the fall in real wage rates, this makes it difficult for them to earn their way out of the in-work poverty that they suffer through no fault of their own.

The current MTB system is obviously targeted according to means. Contrary to popular expectation, rather than protecting the poorest people, it segregates them. Social attitudes are changing and the rhetoric of politicians and the media is also changing (Bamberg *et al*, 2013). Targeting makes it easier to stigmatise and humiliate the poorest people, leading to a lower take-up of the benefits to which they are entitled.

Another structural fault is the fact that the entitlement to benefits is based on a joint application by a couple, (compared with the individual basis for assessment for income tax since 1990–91). This can lead to a state in which many adults, mainly women caring for children or adults, living with their wealthier partners, often have no recourse to an income of their own, except Child Benefit. Family law requires partners to aliment each other, that is, to make sure that they are provided for appropriately, but it does not guarantee an income to the poorer partner, who is not legally entitled to any part of his or her wealthier partner's income. A poorer partner is designated a 'financial dependent'. Surely, the concept of a 'financially-dependent adult', when applied to anyone who has not been so designated by a court, is an anathema in the UK in the 21st century.

Lastly, the extra conditions imposed on the poorest and most vulnerable members of society add to their stress levels as they struggle to keep their heads above water. The main condition used to be 'being available for work'. This has now been replaced by 'being able to provide evidence of having been actively seeking work for 35 hours per week'. Failure to meet the conditions can lead to sanctions that can threaten to make them destitute. In addition, conditionality requires extensive administration, and increases the risk of fraud and error by both recipients and staff.

Our social security system is not fit for purpose – cut the Gordian knot

The UK Social Security system, then, can be described as being in a parlous state. It makes it far more difficult for poorer members of society to earn their way out of poverty, with little or no financial security, leading to anxiety and stress, which undermines their health, which in turn increases demands on the NHS. The fear of unemployment hangs over workers, and of losing home and family, or ending up on the streets, again through no fault of their own.

The recently introduced means-tested Universal Credit (UC) is a slight simplification of the system in some ways. It still contains many of the structural problems of the previous MTBs that it replaces, to which is added fierce conditionality and savage sanctions. It has combined six MTBs and reduced from four to one the number of agencies that may be involved for a single applicant, reducing the risk of error and fraud by either staff or claimant. It eases the transition between in and out of work. The single taper of the UC reduces the MDR to 63 per cent for people with income less than the Personal Allowance and to 75 per cent for those with incomes higher than this, but it is still very high and the resultant system is still highly regressive (Miller, 2011). It is not based on individual assessment, nor is it universal or unconditional. It is still a complex MTB system, the administration of which relies on data that is the result of the integration of several different, real-time computer systems, which often cannot cope.

If we were starting from scratch to design a Social Security system suitable for today's society, it is unlikely that we would choose the current UK system, which is complex, unjust, unwieldy, inefficient and not fit for purpose. It is a Gordian Knot that cannot be unravelled and is beyond reform. It needs to be cut through and replaced by a radical alternative that is fit for the 21st century. A BI is just such an alternative. It disconnects the one-to-one relationship between paid work and income, and thus helps people to be better placed to cope with either an improvement or a worsening of the employment situation. A BI, along with other essential conditions, would contribute to the foundation of a different, better society, representing a new relationship between the state, society and its citizens.

In Part II, this book will compare the structure of the current means-tested benefit system with that of a BI system, through which many of the above complications will be smoothed out.

CHAPTER 2

Values and Vision: the objectives

What sort of society?

BEFORE EMBARKING on any major change, it is important to have a vision of the preferred outcome, so that, even if it is not achieved immediately, at least one can assess whether the proposed changes are moving in the right direction. What sort of society do we wish to create for ourselves and for future generations?

HM the Queen presented a mace, designed and crafted by Michael Lloyd, to the Scottish Parliament at its opening ceremony on 1 July 1999. Engraved on the head of the Scottish Mace are the words: *wisdom, justice, compassion* and *integrity*. These are the ideals to which the people of Scotland aspire for their Members of the Scottish Parliament. These values have not always been evident in the current Social Security system, but they would make a tremendous foundation for a replacement income maintenance system.

One might go further and claim that the first duty of government is to provide the means for every individual to meet their basic needs for a dignified, if modest, standard of living, that includes participation in public life, and enables them to develop and flourish in a sustainable economy as a human right. The right to life is a matter of ethics and takes precedence over economic matters.

Often when conversation turns to tax and benefit systems, a glazed look crosses the listener's face. Yet, the benefit and tax systems are microcosms of society and reward greater examination. It reveals how those who control society regard its lesser members. Note the subtitle of Richard Murphy's new book (2015), *The Joy of Tax: How a fair tax system can create a better society*. To this should be added 'how a fair *social security system* can create a better society'. He quotes four principles that are the underpinnings of a good tax system: peace, equality, truth and simplicity, which are the subject matter of his chapter 6. Both a fair income maintenance system and a fair tax system are absolute essentials for creating a better society. These systems are so fundamental that they can affect every area of people's lives.

Justification for a social security system

What arguments can be put forward to justify a social security system?

- 'Everyone has the right to a standard of living adequate for the health and well-being of himself and of his family, including food, clothing, housing and medical care and necessary social services, and the right to security in the event of unemployment, sickness, disability, widowhood, old age or other lack of livelihood in circumstances beyond his control.' *Universal Declaration of Human Rights*, Article 25 (1), adopted by the General Assembly of the United Nations on 10 December 1945 (United Nations, 1945).

- Thomas Paine, 1796, argued that the land and natural resources belong to the people. When land is appropriated for private use, the owners owe a rent to the whole population who have been excluded (Paine, 1974).

- 'A 2005 World Bank study concluded that most of a nation's wealth derives from intangible capital; that is, from human capital and the quality of institutions, especially the rule of law. The wealthier the nation, the more this is so.' (Bennett, 2009).

- 'No man is an island' (Donne, 1624). We all are dependent on many others. Our decisions and actions affect other people. Thus we are interdependent and therefore mutually responsible for each other.

What objectives and outcomes could an income maintenance system help to achieve?

A list of broad short-term objectives and long-run outcomes to which an income maintenance system could contribute includes the following:

- Value individuals for their own sakes; allow them respect, dignity, privacy and financial autonomy. Emancipate and empower individual adults, reducing unequal power relationships, to enable more fulfilling relationships and increase their life choices. Give them more control over their lives and the freedom to flourish, thus improving their quality of life. Emancipation is worth far more than the monetary value of the benefit.

- Help to provide financial security and prevent income poverty, or at least reduce its incidence and depth, granting the right not to be destitute. The right to life is a matter of ethics and is not an optional extra. Protect financially vulnerable adults who experience discrimination in the labour market, and families with children. These include those over pension-entitlement age, the primary care-giving parent of a dependent child (the parent with care), their dependent children, disabled people, those with chronic illnesses, and unpaid carers. In the long run, it could increase well-being in terms of security, health and educational opportunities, helping people to develop to their full potentials.

- Reduce income inequalities by redistributing income, and heal our divided society. By itself, a BI scheme would not reduce very much the inequalities between rich and poor, men and women, families without and those with dependent children, and geographically. For this to be achieved, it would have to be financed by a restructured income tax system. Invest in people in a sustainable economy, not just in major infrastructure projects; help to regenerate economically deprived areas by putting income into people's wallets and purses and helping to create demand in those areas. Eventually a BI system could help to create a just, united and inclusive society. (Inequality in wealth should also be reduced, but that is beyond the scope of this book).

- Restore the incentives to work-for-pay, by reducing the number and cost of MTBs, and their aggregated withdrawal tapers. Provide more security and stability for self-employed people, small firms and workers co-operatives, unlocking their creativity. Reduce the inequality of power relationships in the workplace, so that workers and their representatives can negotiate for reasonable pay and better working conditions. Give people more choice over their work-life balance, and the opportunity to take time out of paid work to study, travel, care for children and elders, to be involved in community or other volunteer work or to achieve some lifetime ambitions. A BI system would work well for either a full employment economy or one affected by loss of jobs as a result of automation. In the long run, it could create a more efficient and flexible labour market with increased creative entrepreneurship and productivity.

- Simplify the social security system, reducing the risk of errors and fraud, by either staff or recipient, leading to more efficient administration, (assessment, delivery, monitoring and compliance systems); reduce the bureaucracy and intrusion into recipients' lives; reduce the current time-consuming personal effort and stress required to apply for benefits. Eventually it could become a more transparent system and thus lead to increased accountability.

A BI scheme appeals across the political spectrum, to both those on the right and those on the left, each prioritising different objectives. The right wing of the spectrum is not homogeneous. The most right-wing of the neoliberals would not want any kind of welfare system at all, and would end universal free education and health services, and any type of social security system. Some slightly less right-wing neoliberals favour a BI scheme as an opportunity to withdraw all other public services including health and education (Murray, 2006). Several of the above objectives – liberty (choices) for all, less intrusion into people's lives, restoring incentives to work, increasing administrative efficiency, and *reducing* poverty – would appeal to those on the centre right, and these objectives are relatively cheap to achieve. These also appeal to the left, together with the further objectives of *preventing* poverty and of redistribution, which are more expensive to achieve (McLean, 2016: 178–79).

The case for vertical redistribution of income

Few would disagree with four of the objectives, but some might baulk at the third one listed above – vertical redistribution, ie from rich to poor. Horizontal redistribution is usually acceptable, that is, taxation during the main working part of one's life, having received support during childhood and in order to receive a pension later, in return. However, there are some compelling reasons for vertical redistribution:

- To counteract the tendency of markets to redistribute from poor to rich. Not even neoclassical economists have put forward a theorem, let alone evidence, to demonstrate that the 'perfect competition model' will redistribute from rich to poor; it merely keeps the *status quo* at best (Kishtainy, 2014: 158). No evidence has been put forward in support of the trickle down 'theory' as an effective mechanism of redistribution.

- To reverse the current tide of increasing inequality since 1979, evidenced by the increased Gini coefficient (a measure of inequality), which successive governments have failed to stem, or have even encouraged.

- The wealth of our current society is based on the accumulation of ideas, labour and capital of earlier generations, and who is to say whose forebears they were? Everyone should be able to benefit from it.

- No-one can claim to be self-made unless they have lived alone on a deserted island from birth. Since this is impossible, everyone will have benefited from society.

- Support for families with dependent children is essential, because children will become the providers of society's pensions and care in old age, both for those who have raised them and for others of their generation.

- In society, everyone is interdependent, and therefore everyone is mutually responsible for other people.

- Those with secure, well-paid employment have a responsibility to those without.

- Many poor people work hard, too, and yet are unable to earn their way out of poverty. The majority of children in poverty live in households where one or both parents are in work (Belfield *et al*, 2016: 43 T4.2).

- More equal societies have been better for everyone, even the better off, as evidenced in Wilkinson and Pickett's *The Spirit Level* (2009).

- In-work poverty can lead to workers being deprived of time and to the inability to achieve an optimal work-life balance. Insecurity can lead to increased stress. These can have many adverse effects on health, which can make increased demands on the NHS.

- 'The best democracy is one with a more equal income distribution.' (White, 2000: 2).

Vertical redistribution implies that poorer people would be better off, and richer people would be worse off financially, although they may still benefit from the non-financial advantages of a BI system, such as better health on average. It is not possible for everyone to be better off financially in the short term, but if the introduction of a BI system leads to increased growth, then everyone could be better off financially in the long run.

Who are the rich?

It is worth asking: who are the rich? For many of us, a rich person is someone who appears to have greater income or wealth than ourselves. It is a loose term and could apply to many different circumstances.

If the population can be divided into poor and rich halves, then every income tax payer would belong to the rich half. Nearly half of the UK's population has paid income tax in recent years. That means that the other half of the population has had too small an income on which to pay tax. The mid-year population in 2014 was 64.597 million (ONS, 'Population Estimates for UK, England and Wales, Scotland and Northern Ireland'. 2015). Some 30.5 million individuals paid income tax in 2014–15 (HMRC, T 2.1). Another 12.153 millions were minors (aged 0–15), and the few of them who have taxable incomes will have paid tax on it, just as required of adults. There were 11.394 million people, aged 65 and over in 2014, of whom 6.070 million paid income tax in 2014–15. This means that the incomes of over 16.6 million working-age adults and over 5.3 million pensioners, some 22 million adults, were so low, (below the Personal Allowance of £10,000), that they did not have to pay income tax in 2014–15.

The average gross income per head of man, woman and child was £20,560 in the UK and £19,306 in Scotland in 2014 (*Blue Book*: 2015 edition, Table 6.1.3 and Scottish National Accounts Project 2015, Table 1). This could be another very simplistic division between rich and poor. Because of the skewed nature of the distribution of gross income in the UK, there are far more people who have less than the average income than have more.

A more sophisticated definition is required. Rowlingson and McKay (2012: chap 5) distinguish between 'the rich', 'the richer' and 'the richest'. 'The rich' are the top 10 per cent by income and assets, which in the UK in 2007–08 represented a taxable income threshold of £44,900 and asset threshold of £251,611. The top 10 per cent would represent some 6.46 million individuals in 2014, and would include the 4.43 million who paid the higher rate of income tax in 2014–15, including the 0.329 million who were liable for the additional rate of tax (HMRC, T 2.1), together with some 2.03 million others. 'The rich' have a comfortable life-style, which protects them from some of the worst aspects of recessions, but they do not regard themselves as rich.

'The richer' were defined as the top one per cent, corresponding to a taxable income threshold of £149,000 and an asset threshold of £895,947 in 2007–08 (Rowlingson *et al*, 2012). One per cent of the population in

2014 would represent 646,000 individuals, but only 329,000 were liable to the additional rate of income tax in 2014–15.

It might be thought that 'the richest' would be the top 0.1% by income and assets, (64,600 individuals). However, due to the difficulties of accessing suitable data, Rowlingson *et al* define 'the richest' as the top 1,000 'super-rich' people living and working in the UK, as identified by *The Sunday Times* Rich List.

It is anticipated that redistribution from rich to poor would mean that only the top 20–30 per cent of individuals in the gross income distribution would experience a fall in their net incomes. The actual loss would depend on several factors, such as the level of a person's gross income, the actual BI scheme and how it was financed. One should bear in mind that while a wealthy individual may suffer a fall in net income, other members of his/her family may experience gains, so that the household may not necessarily be worse off financially. Sample schemes are developed in Part III.

PART II
Theory and Evidence

CHAPTER 3

The internal structure and design features of income maintenance systems

Townsend's three principles

TOWNSEND (1979: 62–63) identified three distinct general principles of social policy to deal with large-scale deprivation or poverty:

- 'Conditional welfare for the few', as represented by the development of the Poor Laws of 1832–4;

- 'Minimum rights for the many' began to be treated seriously as a basis for social policy in Britain at the turn of the 20th century, and was taken up with renewed vigour in the Beveridge Report of 1942; and

- 'Distributional justice for all', which he said 'has not yet been clearly articulated or tried in Britain'.

The first two having failed, it is now time to pursue the third principle. This will involve reform of both the social security and income tax systems.

The design features of income maintenance systems

An income maintenance system is a set of instruments rather than a program of policy objectives. That is, it is a means towards ends. Each system has an internal structure comprising a set of design features, which are its building blocks. The choices with respect to those design features will both reflect the values of the elite or establishment in society and influence the nature of the society that results.

Even before an income maintenance system can be designed, its intended population must be defined. This is likely to be based on a combination of geographical area and legal, including citizenship, rights.

Any system must first of all specify its unit for the assessment and delivery of its benefits and secondly define who is eligible to receive the benefits. Thirdly, it must decide whether everyone who is eligible should be entitled to receive the same level of benefit or whether entitlement is differentiated. Lastly, it must stipulate whether entitlement is conditional or unconditional. These four design features, *the benefit unit, eligibility, entitlement and contingency*, together create the internal structure of any income maintenance systems. Different taxonomies can be used to define income maintenance systems, based on different combinations of these building blocks (Miller, 1990).

The **unit for assessment and delivery** of benefits could be based on any of the following: the individual (man, woman or child), the individual adult, a couple (married, in a civil partnership, or otherwise cohabiting), a family unit, or a household. The benefit paid could include extra elements to cover dependents of the assessment unit. This is discussed further in chapter 4.

Eligibility defines *who* has the legal right to receive a benefit. Eligibility can be universal, which covers everyone in the defined population, or it can be targeted, where only certain sections of the population are included. Targeting could be based on single or combined criteria, such as: age, need, means, or contribution record (together with the situation of being unable to earn due to certain circumstances, such as Maternity, Invalidity, Sickness, Unemployment or Retirement). It could also include worth or desert (for example, the 'deserving' widowed mother as opposed to the 'undeserving' unmarried mother), capacity (as in the award of scholarships), or merit (as in the allocation of prizes and rewards), among other things. See chapter 5.

Means-testing of benefits is a mixture of targeting based on low means, (on the income or wealth of either the recipient or that of another family or household member), and of selectivity (see below), since the entitlement decreases inversely with means.

Entitlement can be non-selective or selective, which could be based on some of the same criteria as for eligibility, such as, need, means, and worth or desert, where value judgements are applied to groups or situations. Selectivity refers to differential levels of entitlement for people who are equally eligible, according to someone's status within a particular base, and indicates *how much* benefit each will receive. Selectivity can be based on a variety of categories. Three main categories can be identified:

- Personal characteristics, over which one usually has little or no control. These include age, gender, sexual orientation, race, chronic illness or disability – physical or mental. At one time, disability benefits were varied by cause, (war-wounded, industrial injury, accident or genetic). Subsequently they were based on degree of impairment, but now they are based on functionality, that is, the degree to which function is lost;

- Household relationships or status, including: blood relationships, marital or other cohabitation status, the number of adults in the household and the number of dependent children. This also includes being the primary care-giving parent, a lone parent, and housing tenure, householder, or lodger. 'Lone Parent' was another category that used to be differentiated into 'deserving' or otherwise by cause (widowhood, divorced or unmarried mother), but is now based on 'presence';
- Regional variations in costs, such as in house prices and rents, or in the cost of childcare services.

Entitlement based on a continuum can be difficult to assess accurately, so categories might be preferable. Similarly, entitlement based on circumstances that can change frequently should be avoided, as they cause additional bureaucracy. 'Non-selective' means that differential entitlement is not applied. Entitlement is discussed further in chapter 6.

Contingency refers to whether or not *external conditions will be imposed* on potential recipients to force them to change their behaviour, often with sanctions imposed if the conditions are not fulfilled. Conditionality is usually applied to those who are not already involved in some approved activity status, such as being involved in voluntary service or behaving according to traditional gender roles. Those affected tend to be unemployed, or in unskilled, low-waged employment and cannot earn enough to keep themselves and their families out of poverty. The notion of applying value judgements about worth or desert can be a major element in conditionality that often leads to discretion in decision–making about entitlement. Conditionality introduces further requirements that claimants must meet in order to qualify, imposing pre-conditions in order to affect the recipient's behaviour. For example, claimants used to have to be 'available for work' but now have to be able to provide evidence of 'having actively sought work for 35 hours per week'. Contingency is discussed further in chapter 7.

In many ways, the terms 'targeting' (who has the right to receive?), 'selectivity' (how much are they entitled to?) and 'conditionality' (what external conditions will be imposed?) are matters of semantics. Each is merely a different way of discriminating between people, with different bases and slightly different intentions. The distinctions cannot be precise and some overlaps will occur. It raises the question of whether the distinctions are artificial rather than substantive, and, as such, whether it would be preferable to try to eliminate them.

A BI scheme is an income maintenance system that can be defined by its design features. It is based on the individual, is universal and not means-tested, is non-selective, except that different levels of BI according to age are generally accepted, and it is unconditional. Thus it removes all other, often artificial or unnecessary, distinctions between people.

Comparison of some different income maintenance systems

As stated above, the current Social Security system in the UK comprises a National Insurance system, a means-tested Social Assistance safety net, and a categorical disability benefits system. A BI would create a fourth system. Each of these income maintenance systems is based on an internal structure comprising the design features described above. This same internal structure can also be detected in the income tax system in the UK, which also has a unit of assessment, an eligibility criterion, and the tax rate is selective depending on the source of the income. The design features of these systems are summarised and compared in Table 3.1 below.

Contributory NI benefits are usually based on the individual adult. Eligibility is based on his or her contribution record, together with being unable to earn, for example, on account of maternity, invalidity, sickness, unemployment or old age. Eligibility is also time-limited for most contributory benefits. For unemployment benefits, selectivity is based on age, and the claimant would be expected to meet the kind of conditionality requirements outlined above.

Social Assistance benefits are among some of the most complex of all benefits. The primary unit for assessment is the couple, (married, in a civil partnership or otherwise cohabiting), followed by individual adults who are not part of such a couple. Eligibility is based on low incomes. A complex selectivity is imposed. It is selective, for instance, according to whether an adult lives alone or as half of a cohabiting couple or with another adult but not as part of a cohabiting couple. This is a major factor contributing to 'the cohabitation rule' in the UK. The main income-replacement MTBs used to be conditional on willingness to work, but latterly this has changed so that the claimant must demonstrate that s/he is 'actively seeking work'. The newly introduced, means-tested Universal Credit in the UK is a working-age benefit for people on low incomes,

Table 3.1
The internal structure of various income maintenance and income tax systems in the UK

	National Insurance	Social Assistance	Disability Benefits	Basic Income	Income Tax
Define population	working and contributing population	geographical and citizenship	geographical and citizenship	Citizenship – right to reside	geographical
Benefit/tax assessment unit	individual adult	a cohabiting couple, or an individual adult.	individual	individual	individual
Eligibility	contribution record, plus not able to work on account of: Maternity Invalidity Sickness Unemployment Retirement	targeted by means-test on those with low incomes	targeted by need	universal	targeted by means, ie taxable income
Benefits means-tested?	no	yes	no	no	No, except for higher-rate income tax payers whose partners receive Child Benefit.
Entitlement – selective?	yes; extra given for dependents, disability, housing costs, childcare costs	yes; extra for dependents. Couples penalised.	yes, by impairment or functionality	non-selective, except by age	yes, via different rates on interest and on dividends
Contingent?	not permitted to work while receiving benefits	yes, work tests		unconditional	yes, via tax loopholes

regardless of whether or not they are in employment. However, a range of selective criteria can apply including: age, whether the claimant is a couple or a singleton, the number of children, disability, childcare costs and housing costs (Miller, 2011).

Some current benefits, such as Carer's Allowance, do not fit into any of the above systems, but their design features (unit for assessment, eligibility, entitlement and contingency) can still be identified.

Basic Incomes

A BI is 'an unconditional, automatic and non-withdrawable payment to each individual as a right of citizenship... subject to a minimum period of legal residency in the UK, and continuing residence in the UK for most of the year' (Citizen's Income Trust, 2015: 3, 5). A BI is defined by its design features: it is based on the individual, is universal and not means-tested, is non-selective except by age, and is unconditional. A BI scheme is a program of tax-exempt cash transfer payments, and thus is a set of instruments rather than a program of policy objectives. It is a means to ends.

A BI can be described as full or partial. A full BI would be paid at a high enough level for a single adult to enjoy a dignified, if modest, standard of living, enabling participation in society. The terms 'full BI' and 'partial BI' can only be meaningful when used with reference to a reputable poverty benchmark, for example, the EU's official poverty benchmark of 0.6 of median equivalised household income (DWP, 2015) or other reputable poverty benchmarks such as Minimum Income Standards (Hirsch *et al*, 2014). A partial BI would need to be topped up by other income, usually earnings. (Sample schemes are developed in Part III.) A BI is designed as an individual benefit, but the primary caregiver would receive the Child BI to administer on behalf of a dependent child, as is the case for Child Benefit in the UK at present. A BI is similar to Child Benefit, but is for every one.

An early debate centred on whether the BIS should be need-based, or whether everyone would receive the same, ie a Social Dividend. One solution would be to distribute a Social Dividend that is sufficiently high to cover most people's basic needs.

Some claim that life is too complex to be serviced only by a simple BI scheme. This is certainly true, and a separate, but parallel system of needs-based, non-means-tested disability benefits must be retained or even enhanced, to enable disabled people to meet the extra costs that they incur due to their ill health or impairment. This is discussed more fully in chapter 6 below.

Similarly, successive governments' housing policies over the last four decades have led to enormous increases in house prices and rents all over the UK and to wide regional variations in housing costs. For people on low incomes, including many who are in employment, housing costs are met in part or in full through the system of Housing Benefits. The variations in costs and lack of affordable housing means that, at present, it is impossible to include an element for housing costs in a BI scheme, so a separate system for Housing Benefit must be retained. This is also discussed in chapter 6.

Also, both the supply side of childcare provision and its cost varies over the UK, which makes it unsuitable for provision via a BI system. In an ideal world, the most efficient method of providing adequate and convenient childcare services would be public provision, perhaps on the same model as in many Scandinavian countries. Childcare services staffed by highly-trained nursery staff are good for the child, the parents and the economy, and the case has been made for access to free childcare for parents on low incomes in Scotland. Alex Salmond himself wrote 'It was Ailsa [McKay] who convinced me that affordable and universal nursery provision was not just a good idea (which just about everyone supports) but one of the essential economic strategies for developed democracies' (Salmond, 2015: 177).

If a BI scheme were to be implemented in the UK, it is assumed that it would replace the main income-replacement means-tested benefits, most contributory benefits, the State Retirement Pension and Child Benefit. It would also be accompanied by the phasing out of some or all of the Personal Allowance and other tax reliefs and allowances in the income tax system. More generous schemes would require more comprehensive changes to the income tax system. A BI by itself could not redistribute much income from rich to poor. For that, a progressive income tax system is needed. A BI is not a panacea for all ills, and although not a sufficient condition, it is necessary for a better society. The more generous the BI levels, the greater the opportunity of fulfilling the objectives outlined in chapter 2 above.

Tables 3.2 and 3.3 summarise the main content of Part II of this book. As indicated above, each design feature of income maintenance schemes offers a variety of options that could be chosen. In the following chapters, each design feature is examined in turn to compare the effect of the Social Assistance choices currently in the UK, which can be identified as the cause of many current problems, with those of a BI scheme. This book indicates how the set of BI design features can help to fulfil the objectives outlined in chapter 2 above, how these may be challenged and gives the counter arguments. The options associated with each design feature lead to very different systems and societies, and ultimately, they are a matter of personal preference and political choice. These options are summarised in Table 3.2 'The structure of income maintenance systems'.

Table 3.3 'The structure of BI and objectives' expands Table 3.2. It repeats column 4, 'the design features of a BI scheme', and expands column 5 into the five objectives listed above in chapter 2. Table 3.3 summarises the analysis that will take place in the following four chapters, enabling the reader to map the relationships between instruments and objectives.

TABLE 3.2. THE STRUCTURE OF INCOME MAINTENANCE SYSTEMS

INSTRUMENTS OR FEATURES	CURRENT MTB SYSTEM	OUTCOME OF CURRENT SYSTEM	DEFINE BI SYSTEM	HELPS TO FULFILL OBJECTIVES	CHALLENGES & FAQs	ADDITIONAL SUPPORTING ARGUMENTS
UNIT for assessment & delivery of benefits	A couple – married, civil partnerships, or otherwise cohabiting, is the primary status – then individuals.	Poorer partners (mainly women) are excluded from social security in their own right. Adults in unequal power relationships – damaging & demeaning.	based on the INDIVIDUAL	Values all individuals for their own sakes. Grants financial autonomy & choices. This is a necessary condition for emancipation & empowerment of all adults.	Can lead to substantial household economies of scale (HES). Who would complain?	HES are lessened with Partial BI. Removes disincentives for parents of dependent children who want to stay together, and for other adults to share accommodation. This could reduce the demand for single-adult housing.
ELIGIBILITY	Targeted benefits, eg. on basis of need; merit, worth/desert, or means.	Divided society – segregates the most vulnerable people – easily stigmatised, humiliated and rejected – very painful. Low take-up of benefits.	UNIVERSAL based on citizenship; legal right to reside in the country, plus residency condition.	Helps to create a more united and inclusive society by reducing inequalities in income. Increases economic demand. Provides a safety net. Helps to reduce the incidence of financial poverty	Do rich people benefit more than the poorest? Why give it to rich people, who don't need it? How to define citizenship and the population?	Universal schemes such as the NHS are inclusive, popular and redistributive. It is more efficient (ie cheaper) to give it to everyone and claw back from the richest via a fairer income tax system.
	Targeting via means-testing benefits (MTBs)	Benefit tapers introduce inherent disincentives to work-for-pay, poverty traps; are very regressive	BASIC INCOME NOT MEANS-TESTED	Restores the incentive to work-for-pay; increases labour market efficiency and flexibility.	'Tax rates' reduce from 0.95 for some; increase from 0.32 for others.	Coupled with wage protection, people could earn their way out of poverty, if necessary.
ENTITLEMENT	Selective, on personal characteristics, often on frequently changing relationships & circumstances.	Discriminating, divides society; couples are penalised; receiving less each than a single-adult; leads to the intrusive and distasteful cohabitation rule; increases admin errors, fraud and costs.	NON-SELECTIVE, – except can be age-related.	Non-discriminating, less divisive, less intrusive. Simpler, more efficient administration reduces risk of error, and fraud, and reduces costs, – should lead to greater transparency and accountability.	Is there a case for selectivity – financially-vulnerable adults and families with children? Disabled people & unpaid carers.	Ends discrimination against couples. Ends the intrusive cohabitation rule. Retain the current disability benefits. (– not means-tested), in parallel with BIs, and provide new gateways, if necessary.
CONTINGENCY	Pre-conditions imposed, eg. availability for work, or demonstrating active search for work.	Restrictions on benefits Harsh conditionality, coercion and savage sanctions imposed Struggles of benefit claimants. No financial security for poorest. Increases risk of administration errors, fraud and costs.	UNCOND-ITIONAL	Gives more choice and flexibility. Reduces inequality of power relationships, – increases industrial democracy. Gives unconditional right not to be destitute; contributes to financial security. Reduces administration errors, fraud and costs. Entrepreneurship.	Why give 'something for nothing'? Reciprocity & Participation Income? What if some people give up working? A subsidy for employers? Free-riders – minimal consumers?	Giving nothing shortens lives. A BI entitles people to necessities. Labour market effects could be mixed – redistribution between paid and unpaid work? Wage rates will adjust. Most people want to work-for-pay, for social & health advantages. Trust people. Index BIs. Tolerate the few free riders.

TABLE 3.3. HOW THE STRUCTURE OF A BASIC INCOME (BI) SCHEME HELPS TO FULFIL THE OBJECTIVES

DEFINE THE BI SYSTEM	Value each individual for his/her own sake; more life choices for adults.	Prevent income poverty; provide financial security; Increase wellbeing.	Reduce income inequality. United, just and inclusive society.	Labour market efficiency & flexibility; sustainable economic growth.	Simplify administration.
based on the **INDIVIDUAL**	Grants financial privacy, autonomy & choices to all adults. It is a necessary condition for emancipation & empowerment.	Would give former 'financial dependents' access to Social Security in their own right, for the first time.	No more financially dependent adults – except where decided legally by a Court.	Household economies of scale provide incentives for adults to share housing, and reduce demand for single person housing.	Simpler administration, but more tax/benefit units to assess. Less intrusive.
UNIVERSAL based on citizenship; legal right to reside in the country, plus residency condition.	Also a necessary condition for emancipation of adults.	Ends stigma and low take-up. All adults eligible for the first time. Necessary condition for a safety net. Helps to reduce the incidence of financial poverty.	Ends discrimination, stigma and division. More inclusive society.	Increases economic demand. Reduction of stress improves health of former claimants & low-paid workers – reduces cost of NHS, personal social services, etc.	It is more efficient (cheaper) to give a BI to all and to assess every person once only pa for a fairer income tax, so that rich people do not profit overall. More units.
BASIC INCOME NOT MEANS-TESTED, but M-T Housing Benefit retained.		Coupled with wage protection, people can earn their way out of poverty, if necessary.	Benefit tapers no longer make the effective income tax system more regressive.	Reduction in marginal deduction rates restores incentives to work-for-pay. Wage rates adjust. Increases labour market efficiency.	Reduces administration.
NON-SELECTIVE, except can be age-related.	Couples no longer discriminated against. Helps to end the cohabitation rule.		Non-discriminating, less divisive. Ends division into deserving and undeserving poor.		Simpler, more efficient administration reduces risk of error and fraud, and reduces costs – should lead to greater transparency/accountability.
UNCOND-ITIONAL	Also a necessary condition for empowerment of adults. Reduces inequality of power relationships – able to negotiate fairer relationships. Gives more choices – re paid and unpaid work, re work-life balance, re household formation.	Creates a safety net. Gives unconditional right not to be destitute. Necessary for financial security. Reduces depth of poverty, and could prevent it, depending on size of the BI. Reduces current time-consuming effort to apply for benefits.	Also ends division into deserving and undeserving poor. Redistribution between paid and unpaid work. Trusts citizens to make their own contributions to society. Quality of life. Supports life-long learning and creative enterprise.	Reduces inequality of power relationship – increases industrial democracy; financial security gives choices – enables workers to negotiate for fair pay and good working conditions. Labour market flexibility for workers. Entrepreneurship.	Decouples income from paid work. No difference between in-work and out-of-work benefits. Reduces risk of administrative and compliance errors by staff or recipient, and fraud. Reduces costs.
FINANCED BY A RESTRUCTURED INCOME TAX SYSTEM		The higher the income tax rates, the greater the BI, and the greater its impact.	Fairer tax reduces income inequalities and helps to create a more unite and inclusive society.	MDR could decrease for many, but increase for others, who could still be better off due to their BIs.	Will require an increased rate of income tax on those with a higher income, to claw back the BI.

CHAPTER 4

The effects of individual assessment on women's lives: the unit for assessment and delivery of benefits – joint or individual?

The Marriage Laws

HELENA KENNEDY, the well-known barrister and broadcaster, wrote 'until the late 19th century, under the Common Law a husband and wife were treated as one person and marriage meant the surrender of separate legal rights for a woman. From this unity of husband and wife sprang all the disabilities of the married woman.' (Kennedy, 1993: 25). Indeed, many of these disabilities survive to this day. It was only as recently as 1990–91 that married women in the UK became entitled to independent taxation of their incomes and chargeable gains under the Finance Act 1988 (Howe, 1980), (HMRC, 2015).

The marriage law, rather than being a contract between the partners, as many assume, is a contract between the state and the couple. The partners agree to aliment each other (literally 'to feed' or to maintain each other) or more generally, to ensure that the poorer partner is maintained to a standard commensurate with the standing of the wealthier partner. This ensures that the poorer partner is not a burden on the state. This is a legacy from the time when a wife was one of a man's chattels, and it was intended to ensure that a wealthy man's legacy was passed only to his own legitimate offspring. However, it effectively puts the right to state benefits out of her reach, except with the participation of her husband. At the same time, she is not legally entitled to any of her husband's income, nor is she even legally entitled to any savings out of money that he gives her for housekeeping. A married woman can have no recourse to an independent income from the state except by termination of the marriage by divorce or widowhood (Thomson, 2002: 47). Separation was often logistically impossible for herself and her children.

The marriage law obviously applies only to married couples, but it was felt (possibly originating from religious bodies) that (undeserving) unmarried couples should not profit through individual assessment for Social Security more than (deserving) married ones through joint assessment. Thus unmarried couples too were subject to this rule, rather than correcting the outdated situation being propagated by the marriage laws. When the Child Benefit Bill 1975 was being debated in Parliament in the 1970s, it was acknowledged that a husband might not provide his wife with enough resources to feed their children, and so purse prevailed over wallet. The default situation since then has been that Child Benefit is paid to the mother as a cash payment, rather than as a tax relief to the father. It was never similarly recognised and acknowledged that he also might not provide his wife with enough resources to maintain herself adequately.

As indicated in chapter 1, under the current SA system in the UK, all couples – married, in a civil partnership or otherwise cohabiting – have to make joint applications for benefits, but not other adults sharing accommodation, such as two siblings, a parent with an adult offspring, or a householder with a lodger, all of whom are entitled to individual assessment. The differential treatment for cohabiting couples again derives from the marriage laws. In effect, the result of this is that most married or cohabiting women with no source of personal income are expected to be financially dependent on their husbands or partners. This is not a gendered provision, because it could also apply to a male partner, but it is gendered in its effect, since the people who are most likely to be affected in this way are women, often caring for children or elders.

Financial dependents

Women are much more likely to work-for-pay today than in the past and many first-time mothers, in the time after their maternity benefits come to an end and before they return to work, may be shocked to find themselves in the unwelcome, novel situation where they have become financial dependents on a partner. They are not entitled to any social assistance in their own right, (except for Child Benefit to administer on behalf of the child), nor are they legally entitled to any of their spouse's or partner's income. This may be repeated with every birth. With just over 55,000 births in Scotland in 2015 (National Records of Scotland, 2016: BT.1), a large number of women may be subject to this experience at any one time. In the current system, adult offspring who live with their parents are entitled to apply for benefits on their own account, while each financially dependent parent is not so entitled. Surely, in a developed society in the

21st century, the status of 'financial dependent' for an adult should be an anachronism?

In contrast, financial dependence would be consigned to history under a BI scheme which would entitle every man, woman and child to a cash payment in his or her own right. Those adults, mainly women, who would otherwise have been financial dependents, could become emancipated. However, the tax/benefit unit for assessment and delivery being based on the individual is a necessary, but not sufficient, condition for full empowerment, which also requires universality and unconditionality. But it could help them to negotiate a better relationship within the household and a fairer sharing of caring responsibilities and domestic tasks, making a difficult situation more tolerable. In this way, the tax/benefit unit being based on the individual could also lead to fewer relationship breakdowns.

The change of the assessment and delivery unit for benefits from cohabiting couple to individual will probably give direct help to more women than men. Yet some feminists reject the idea of a BI scheme. The feminist movement is not a homogeneous body and at least two wings can be discerned. Some women are fighting for women's emancipation and equal rights in the labour market – for the right of women to adopt men's life-styles. Other women are fighting for the rights for women who are not in the labour market, who would like to give men the opportunity to adopt their life-styles. The women's emancipation wing regards a BI scheme as forcing women back into traditional roles in the home. However, it gives women more choices over their lifestyles and work-life balance, including not being forced to work in unsatisfying drudge jobs at minimal wage rates. The answer is not to reject a BI scheme, but to ensure that more women receive a better education and training, and can therefore command better wages in the workplace.

In a recent basic income pilot project in India, it was ensured that everyone in the pilot communities had his or her own bank account into which the BI could be paid, and women's status was reported to be enhanced by their new financial independence (Davala *et al*, 2015). It follows that a BI would be paid only into a single person account, rather than joint accounts, unless authorised by a court order, for instance where a *curator bonis* was appointed. Individuals could subsequently pool some or all of their BI with a partner if they wish, but it is not up to the state to do this for them.

Household Economies of Scale – incentive to share accommodation

As a… firm produces more [units], the average cost of production per [unit] varies. Increasing production from low levels, the average cost per unit will fall – a phenomenon known as economies of scale

KISHTAINY, 2014: 152

Hirsch (2015) has criticised BI schemes because individual assessment means that couples will receive twice as much as a singleton, when they could manage on less than that. In other words, a couple would receive more than they need, and would be able to take advantage of household economies of scale (HES).

Under the current Social Assistance system in the UK, married and other cohabiting couples are discriminated against, getting less between them than twice what a singleton receives. Thus, all the advantages that they might have gained from HES are removed. However, HES are tolerated where other adults share accommodation, such as, again, two siblings, a parent with an adult offspring, or a householder with a lodger, none of whom is penalised in this way.

This results from a combination of the primary unit of assessment and delivery being the couple, and selectivity based on a less favourable entitlement for each partner of a couple. This is explored further in chapter 6. The current UK system could be driving apart claimant couples with financial problems, because they can receive more between them apart than together. Thus, changing this situation could also lead to less financial stress, resulting in fewer relationship break-ups.

The BI would be the same for people in the same age group, resulting in HES for couples. However, HES could provide an incentive for adults to share accommodation, both for two individuals to form a household together, or, for example, enabling those parents who wish to do so to afford to stay together with their dependent children. The financial disincentive effects of assessment based on the couple can affect household formation (Torry, 2013: 102–3). Building more housing, especially affordable social housing, is a longer-term solution to the housing problem, but HES could help to reduce the current demand for single-person housing in the short term.

The Social Assistance system provides a ceiling for the benefit system based on the principle that no-one should get more than they need, even if some do not receive enough. A BI scheme provides a floor on the principle that it is important that everyone gets sufficient to meet basic needs, even if it means that some could receive more than enough, for instance, through HES.

Ultimately, the choice is between, on the one hand, joint assessment, thus maintaining the status of 'financial dependent', which affects more women than men, together with discrimination against the partners in a couple in order to avoid HES. On the other hand, individual assessment for all, whether single, married or otherwise cohabiting, contributes to greater financial independence, and, with the same level of BI for all in the same age group, leads to HES for those in shared accommodation, who would be able to manage financially more easily compared with a singleton. Most people who are currently financial dependents would be better off financially under the latter system, as would all cohabiting couples. A method that can ameliorate HES (again via selectivity) is discussed in chapter 14.

Effect of BI on women's lives

The unit being the individual rather than the couple would probably affect more women than men, and arguably this is the single change that would have the most profound effect on women. This may sound as though a BI scheme favours women. In fact it is just remedying the effects of the current social security system, which in so many ways ignore women's needs.

Women are at a disadvantage in many ways in the UK, including:

- The responsibility for child and elder care falls mainly on women.
- The primary care-giving parent is discriminated against in the labour market.
- Women tend to be encouraged to go into gendered types of employment that are often part-time, low-paid and insecure.
- The gender pay gap persists, in spite of the Equal Pay Act 1970, and the Equality Act 2010
- Both NI benefits and means-tested Social Assistance benefits are designed to meet the needs of men's working lives.
- Women have less opportunity to contribute to pensions and more women than men suffer poverty in old age.

Gillespie shows that women have been particularly disadvantaged: by public spending cuts in terms of job losses in the public sector where women predominate; their greater likelihood of being underemployed and in insecure forms of work; and their greater use of public services (Gillespie, 2016: 193).

Universality and unconditionality are also likely to have a profound effect on people's lives, enabling emancipation and empowerment. Arguably this also will be greater for women than for men. The prevention or reduction in poverty, and the reduction in income inequality, leading to the creation of a united and inclusive society, could also transform women's lives.

INDIA 2011–13

The outcomes of some BI pilot studies in India in 2011–13 are particularly heart-warming, and illustrate the extra beneficial emancipatory effects of the scheme for women.

In spite of thousands of anti-poverty schemes having been launched across India over the years, poverty and deprivation are still visible everywhere. One of these schemes is the Public Distribution System that provides subsidised food, (wheat, rice, sugar – and kerosene). The inefficiency of this system leads to immense material wastage and financial leakage, and prevents the intended beneficiaries from receiving their entitlements (Davala et al, 2015: 4). However, the Delhi government decided in 2010 to take a new approach and

> ... appointed the Self-Employed Women's Association (SEWA) and the Indian Development Foundation to conduct a pilot study into cash transfers as a possible alternative to the Public Distribution System (PDS). The pilot, which began in January 2011, will run for one year in West Delhi's Raghubir Nagar Slum

SHRINIVASAN, 2012: 7

The project was funded by the United Nations Development Programme.

Two other pilot studies were set up in Indore District in Madhya Pradesh, (one of India's most under-developed regions), with financial help from the United Nations Children's Emergency Fund, UNICEF. The larger one started in June 2011 and ran until May 2012, and was then extended for a further six months. A sample was drawn up of 50 villages, with about 100 households in each, from which eight villages were selected for receipt of the cash transfers, and a further 12 villages acted as controls.

The main activity was farm labouring. SEWA was already operative in half of the villages. All the men, women and children listed as usually resident in the household, ie usually sleeping there for at least four nights a week, were eligible. Those who were already listed as resident at the beginning could form independent households within their village and remain in the sample. Newly married women and new babies could be added to the sample, but no others. This led to a total sample of 5,547 individuals who were eligible for the cash transfer in 938 households. There were another 1,096 households in the control villages, and altogether 11,231 individuals were involved in both pilot and control samples.

A basic income of 200 rupees per adult per month and 100 rupees per child was paid for the first 12 months, after which it was adjusted for inflation and increased by 50 per cent for the last six months. For the 30 per cent of the population whose income was below the poverty line, this represented about 30 per cent of their expenditure – on bare subsistence. For the 20 per cent whose income was above the poverty line, but who were still regarded as vulnerable, the BI represented less than 20 per cent of average income. The basic incomes replaced the food and fuel subsidies. Members of SEWA helped women to open bank accounts in the SEWA villages. A cash transfer team helped the other villagers to open their bank accounts.

A baseline survey or census was carried out in all 20 villages before the start of the pilot study, together with a Community Survey. An Interim Evaluation Survey was conducted half way through the pilot, and a Final Evaluation Survey and another Community Survey carried out at the end. A Post-Final Evaluation was made some months after the end of the pilot. The survey data was supported by 100 case studies of families, and specialist information was collected from designated key informants (Davala *et al*, 2015: 40).

The smaller of the two pilot studies in Madhya Pradesh involved one tribal village of 127 households with 756 residents, and one similar control village of 97 households with 817 inhabitants. The pilot lasted from February 2012 to January 2013. Adults received Rs 300 per month each, and children Rs 150 each, paid to the mother. The average amount received per household was Rs 1,276 per month. A similar set of surveys was carried out as for the larger project.

The results were very positive. The outcomes fell into three areas – an emancipatory effect, improvement in well being, and an increase in productivity. The cash transfer payments had an emancipatory effect on many who had a low status in their communities, even apart from the caste system. Women were the immediately obvious examples in a society where the women were second-class citizens with no citizenship rights (even in high caste households), with no identity, and no empowerment. Their first problem was to establish that they existed, in order to open a bank account. This could take several weeks, but SEWA helped in the SEWA villages. The individualisation of the BI meant that for the first time women had some control over their lives and influence in the household. Both men and women agreed that women had been major beneficiaries of the advantages offered by the cash transfers. BI was emancipatory for two other groups – disabled people and the elderly, who tended to be marginalised within their households when food and money were tight. Both groups benefitted from better nutrition and easier access to healthcare services. Another example of the emancipatory nature of BIS occurred when it helped some families, who, by pooling their BIS, were able to buy a family member out of bonded labour.

Well-being covers such matters as living conditions, nutrition, health and education. It was found that some of the cash transfers were used by the villagers to improve their living standards by pooling them to install a latrine in their dwelling, which had a knock-on effect on the health of its members. A second improvement was that of many households installing a tube well for irrigation, or having a private tap or pump in the house for drinking water, the effects of which would continue after the end of the project. Another improvement came from the increased use of electricity for cooking and lighting, and others were able to make repairs to their dwellings, while a few built new ones. Some households bought useful assets such as furniture, or items of transport such as bicycles, scooters or motorbikes, or mobile phones, an electric fan, a TV, or changed to using modern methods of protection against mosquitos.

Improvements in nutrition came about by people being able to widen their diets to include fresh vegetables and fruit, milk, eggs and fish: 'the establishment of a fishing cooperative in the tribal village led to a transformation of the diet of the villagers' (Davala, 2015: 96). Some of the improved nutrition was directly due to their being able to buy food with cash rather than credit and thus avoid the high interest rates. Others were able to buy in bulk and avoid the time and transport costs of frequent trips to the market. It had a substantial effect on children, in that height-for-age and weight-for-age distributions increased towards the standards recommended by the World Health Organisation, and this improvement was even more marked for girls than for boys.

The health effects that were observed 'may be four-fold. First, basic income may improve resilience to sickness... Second, it may improve preparedness, the ability to respond in a timely manner to an illness or accident... Third, there may be a reduction of debt incurred to fund medical expenses... Fourth... is that besides the effect of cash or income in itself there is a powerful positive effect of income security' (Davala *et al*, 2015: 99–100). One outcome was the preference of the villagers to use private healthcare services rather than public health facilities, but this was mainly on account of the poor quality of the services provided by the latter.

Basic incomes also had a significant effect on education: 'it may enable some families to spend on essential or useful items that enable their children to go to school more easily or cheaply. It may facilitate better eating habits... giving children more energy and health, and thus making it more likely they will go to school and be able to learn properly while there' (Davala *et al*, 2015: 115). It might also enable families to send their children to a better school, or to pay for private tuition outside school. It could also release the children from working on their family farm or from other paid labour. Basic incomes were associated with increased enrolment, attendance and performance at school, and more school-related spending, on uniforms, shoes, tuition fees, books and transport to school: 'a particularly encouraging sign was that expenditure on schooling for girls was decidedly higher among households receiving the basic income. This effect was even greater among those in SEWA villages, where spending on girls' schooling increased by over 100 per cent...' (Davala *et al*, 2015: 119).

Basic incomes were also found to have a positive effect on work, productivity and growth 'in and around agriculture and small-scale production of basic goods and services' (Davala *et al*, 2015: 137). It reduced child labour both in waged work and on the farm, in favour of education.

Time spent on labour can be divided into its components: caring for children and others, 'housework', own-account work for oneself or for family, non-farming income-earning activity, and labour for wages or some non-monetary payment. Participants in the pilot studies often had a main and a second labour activity, the two sources of income together giving greater protection. The BI often enabled that dual activity to occur, especially for women. There was also a shift to own-account work from the casual wage labour that had involved competing for limited opportunities. This enabled them to strengthen their bargaining power in the market for wage labour. Women were the primary beneficiaries of growth in secondary economic activities. The individualised cash transfer led to independent work opportunities. Several groups of women pooled their

BIS to buy sewing machines to make clothes for their families and for others.

The cash transfer enabled the villagers to farm their land more intensively. They bought assets: small or large livestock, seeds, fertiliser, pesticides, tools and equipment, tube wells and electric pumps for irrigation, the effect of which would continue after the end of the pilot. In the tribal village, a cooperative fish farm was set up, which helped to improve their own and others' diets. Together with their improved nutrition and health, the BI provided a safety valve. The steady predictable income reduced the adverse shock of temporary unemployment, and people were less likely to default on debt payments. This also had an emancipatory effect, as the villagers had greater control over their lives. The economic value of the positive effects exceeded the value of the transfer.

The pilot project was such a success that several political parties wanted to get in on the act before the election in 2014. In their haste, they were intending to reduce the subsidies before the infrastructure of individualised bank accounts had been set up, and the people were able to receive their transfers, which would have been absolutely disastrous (Standing, 2013). 'In 2014, the Indian population elected a new government, the first with an absolute majority of seats for 30 years... Reforms should start soon and be what is called 'evidence-based'. All the old policies seem set for review' (Davala *et al*, 2015:196).

The three areas into which the outcomes fell – an emancipatory effect, improvement in wellbeing, and an increase in productivity – are precisely three of the objectives identified in chapter 2 to which an income maintenance system, such as a BI scheme, can contribute. The same broad outcomes can be expected from BI pilot schemes in Scotland or the UK.

CHAPTER 5

Migration – and giving a BI to rich people

Defining the population

ALTHOUGH IT IS claimed that universality is a defining feature of a BI scheme, it cannot exist in reality. Atkinson (2015: 221) argues that 'A universal income is... a chimera. Any actual scheme would involve a condition of eligibility and hence the risk of exclusion'. The population must be defined, and eligibility criteria are required. These are likely to be based on a combination of geographical area and legal, including citizenship, rights, so that recipients can be identified. This will inevitably exclude some people and needs to be addressed, whatever income maintenance system is adopted.

Torry points out that 'citizenship' is a multifaceted concept, involving civil, political, social and economic rights and duties, and involving rights and duties in relation to cultural, local, national, regional and global levels' (Torry, 2013: 209). For BI purposes, it should be defined in an inclusive way.

The Citizen's Income Trust (CIT) (2015: 5) states '*citizenship becomes the basis of entitlement,* subject to a minimum period of legal residency in the UK, and continuing residence in the UK for most of the year' (italics in original). CIT's definition of citizenship is based on the legal right to permanent residence in the UK.

Thus, a BI scheme in a country could be paid as a right of citizenship, for those:

- With the legal right to permanent residence in the country; and
- Who have fulfilled a minimum period of *continuous* legal residency in the country prior to the commencement of payment; and
- Who maintain a continuing physical presence in the country for most of each subsequent year, while in receipt of the BI.

It soon becomes clear that the design and administration of a universal BI scheme could be more problematic than at first thought. This is discussed in more detail in chapter 8.

Criteria would also be needed to address specific residence situations to stipulate the conditions in which the following four groups of people are included:

- People who have the legal right to permanent residence in the UK, but who have relocated abroad, and so have not exercised that right for certain periods in their lives;
- Migrants to the UK from parts of the EU, depending on the UK's relationship with the EU;
- Asylum seekers who seek refugee status on account of persecution, war or natural disasters in their own countries; and
- Other migrants who do not fall within any of the above categories.

There are many people around the world with the legal right to permanent residence in the UK who choose not live in this country. UK citizens who spend their working lives abroad and then retire here would have to fulfil the minimum period of residency requirements described above. Would UK citizens who spend their working lives here and wish to retire abroad be eligible? Obviously, NI pension rights should be honoured, as now.

Then, how should residents based in the UK whose work takes them abroad for much of the year, or on one- or two-year contracts for instance, be treated? Should it be based on whether they pay taxes in the UK, – on all of their income, or just income arising in the UK? Should UK students studying abroad be eligible? Should there be special provisions for students wishing to take a gap-year?

If residence is to be the basis of entitlement, how will homeless people and travellers be included? Prisoners should be eligible, but some of their BIS may have to be put towards their subsistence, and some for pocket money. Maybe some could be set aside so that there would be a small nest egg to help them to get back on their feet when they are discharged, and thus reduce the risk of recidivism.

Currently (in 2017), the UK has agreements with the other 27 countries in the EU that deal with migration within the EU, but these are likely to change as a result of the 'Brexit' negotiations following the Referendum on the EU on 23 June 2016. The agreements lay out the UK's responsibilities to immigrants from the other countries and their responsibilities to UK citizens residing in their country. Atkinson (2015: 220) points out that:

> One country cannot exclude the citizens of other EU member states that come to that country to work. According to Article 45 of the Treaty on

the functioning of the European Union, such persons should enjoy 'equal treatment with nationals in access to employment, working conditions and all other social and tax advantages.

If the EU Referendum result was mainly about the UK public wanting to give the Establishment a bloody nose for enriching themselves while impoverishing many, one might wonder whether its outcome might have been different if a good BI scheme had already been implemented?

The third group to consider is that of asylum seekers from outwith the EU, who are escaping from countries where they may have experienced persecution or conflict. Many migrants have escaped from war-torn countries, into the affairs of which the UK has involved itself in recent decades, notably Afghanistan, Iraq and Libya. Many others in Syria and elsewhere believed that the UK would support those who rose up against their governments in the name of democracy during the 'Arab Spring' in 2011. Currently, asylum seekers in the UK receive little help from the state, and some are left destitute, but may receive support from charities. They are not allowed to work, and they can be left in limbo for many months while their cases are being examined, due to inadequate resources for the task, leading to the build-up of a backlog of cases. A case can be made for treating asylum seekers more humanely, by granting a BI on registration on compassionate grounds and speeding up the process of assessing the claim for refugee status. The BI would only be withdrawn a few weeks after his or her application or appeal has been rejected, when she/he is required to depart (Refugee Council, 2016).

Migration

The fourth group is that of economic migrants. How does one distinguish between the anguish of an asylum seeker and an economic migrant who may be trying to avoid poverty and hunger in their own country, which can be equally threatening to life? What compassionate rights, if any, should such illegal migrants have in the host country that would not encourage an overwhelming tide? There are others who are better qualified than I am to give answers.

The UK attracts fewer migrants per head of population than Germany or Sweden, where wage rates are higher and working conditions are better than in the UK. Even though the UK benefit system is less generous than those of many other European countries, the UK still remains attractive for several reasons. Firstly, English is more common as a second language than many continental European languages, especially for migrants from

Commonwealth countries. Secondly, our Social Assistance system is not contribution-based, so, in theory, migrants would not have to wait to build up eligibility. Lastly, UK citizens do not currently have to carry identity papers with them at all times, as in many continental European countries.

The surge in migrants into Europe in 2015 and 2016, especially from Afghanistan, Pakistan, Iraq, Syria and Libya, gives us pause to consider migration from a worldwide perspective, not just a UK one.

- Highly-skilled migrants (doctors, nurses, etc) can fill in gaps in the host country's skill base, giving great benefit to the host country, but can create an expensive brain drain for the country of origin.

- Evidence indicates that immigrants have contributed more to the UK economy than they have gained in benefits (Travis, 2014).

- Growth in the UK economy tends to benefit the wealthier part of society

- Low-skilled and unskilled migrants will often take on low-paid, more unpleasant work that the local people eschew, (or which the disincentives inherent in the host MTB system discourage locals from undertaking).

- The presence of low-skilled workers can have the knock-on effect of keeping unemployment high and thus wage-rates low.

- Migrants can find themselves in competition with the poorer local residents for lower paid work and for services such as housing, health and education.

- The main factor influencing the rate of migration in the world for economic reasons is the differential between wage-rates in the destination and source countries.

Reluctant migrants, who feel compelled by circumstances to emigrate, would prefer to stay in their own home countries to build up their economies if opportunities allowed. This could also help to prevent the brain drain of expensively trained personnel from poorer countries to more developed ones. A well-administered international BI system, that delivered a BI to each individual, with no opportunity for corruption, might help to redistribute incomes from richer to poorer countries and create a more optimistic environment in the latter. A hypothetical example is illustrated in Appendix B. Further, if a migrant, who wished to move from one BI domain to another, were to be eligible only for the lesser BI of the two domains, this might discourage mass migration in the future.

Giving a BI to rich people to protect the poor: Eligibility – targeted or universal?

Eligibility defines *who* should receive a benefit. The whole population must be defined, whether a system is based on universal or targeted benefits. Universality in this context includes everyone in the defined population. Targeting excludes some members of the defined population from eligibility. Eligibility for current Social Assistance benefits in the UK is targeted on people with low incomes.

Targeting within the UK social security system divides the country into those who receive means-tested Social Assistance benefits and those who do not. Sometimes this is interpreted as a division of the population into those who only receive from the welfare state and those who only contribute to it. Recent work reveals that most of the population in the UK has benefited from the welfare state, (health, education, and benefits or tax breaks), and so this distinction is not valid (Hills, 2014).

People on low incomes in the UK can apply for means-tested benefits. At one time, Social Assistance claimants were divided into deserving and undeserving poor. Now the media and government ministers seem to insist on castigating/demonising *all* low-income claimants unfairly as being 'skivers', 'scroungers' and 'spongers', for which there is no evidence (Bamberg *et al*, 2013).

Universality means that everyone is included, and by avoiding the division created by targeting, it could lead to a more united, inclusive and harmonious society. If those who were formerly excluded from any state benefits were to be included, then it could help to reduce the *incidence* of income poverty, depending on the generosity of the BI. This is especially important for working-age adults for whom there is no universal provision at the moment.

Child Benefit (CB) is the closest to a universal benefit that has been implemented in the UK so far, but technically it is targeted by age, or by being a full-time school pupil, and is selective by position in the family. Although there were proposals to remove CB from those families where one partner is taxed at the higher rate of income tax, it remains intact. This is fair, because the CB could be the only source of income to which this partner has access. Meanwhile the high-earning partner is taxed on income at a rate of 50 per cent until the equivalent amount of CB has been withdrawn.

A potential criticism of BI is that its universality includes rich people, who do not need it, and may even appear to benefit more from it than poor people. This claim is also made about free bus passes for the elderly. So why give a BI to rich people, who don't need it?

There are three good reasons. Systems designed only for poor people are divisive and create the potential for recipients to be segregated, labelled as undeserving and for their entitlements to be eroded over time. Benefits claimants feel this humiliation and rejection by their peers even more painfully than the problem of living on below poverty-level benefits. The stigma leads to low take-up of the benefits to which many financially vulnerable people are entitled (Bamberg *et al*, 2013). In other words, targeting benefits only on the poorest does not protect them but, rather, increases their vulnerability. A case can be made for a universal system, from which everyone can benefit, because not only will rich people protect it for their own sakes, but it will also protect poor people more effectively (Danson *et al*, 2012).

Secondly, a universal system that gives the same amount of BI to both rich and poor is redistributive in the sense that it has a greater positive impact on the lives of the poorest than on the richest.

Thirdly, it is much more efficient (and therefore cheaper) to give a BI to everyone, and to assess individuals for their means once only each year for income tax purposes. Building progressivity into the income tax system could ensure that the wealthy are no better off as a result of the introduction of a BI scheme. Other universal systems, such as the NHS in the UK, are inclusive, popular and redistributive.

Those who argue against giving a BI to rich people, might like to consider whether the wealthy should be means-tested for NHS services, which effectively implies that everyone would have to be means-tested, and where should such a threshold start? Similarly, if being consistent, they would have to agree that the enormous subsidies for the wealthy through tax allowances, reliefs and exemptions are insupportable.

Eligibility offers a choice between: targeting, which can clearly be seen as divisive and can be stigmatising, leading to low take-up of MTBs; and universality, which can help to create a more united and inclusive society, and helps to reduce the *incidence* of income poverty. A reduction in the *depth* of income poverty will require the levels of the BIs to be greater than the real value of the out-of-work Social Assistance benefits that they replace.

Why benefits should not be means-tested

Means-testing of benefits in the UK is based on a combination of targeting and selectivity. Recipients are targeted according to low incomes, and selectivity occurs because entitlement decreases inversely with income. All MTBs embody an inherent disincentive to work-for-pay. When unemployed or low-paid workers in the UK try to earn their way out of poverty, not only do they face deductions of income tax and employees' National Insurance Contributions (NICs) from their earnings, but the tapers (withdrawal rates) of their various MTBs are aggregated and also deducted.

This creates a Marginal Deduction Rate that acts like a tax rate and it can be nearly 96 per cent (DWP, 2010: 8, para 14). The high Marginal Deduction Rates facing most low-income people as a result of the withdrawal of MTBs are much higher than those facing high income taxpayers, whose Marginal Deduction Rates are only 42 per cent or 47 per cent at most. These resultant effective tax rates are very regressive. A worker on the National Living Wage (NLW) of £7.50 per hour in 2017–18 could have been working for as little as 30p per hour once all the deductions had been made. However, not all claimants face these highest Marginal Deduction Rates. It depends on which combination of means-tested benefits they are claiming.

The high Marginal Deduction Rates inherent in MTBs have a disproportionate effect in depressing the net incomes of low- and middle-income families, who would be the obvious beneficiaries from the replacement of MTBs by a BI. Unemployed workers contemplating a return to the workplace in low-paid jobs also face this problem. Those not in the workplace would not necessarily benefit from the implementation of a BI scheme unless the amount of the BI was greater than the real value of their current benefit levels. Coupled with the erosion of the National Minimum Wage in real terms over time, it is now more difficult, though not impossible, for low-paid workers to earn their way out of poverty in the UK.

The introduction of means-tested Universal Credit (UC), the new unified working-age benefit, reduced the Marginal Deduction Rate to 65 per cent for those with incomes less than the Personal Allowance, and 76 per cent for those with incomes above it, but it still creates very regressive effective tax rates (Miller, 2011). Entitlement to Basic Income will not be means-tested, either on the income or wealth of the recipient, or on that of another family or household member.

To summarise, means-tested benefits targeted towards people on low income create an inherent disincentive to work-for-pay. They depress the net pay of low-paid workers, and make it almost impossible for unemployed and low-waged claimants to earn their way out of poverty. MTBs effectively create a highly regressive income tax system. Benefits that are not means-tested restore the incentive to work-for-pay provided by the gross wage rates, even for individuals on low earnings. It increases labour market efficiency and avoids introducing regressive tendencies into the income tax system.

ALASKA 1976 –

Alaska provides an example of a BI scheme that has survived for more than three decades. It is a genuine BI, being based on the individual, is universal for all who have resided for at least one year in Alaska, gives the same to everyone and is unconditional. It differs in two ways from proposals for the UK. First of all, the BIS are small in amount and are not intended as a social security system. Second, they are financed out of oil revenues accumulated over the past 40 years.

In 1955, Alaska called a constitutional convention in advance of statehood, which led to the proclamation that all of the natural resources of Alaska belong to the state for the benefit of the people. Oil was then discovered in 1967 on its northern shore near Prudhoe Bay. The Alaska Permanent Fund (APF) was set up in 1976, due in large part to the single-minded determination of Jay Hammond, governor from 1974–82 (Hammond, 1994). At least 25 per cent of each year's oil *royalties* would be dedicated to the new APF. Hammond had hoped that at least 50 per cent of *all* oil revenues would be dedicated, which would have been four times larger than was finally agreed. The APF was set up as a fund of income-producing investments, but there was no mention of how it would be used.

The Dividend Bill was passed in 1982, again due to Hammond's persistence. David Rose became the first executive director (1982–92) of the APF Corporation, the body created in 1980 to manage the fund and dividend. His goal was to follow the 'prudent investor rule', which set a precedent for it (Rose *et al*, 2008). 'These two books together lay out the long series of events between 1955 to 1992 that led to the APF being established in the Alaskan state constitution; the PFD [Permanent Fund Dividend] being established by law; the prudent investor rule being established by law and precedent; and all being protected by public opinion' (Widerquist, 2011: 10). Widerquist speculates on the outcome, had Governor Hammond had his way, and thus four times the amounts would have been dedicated to the APF. The best-case scenario could have led to a $400 billion fund in 2010. 'Suppose the state was able to withdraw five per cent each year, using half of it for dividends and half for the state's operating budget. That would produce a dividend of $15,000 per person a year and $10 billion for the state budget' (Widerquist, 2011: 11).

The Alaska Dividend continues to be extremely popular. It 'distributes a yearly dividend to every man, woman and child in Alaska without any conditions whatsoever. It has helped Alaska maintain one of the lowest poverty rates in the United States. It has helped Alaska become the most economically equal of all 50 states. And it has helped Alaska become the only US state in which equality has risen rather than fallen over the past 20 years. Certainly Alaska is doing something right' (Widerquist, 2010: 13). The annual dividend has varied between US$1,000 and US$2,000 depending on the international financial markets.

Widerquist continues with a discussion about sovereign wealth funds based on community control over community-owned resources, the income stream of which is invested in international shares. He writes convincingly about the advantages of such funds and how to go about setting them up. He offers six lessons that can be learned from the Alaskan experience:

- Resource dividends are popular once they are in place.
- The Alaska model can be exported. He notes that you do not have to be resource-rich to have a resource dividend. Alaska is not unusually rich. It uses only a fraction of its resource wealth to fund the entire dividend. Every country, state, and region has resources. He cites Singapore and Hong Kong as being probably the most resource-poor in the world, and yet they have fabulously valuable real estate.
- Look for, and take advantage of, opportunities.
- Think like a monopolist; once community control is asserted over resources, the members of the community have a monopoly over the resources.
- Build a large constituency in favour of the project.
- Avoid creating an opposition.

Lessons from the APF Dividend can be found in Widerquist's two co-edited books (Widerquist *et al*, 2012a and 2012b), reviewed by Torry (2013b: 8–9) and (2014: 8–9) respectively. These edited volumes make a valuable companion set.

At a conference celebrating the 30th anniversary of the foundation of BIEN, at Louvain-La-Neuve, 1 October 2016, Karl Widerquist reported that, sadly, the happy situation of the APF Dividend is now under threat. In the past, Alaskans, in their wisdom, voted to use the rest of the income from the APF to finance public expenditure and to abolish all taxes, including sales and income tax. With the financial crisis in world markets, and the fall in the oil price, the return on the APF has dwindled, and Alaska is facing budget problems. Now there are proposals to divert the returns used to finance the APF Dividend to use it to fund public expenditure, rather than re-introduce taxes, such as income tax. This proposal would favour wealthier people at the expense of the poorest.

CHAPTER 6

When is discrimination justified? Entitlement: selective or non-selective benefits

Selectivity

SELECTIVITY REFERS to the practice of granting *differential levels of entitlement* to people who are otherwise equally eligible. The amounts of benefits could vary according to personal attributes (age, gender, sexual orientation or race), or according to household relationships or status (blood relationship, marital or other cohabitation status, the number of adults in the household, the number of dependent children, householder status, or housing tenure) or according to regional variations in costs (housing or childcare provision). 'Non-selective' means that the amounts do not differ. The administration of selective schemes can be relatively straightforward when entitlement is based on distinct categories. It can become much more complex where it is based on circumstances that can change frequently, or on attributes that change along a continuum, such as 'living together', or where it can be difficult to define a threshold.

The variety of categorical benefits on which selectivity has been based has decreased over recent decades. Notions of worth and desert used to lead to differential entitlement, such that a 'deserving' widow received higher benefits than an 'undeserving' unmarried mother. At one time the entitlements of people to disability benefits were based on cause, so that war-disabled people received more in benefits than those disabled at work, who received more than those disabled by other types of accident, or from birth. This distinction is less obvious today in the actual level of benefits.

Discrimination against couples

A significant current practice, however, is to claw back household economies of scale (HES) from married, civil partnership, or otherwise cohabiting couples. The couple as assessment unit, rather than the individual, contributes to this. But even with an individual basis for assessment and delivery, it would still be possible to use selective benefits as now to penalise cohabiting couples, by granting a lesser amount for each cohabiting adult, compared with other two-adult households or single adults.

Calls for the system to change have covered at least three decades (Miller, 1986) culminating in Baroness Stroud, Director of the Centre for Social Justice, in an open letter to the Chancellor of the Exchequer, George Osborne, writing to ask him to take steps to:

> Eradicate the couple penalty: There is a disincentive in the welfare system for couples to build long term stable families... some couples can still receive more living apart than living together. This is particularly concerning where children are involved, given the importance of long term family stability for the wellbeing and life chances of children.
>
> STROUD, 2016

The current system claws back HES from all cohabiting couples, but not other adult couples, such as two siblings sharing accommodation, a parent with an adult offspring, or a householder with a lodger. Nor does it penalise young adults, such as students, who share accommodation, or people living in a hostel or a residential home who are also likely to experience HES. If the principle is that HES should be clawed back, then surely it should be applied to all adults in shared accommodation, otherwise it is discriminatory? However, not only is this idea likely to prove unpopular, but there would be insurmountable administrative problems. These problems would be compounded by the fact that individuals may change their singleton/sharing status fairly frequently. It would defeat the objective of simplifying the administrative system.

Possibly the worst outcome of the current differential entitlement is the intrusive and distasteful 'cohabitation rule' (Kelly, 2011). The role of selectivity in this is discussed in chapter 7.

A 'pure' BI scheme would be non-selective, except that the amounts could be age-related, for instance, giving different amounts for a child, young adult, other working-age adult, and for those over pension-entitlement age.

Early discussions about BI schemes centred on whether a BI would be needs-based, ie selective, or whether it would be a 'social dividend', where everyone would receive the same amount regardless of need. One solution is to make a social dividend sufficiently high so that it will cover most people's necessities.

Non-selective benefits are simpler than selective ones, and are therefore expected to reduce administration and compliance errors by both recipients and staff. They would also be simpler and cheaper to administer and monitor, and would be expected to lead to a more transparent and accountable system. It could reduce the current time-consuming personal effort required of claimants who apply for benefits.

Can a case be made for selective benefits?

It is worth asking whether some selective benefits can be justified?

The people most at risk of income poverty are financially vulnerable adults and families with children. They comprise:

- those over pension-entitlement age,
- dependent children aged 0–15,
- the primary care-giving parent or Parent with Care (PWC), including lone parents,
- people with disabilities or chronic illnesses, or who are frail
- those who are incapable of working-for-pay, and
- unpaid volunteer carers of adults, that is, not earning a wage for their caring services.

All of these adults face discrimination in the labour market. To what extent is it possible to protect the people in these categories without introducing further selectivity (in addition to age-based selectivity)? The first three categories can be accommodated easily. The latter three are discussed under the heading 'the needs of disabled people' below. Age-related selection is acceptable in BI schemes, and seniors and dependent children can be identified by their date of birth. Those over pension-entitlement age should receive a full BI (which may be defined with reference to a chosen poverty benchmark).

Similarly, BI levels for PWCs and children should be designed such that families with children receive at least the full relevant amount for their household type, as indicated by the chosen poverty benchmark. If those over pension-entitlement age and families with children were protected, regardless of their individual circumstances, then the only people to whom it would be possible to give a *partial* BI would be working-age adults who are not primary care-giving parents. This is discussed further in chapters 10 and 14.

More on economies of scale

If a *full* BI were granted to every adult, then HES would be evident in households containing two or more adults. A partial BI for all working-age adults reduces the HES for couples, but it could be difficult for single-tons, and especially lone parents, to manage, unless they earned extra income or reduced their general level of consumption.

However, if a partial BI is granted to all working-age adults in order to reduce HES, then, in order to protect families with children, a premium for 14–15 year olds could be introduced. However, this can lead to Family Economies of Scale (FES), where large families receive increasingly more than necessary to meet their needs.

A case might be made for further selectivity (in addition to age-based selectivity) in the form of a PWC premium, in order to reduce both HES and FES.

This could take the form of topping up a partial BI for working-age adults to a full BI for *all* primary care-giving parents. Also PWCs can easily be identified administratively, since they are the ones to whom Child BI is entrusted. This arrangement appears to reduce the FES at little or no extra cost, and it avoids the more expensive HES when all working-age adults receive a full BI. This arrangement protects all families with children, including single parents, both male and female, without having to distinguish between lone and other parents. Neither of these conditions (date of birth, and being a primary care-giving parent) changes frequently, and therefore should not be difficult to administer.

On the other hand, HES can provide an incentive for adults to share accommodation and thus reduce the demand for single-person housing. Acceptance that HES is a consequence of BI schemes also acknowledges the fact that sharing accommodation is not always easy – it can be stressful, and compromises often have to be made.

Selectivity by age is acceptable in a BI scheme; 'children are entitled to a lower income than the elderly' (Van Parijs, 1988: 6). Other differences within an age group are not acceptable, except for the introduction of a premium for all PWCs to top up their partial BIs to full ones, as described above. This would reduce both FES and HES, while protecting families with children.

In essence, selectivity can be described as discriminatory and divisive. The choice between selective and non-selective benefits is that between a further divided society, (possibly with an intrusive cohabitation rule), and a less divisive or intrusive society with a simpler, more efficient administration system.

Even a relatively low partial BI, being universal and based on the individual, would benefit those who are currently excluded by our targeted means-tested system. It can provide some financial security both to former 'financial dependents' and to many others now struggling as reluctant, self-employed workers. It will not prevent poverty, but it can help to reduce the depth of both out-of-work and in-work financial poverty. It can provide a springboard for part-time work and help industrial democracy by giving a better platform for employees and their trades unions to negotiate for reasonable pay and good working conditions. Those receiving a partial BI will still have an incentive to work-for-pay, at least to top up to the level of a full BI. A reduction in the means-testing of benefits, and thus the Marginal Deduction Rate, will also improve incentives to work-for-pay. Even for those whose current benefit levels do not increase, the lifting of conditionality can lead to more freedom of choice for many. These effects increase with the generosity of the BI. Realistic wage protection would certainly still be required. Partial BIs help to reduce household economies of scale, and provide an opportunity for the introduction of income/earnings disregards, where the first tranche of gross income is free of income tax or NICs. (This will be discussed later in chapters 13 and 14).

A BI is not a panacea for all ills, and, as some critics claim, life is too complex and diverse for a simple BI scheme to meet everyone's needs, preferring a series of benefits each designed to meet a particular set of circumstances. An income payment that tried to cover everything would be too blunt an instrument. At the other extreme, too many different benefits could lead to the danger of trying to micro-manage people's lives, leaving them without elements of personal choice. Depending on the generosity of the type of BI scheme defined here, it has the potential to meet the needs both of those over pension-entitlement age and of dependent children.

However, there are at least three areas that a BI scheme will not address:

- The problem of high and variable housing costs across the UK, as a result of government policy leading to far too-little house-building over several decades coupled with its policy of encouraging speculative investment in housing;
- The extra costs incurred by disabled people, which will have to be met separately, as with any income maintenance system;
- State-provided, or at least state-funded convenient childcare will still be needed. As Alex Salmond acknowledges, good quality childcare provision is good for the child, the parent and the economy (Salmond, 2015: 177).

These will have to be addressed by separate but parallel systems, in addition to the BI scheme.

Housing costs

The current, means-tested Social Assistance benefits in the UK and the National Living Wage (NLW) have been declining since a peak in 1965 (Atkinson, 2015: 226, Fig 8.4) and are recognised by many authorities as being far too low, not even having kept up with inflation, let alone the prosperity of society. This has led to widespread in-work and out-of-work poverty. Receipt of SA benefits usually entitles the recipient to a means-tested Housing Benefit. A BI is not a panacea for all ills, and it will not heal the harm that has resulted from the housing policy of consecutive governments since 1979. The lack of house-building, together with encouraging those with deposits and high incomes to treat houses as speculative investments, has led to large increases in house prices and therefore rents, but varying across the country. This policy guarantees that wealth is siphoned off from aspirant first-time buyers into the pockets of current homeowners, (although this is only realised when the property is sold). Tax revenues are channelled via private-rented sector tenants to their landlords' pockets. A tenant's right to buy his/her council house since the 1980s has discouraged local authorities from building new social housing. These, together with a chronic dearth of new private house-building for decades, and an increased demand due to people living longer and the break-up of families, has pumped up house prices and rents, especially in London and the south east of England. But it has had a knock-on effect elsewhere, including in Scotland. Not only are house prices and rents high compared with average incomes, but there are wide regional variations around the UK.

This means that it is impossible to include an element for housing costs within the BI without leaving many of the poorest in high rent areas with too little to cover their housing costs. The obvious solution to the housing crisis would be a major house-building program, including investing in more affordable social housing, such as took place after WWII, but that will take time. A more immediate solution might be to introduce a Land Value Tax, taxing the rental value of the land, but not any buildings or other structures on it. This could have the effect of gradually reducing house prices (Wightman, 2009). This could be distributed equally to everyone as a housing-cost BI in the region in which it is levied. In the meantime, if a BI scheme is introduced in conjunction with the current housing policy, the poorest will have to rely on a separate individualised, means-tested Housing Benefit system, covering both rent and mortgage interest up to a given level (but not repayment of capital) and Council Tax

Relief/Support, including water rates. It means that even those receiving a full BI could effectively still be dependent on means-testing for housing costs, but to a lesser extent than now. The need to retain a separate Housing Benefit system is not a problem caused by, or inherent in, the BI system, but rather is one caused by historical and current housing policy and it can only be cured by a change to an appropriate housing policy. The current housing policy undermines the objective of ending MTBs and thus of obtaining labour market efficiency.

The needs of disabled people

Disability Benefits (DBs) are based on need, and it is therefore a different system from BIs. In the past, disabled people used to self-assess their needs based on 'impairment', supported with evidence from their GPs, consultants, and other health professionals. This is still their preferred system. Latterly, this approach has been replaced by a process of assessment of 'functionality' by external companies employing people without health qualifications, and who did not have details of the applicant's history or background.

If a BI system were introduced in the UK, or in Scotland, a disabled person would automatically receive a BI on the same basis as others. In addition, s/he should continue to receive tax-exempt, non-means-tested, DBs based on need as now. This would comprise a parallel, but separate, system from the BI scheme. This group of people should include those acknowledged as being incapable of working-for-pay. Retaining all of the current disability benefits would ensure that no disabled person is worse off under the new system. Some Social Assistance benefits include DBs, thus providing automatic gateways to them. Where a BI replaces these MTBs, then new gateways may need to be devised, that automatically entitle them to their disability benefits.

Ideally, each person with disabilities or a chronic illness should receive a package of payments that would cover any shortfall if s/he receives only a partial BI. It would also cover the extra costs that are incurred by disabled people, including for care, mobility, special equipment, special diets, extra heating and laundry costs. It would also cover the general increase in their living costs, due to the fact that many cannot take advantage of the cost-saving methods that others employ. For instance, someone whose disability means that they cannot cook for themselves will face extra costs from having to buy more processed foods than others. Further, on the grounds of equity, disabled people who are able to undertake paid work should not have to use their earnings to cover the costs of disability (that are necessities to them), while other people can use theirs for luxuries (Spicker, 2015).

Marilyn Waring describes aspects of the unpaid care economy from her own experience, and explores the relationship between those carrying out unpaid domestic work and other care work with those in the paid economy who benefit from it (Waring, 2016: 17–21).

A full BI, or reasonably generous partial BI (of about 75–80 per cent of a full BI), for working-age adults could enable some of them to offer to be informal *unpaid carers*, for family and friends, without risking making themselves destitute, and without having to be nominated or approved officially. This would avoid the bureaucracy involved in associating a particular unpaid carer with the disabled person. Full-time paid carers of a disabled person would have to be registered as such, and their costs would be included in the package of payments for the person with disabilities. If costs are incurred on account of a caring role, such as fares to accompany the disabled person on a hospital visit, then ideally this should be provided for as part of his or her 'costs of disability' package.

Both housing and disability benefits are very much in need of revision, but are beyond the scope of this book. The interaction between BI and support for these costs (and between them) would need to be considered in developing policy in each area.

Childcare costs and other public services

Similarly, a BI scheme is not a panacea in the sense that it should or could replace all other benefits and public services. Investment will still be needed in services such as health and social care, childcare, education, social housing, public transport and other infrastructure. However, by reducing the stresses and anxieties of modern life, a BI scheme would help to reduce the indirect costs of poverty on the health service, personal social services and the justice system.

Childcare facilities for pre-school children are essential for many working parents. However, it is often extremely difficult to meet the costs of childcare from typical levels of earnings, especially when there are several children in the same family requiring childcare. The provision of childcare for pre-school children can take the form, amongst others, of:

- unpaid parental childcare;
- childcare by a close family member, friend or neighbour, with or without a private financial arrangement;

- registered child-minder;
- registered private nursery;
- registered nursery provided by an employer on the premises,
- state-run nursery;
- nursery (childcare) classes for 2–4 year-olds at primary schools.

The costs of childcare services in the UK are not only some of the highest in Europe (Gillespie *et al*, 2016: 101), but the current state support for them is a complex mixture. Wadsworth presents a comprehensive picture of the numbers of children of different ages involved, the average weekly cost before subsidies, and the total government spending on childcare via various schemes (Wadsworth, 2016). These range from Free Early Education for children aged three and four, and some aged two years, (which entitled them in 2014–15 to 15 hours per week of free care for 38 weeks a year at £5.49 per hour), to the Childcare Element of Working Tax Credit, Employer Supported Childcare Vouchers and Tax Free Childcare, each of which represents a different level of subsidy. The latter three are largely mutually exclusive. Wadsworth notes that current schemes for supporting childcare by registered child-minders and private nurseries have had the unintended consequences of increasing their wages and fees (Wadsworth, 2016: 6), which maybe is not a bad thing for a chronically poorly paid, but very important, service (Gillespie *et al*, 2016: 101).

The actual subsidy claimed depends on the age of the child, the household composition, the working hours of a lone parent or both parents in a couple, and their earnings level, and whether they claim any of the main income-replacement benefits, among other things. The actual costs of the different schemes vary widely. For 2014–15, Wadsworth calculates that the *average* total claim per child is between £79 and £98 per week (Wadsworth, 2016: 8). He proposes a harmonisation of rates by increasing the Free Early Education vouchers to £85 per week for 48 weeks a year for all children aged two, three, and four-years. However, he concludes that 'a slightly more radical proposal would be to spend £6.4 billion on providing nursery classes at state primary schools for children aged two to four. This will take time to implement but simplifies things for parents and does not have the unintended consequences of pushing up childcare costs' (Wadsworth, 2016: 8).

A full BI for all primary care-givers would provide them with an easier choice between caring for her/his children at home during the pre-compulsory school years without being destitute, or working for pay. It could enable a private financial arrangement with a close relative or friend for childcare services to be made. Similarly, even a relatively generous partial BI would make kinship childcare more feasible. It enables a grandparent or other close family-members to take on the childcare, either freely or paid for out of the PWC premium in a private arrangement, and thus without the family-members leaving themselves destitute. The BI is unlikely to make much difference to either private registered child-minders or private nurseries.

Clearly, it would be beyond the scope of a BI scheme to include a component to cover the childcare cost for every child aged 0–4. Any schemes for supporting private registered services would be separate from and in addition to the BI scheme, and should be designed to be as simple and fair as possible.

A BI cannot replace good quality, free, publically-funded childcare services, which would be the most economically efficient and which are good for the wellbeing of children and their parents and good for the economy (Salmond, 2015: 177). Nursery classes for 2–4 year olds in all primary schools could be an excellent way of investing in the early years of our future generations. The Nordic countries routinely provide publically provided nurseries, by highly trained nursery staff with a background in child development.

Of course, as every parent knows, childcare requirements do not stop at the age of five. The provision of daily pre-school breakfast clubs, after-school homework classes and holiday play clubs would still be required in many cases. Similarly, parental holidays do not always coincide with school holidays. If a BI scheme were to lead to a reduction in the working week, and/or more equal sharing of paid and unpaid work, then this problem would be reduced.

IRAN 2010–

In December 2010, Iran nearly became the first country in the world to establish a nationwide Citizen's or Basic Income scheme. Interestingly, the scheme did not emerge by design, but by default: it was the by-product of an effort to reform an out-dated system of price subsidies that concerned primarily fuel products. A basic income proved to be the most practical way of compensating the population for the loss of subsidies that had been costing some US$100–120 billion a year (Tabatabai, 2012: 2).

Iran used to subsidise some food products, but mainly fuel, using its substantial oil revenues. Not only were these subsidies regarded as both inefficient and unfair, but it led to wasteful use of petrol that caused an increase in air pollution. It was decided to end these subsidies over a five-year period, gradually increasing fuel prices towards market rates, but to compensate the population by granting direct cash transfers instead, under the Subsidy Reform Law of January 2010. This became the main component of Iran's economic reform plan. At first the government tried to compensate the population via a needs-based system, but this caused a lot of friction and frustration as people complained that it too was unfair. In the end, the government decided to give the same to every Iranian. When the first phase of the reform process became operational on 19 December 2010, just over 80 per cent of the population of 75 million started to receive 810,000 rials (about $80) every two months. However, the entitlements of all household members are payable to the head of the household alone, not to individual members, *even if adult*. Thus, Iran almost became the first country to establish an authentic universal, unconditional and regular *de facto* Citizen's Income, not by design, but as a by-product of an attempt to transform an inefficient and unfair system of sharing the country's oil wealth.

In the first year, about US$40 billion was paid out to households. Some 1–2 million households have decided not to claim the BI: 'the objective is twofold: improving economic efficiency through rationalisation of subsidised prices, and reducing income disparities through cash transfers' (Tabatabai, 2012: 2). Two effects have been noted. The prices of the previously subsidised commodities rose by one percentage point per month initially for the first year, but this was as expected. Secondly, there has been a decline in the consumption of fuel – again to be expected. The impact of the reform is expected to be egalitarian, because the withdrawal of subsidies would be in proportion to their consumption of the subsidised goods, and thus related to income size. However, the flat rate BI would have a greater impact on low-income people than wealthier individuals.

Tabatabai draws some lessons from this experience. The source of funding for a BI scheme can be a major issue. In this case, the oil revenues provided the source, and the concern facing the population was that of making sure that they received their fair share. Tabatabai points out that this source of funding makes it easier to adopt a BI than if a rights or entitlement approach is made, with talk of reciprocity. He contrasts the Iranian BI scheme based on sharing the current oil revenues with Alaska's sovereign wealth fund built up over the years, and which should last for longer. A second lesson comes from the observation that the flow of funds in Iran is restricted in any given time period, and universality means that the share going to the poorer sections of the community is less than if eligibility had been targeted at them. A move has already started to urge higher income households to withdraw from the cash transfer scheme. He concludes that the 'success of the reform depends on the vast majority of the people feeling that they are not being cheated out of their fair share of the oil wealth'.

Oil resources may be less controversial sources for funding a BI scheme initially, but they are not without their problems. Iran is also currently being hit by the fall in oil prices, and faces problems financing the cash transfer program, and so it is proposing to withdraw this scheme from roughly one third of the wealthiest of the population (BIEN, 2016; Iran).

The BI schemes in Iran and Alaska are similar in being financed from oil wealth, are universal and non-selective, and despite being relatively small in amount they are very popular with their residents.

CHAPTER 7

More control over our lives
Contingency: conditionality or unconditionality?

Conditionality and sanctions

CONTINGENCY REFERS to the practice of imposing pre-conditions on potential recipients which affect their entitlement to benefits, such as work tests, being involved in voluntary service, or behaving according to traditional gender roles, in order to influence their behaviour. UK Social Assistance benefits used to be conditional on willingness-to-work tests, or 'being available for work', but in recent times, this has been replaced by the more stringent condition of the claimant having to provide evidence of having actively sought work for 35 hours per week (Watts *et al*, 2014). This fierce conditionality has often been accompanied by savage sanctions being placed on each claimant for even quite minor misdemeanours. If late for an appointment at the benefit office, due to their child-minding arrangements having fallen through at the last minute, for instance, the claimant can be sanctioned by the loss of two weeks benefit. The implementation and enforcement of conditionality requires extra monitoring and administration compared with a system without conditions, leading to an increased risk of error and fraud. It is often completely lacking in compassion, or even a simple understanding of the effect that these conditions and sanctions have on the families who run the risk of destitution. It is not just the adults who suffer, but their children too. Most poor people do not have savings on which to rely in emergencies, and they do not survive the hardships endured unscathed. One might wonder whether the design of the current social security rules, which fails the most vulnerable in society, is the result of ignorance, incompetence, or is in fact fulfilling its purpose?

A relic from earlier times is the conditionality currently imposed on lone parents and other single women. In theory, this is gender-neutral, but, in practice, it affects many more women than men. 'The cohabitation rule' is the outcome of two features. Selectivity entitles a single adult to an enhanced benefit (chapter 6), but it is also conditional on her not living together with anyone as husband and wife. Evidence of a regular male over-night visitor to a singleton female home can lead to the withdrawal of benefit on the assumption that the regular visitor is supporting the single resident financially, even if he is not. Conditionality is used to impose traditional gender roles by casting him into the role of breadwinner and her into that of dependent home-maker (Kelly, 2011).

In contrast, unconditionality could help to reduce the inequality of power relationships. Together with the assessment being based on the individual and with universal eligibility, unconditionality could help to emancipate and empower adults. It could enhance industrial democracy by reducing inequality in the work place, and give workers and their trades unions the security to be able to negotiate co-operatively for fair pay and good working conditions. It grants the unconditional right not to be destitute, and contributes to financial security. Unconditionality gives people more choices and flexibility in life, helping them to develop to their full potential. It is simpler and cheaper to deliver and monitor than conditionality, and should help to make the administration system more transparent, and therefore more accountable.

Free riders and reciprocity

Despite bestowing such key advantages, unconditionality could be the most difficult aspect of a BI system for many to accept, for two reasons. First is the concern that everyone will give up working-for-pay altogether and that the economy will plunge into a downward spiral. The second is that, even if this did not occur, some abhor the idea of giving 'something for nothing', which could encourage 'free riders', who choose not to work, but rather to enjoy, for example, sea, sun and surf all the time. However, many of these people who are perceived as 'free riders' are doing activities that are valuable to society, but are invisible – particularly care and community work.

Moreover, as Carole Pateman points out:

> The mutual reinforcement of marriage and employment explains why husbands can take advantage of the unpaid work of wives and avoid doing their fair share of the caring work. That is why there is massive free riding in the household – by husbands.

PATEMAN, 2004: 99

Those who abhor giving 'something for nothing' believe that everyone should contribute to society in some proscribed way. In other words, if a benefit is granted, then some form of service should be provided in exchange, such as that given by those who are already caring for an adult or a dependent child, or having to work in some proscribed employment, or in an acceptable form of voluntary service.

This exchange is known as '*reciprocity*', but reciprocity is a two-way street. There is some debate as to which part of the exchange should take place first. Should the service be granted before the benefit is received, or, if the benefit is granted first, might it induce such a feeling of gratitude that it subsequently leads to a service being provided voluntarily? Antipathy to 'something for nothing' may be understandable where a BI scheme is financed out of income tax, but reciprocity could hardly be justified if it were financed out of a sovereign wealth fund, for instance. It is as well that not everyone demands reciprocity for a charitable act, such that, before saving someone from drowning, say, a verbal contract has to be negotiated.

Individuals should be entitled to their necessities on the grounds of compassion, but they should have to earn their luxuries. People living in multi-deprived areas have measurably fewer years of life expectancy than their wealthy neighbours (Marmot, 2015: 24–27). Is the crime of being poor really so terrible as to be punishable by an early death? Even prisoners in the UK usually receive three meals each day. Could this be one reason why our prisons are over-flowing?

If the current technological revolution continues to automate processes and replace workers with robots, then the need for a BI system will be even more urgent. If large numbers of people have no employment, and little possibility of paid work, then a full BI, or a generous partial BI (of say at least 75–80 per cent of a full BI) will be essential for people to be able to maintain themselves adequately. There will still be demand for highly-skilled labour in the innovative, high-technology industries. There will always be demand for workers in jobs that require the personal touch, such as the caring professions, complementary therapies and other personal services, and the creative arts. The amount of part-time work could increase. With a better work-life balance, people could occupy themselves as described above in studying for pleasure or as an investment in their future, travelling, doing voluntary work, caring for a child or an elder, or spending time fulfilling a creative arts or other personal ambition. With a better work-life balance, people will have more time to enjoy keeping fit and maintaining better health. The education sector and leisure will be growth industries. A BI gives people the opportunity to make their contributions to society in a way that is important to them (Geoghegan, 2015).

Participation Incomes

Some who are interested in Basic Income schemes would be prepared to accept a version known as *Participation Income* (PI). Tony Atkinson makes a case for PI, which he believes will be more politically acceptable than an unconditional BI. He lists those who would qualify:

> ... people working as an employee or self-employed, absent from work on grounds of sickness and injury, unable to work on grounds of disability and unemployed but available for work, it would also include people engaging in approved forms of education and training, caring for young, elderly or disabled dependents or undertaking approved forms of voluntary work, etc. The condition involves neither *payment* nor *work*: it is a wider definition of social contribution.
>
> ATKINSON, 1996: 68–69

The financially vulnerable adults and families with children, who were discussed in chapter 6 above, would qualify. However, might participation just be a means of preserving 'deserving' and 'undeserving' categories, with all the problems of division, humiliation and rejection to which they lead, as discussed in chapter 5 above?

Atkinson (2015: 219) again proposes 'a benefit to be paid on the basis not of citizenship, but of "participation"'. He would exclude from his PI those who devoted their lives to pure leisure (Atkinson, 2015: 221), while Van Parijs (1991) makes the opposite case for 'why surfers should be fed'. In fact, surfers are likely to have to work-for-pay, in order to buy their expensive equipment and pay for travel costs. Perhaps society should celebrate the fact that some would willingly embrace a minimal consumption life-style, gaining enjoyment from living on a very modest, unconditional BI. This could be one of the factors leading to 'prosperity without material growth'. It may well be cheaper to tolerate free riders, rather than try to foist reluctant workers onto otherwise efficient companies, so long as they cause no harm, and their critics can choose to do likewise.

Atkinson clearly wishes the criteria for PI to be very inclusive and recognise the wide range of activities that contribute socially, so 'in reality, very few people would be excluded' (page 221). Thus, it is likely that the number of free riders would be relatively small. De Wispelaere and Stirton (2008) criticise a PI system, because it will require a more extensive, intrusive and expensive bureaucracy to monitor for the participation criteria, than for an unconditional BI. It would exclude only a minority of people who reside in the UK (see chapter 8), but who for some reason choose only leisure and thus do not comply, and who would receive 'nothing for nothing'. Maybe it is assumed that those excluded will be forced to take up employment that is well enough paid to prevent poverty, but times have changed and there is no guarantee that there will be enough employment for everyone. Would it be feasible or wise for a government to act as 'employer of last resort'? However the exclusion criteria might be designed, 'nothing for nothing' would inevitably lead to poverty for some people, which would undermine health and shorten lives. This would be tantamount to a policy of a lower life expectancy for the crime of being both poor and non-compliant, and should be challenged on the grounds of compassion. Also, it is based on subjective value judgements of what participation is 'acceptable' and what counts as leisure.

One of the defining features of a BI is that of unconditionality. However, it is possible to envisage a PI, which has all the features of a BI except for unconditionality. Similarly, MTBs are associated with work-test conditionality, but an example of an unconditional MTB is that of Pension Credit, for people of pension-entitlement age or over, who are not required to work-for-pay.

Effects of unconditionality on incentives to work

This section is based on economic theory and may be skipped by the non-specialist if preferred. Its main message is that most people want to work, and that fears of an unconditional BI scheme sending the economy plunging into a downward spiral are misplaced. Economic theory recognises two incentives that influence the number of hours that individuals are willing to offer in the labour market, (their 'labour supply'). One is the amount of their unearned income, including a BI, and the other is the real wage rate net of all deductions, (such as income tax, NICs and benefit withdrawal tapers), that they face, (Borgas, 2009). However, there is also a *reservation wage* below which a worker is unwilling to offer his labour in a particular type of work. In these circumstances, governments use conditionality to over-ride the natural (dis)incentives of the market. With a BI, low paid workers can avoid unsatisfying, unpleasant drudge work at rock bottom wages. In neoclassical labour supply theory, it is assumed that an individual chooses between their time and income. Time that is not used to earn income is labelled 'leisure', which is a narrow and gender-blind definition of the term.

Recent theoretical research (Miller, 2015) predicts that a very low *unearned income* or BI will divide society into two. There are those on relatively high wages who are overworked and deprived of 'leisure', and those who face only wages lower than their reservation wage, which is the lowest acceptable wage at which they will offer work in a given job, so they have no work and are deprived of income. It also predicts that a slightly larger unearned income could lead to a relatively large reduction in the labour supply of an individual who is deprived of 'leisure', but it could shift the labour supply curve of an individual who is deprived of income in a positive direction and even propel him or her from no work to some work-for-pay. The labour supply of both of these groups is said to be elastic. Granting this same level of unearned income or BI would have a comparatively small (inelastic) negative effect on the labour supply of an individual who is deprived of neither 'leisure' nor income.

Economists may be interested to learn that the same theoretical research derives backward-bending labour supply curves from a utility function (Miller, 2015). This predicts that for a given BI, if the *real net wage* increases, then low-waged earners will increase their hours, while higher-waged individuals would decrease theirs, but only slightly. The replacement of MTBs by universal benefits would lower the Marginal Deduction Rates facing many low-waged workers. The resultant increased real net wage rate could rise above their reservation wage rates, potentially increasing their paid hours markedly (Pasma, 2009). However, if high-waged earners were to face slightly higher income tax rates, thus decreasing their real net wage rates, then they, too, for a given BI level, are likely to increase their hours, but only slightly.

The interplay of changes in BI and net wage rates can have fairly complex effects. The changes in labour market behaviour in response to changes in benefit rates, such as the introduction of a BI scheme, and possible changes in effective tax rates on income, are called endogenous changes.

The theoretical case for the effect of the introduction of a BI scheme on the labour market is as follows:

- The introduction of even a full BI will only ever cover an individual's necessities (excluding housing costs, the extra costs incurred by disabled people and childcare costs), and is unlikely to be sufficient to allow people to abandon their jobs. Luxuries will still have to be earned.

- This is even more relevant if working-age individuals were to receive only a partial BI, which will not even cover their necessities.

- Layard (2014: 67–68) reports that work is the third most important factor affecting happiness after family relationships and financial situation. Thus, it would appear that most people want to work-for-pay, not just for the earnings, but for the social and health advantages it brings. These include job satisfaction and fulfilment from the work, the opportunity to make friends, providing a structure for one's time, and from gaining the status of one who is acknowledged as contributing to society. The problem is not so much one of people wanting to avoid work, but of there not being available enough good quality work for fair wages, or of workers not having the necessary skills for the jobs that are available.

- Many people who currently have an unconditional, unearned income still choose to carry on earning.

- Some may take the opportunity to reduce their working hours to achieve a better work-life balance, reducing the stresses of modern life. Others, who are not in paid employment currently, might move into part-time work. There could be redistribution between unpaid and paid working hours. Thus, the introduction of a BI system could lead to an improvement in the quality of life of the population.

- It might eventually be possible to move to a standard 30-hour working week, although the New Economics Foundation argued for a 21-hour week, and a 15-hour week was imagined as likely by the 21st century by J.M. Keynes (Coote *et al*, 2013: 156–7). Productivity could increase with a shorter working week as demonstrated during the oil crisis of 1973, when the economy was limited to a three-day working week, but productivity was not reduced proportionately.

- Some may take the occasional sabbatical to study, train to increase their skills base, travel, do voluntary work, care for a child or an elder, or spend time to fulfil a creative arts or other personal ambition.

- The financial security of the BI would enable low-paid workers to eschew unpleasant drudge jobs until wage rates increase.

- A BI can lead to greater industrial democracy by providing the security that enables workers and their trades unions to negotiate co-operatively for fair pay and better working conditions.

- Wage-rates are likely to adjust, so that those of popular jobs would fall, and those of unpleasant jobs would rise, unless they could be mechanised. It is expected that wage-rates would normally be determined by supply and demand, but wage protection could still be necessary to protect workers from unscrupulous employers cutting wages drastically.

- If a partial BI were paid to working-age adults, then wage protection would certainly be necessary in order to ensure that they would be able to earn their way out of poverty.

Indexing the levels of the BIS to mean income per head, for the term of a Parliament, would reflect the prosperity of society, and provide a self-stabilising mechanism for the economy. If people worked fewer hours on account of the BI, and mean income per head fell, then the level of the BI in the following time period, (as the same proportion of a lower mean income per head), would be lower. This in turn might increase the incentive for people to seek to increase their work effort and earnings.

It can be claimed that in-work, means-tested benefits, such as Working Tax Credits, subsidise the profits of employers, because if an employer reduces wage, then the workers' MTBs will increase, thus partially compensating the workers for the reduction. Some people fear that the implementation of a BI scheme would similarly push down wages and serve the same purpose. However, there is a difference. The amount of a BI does not change with a change in earnings. Also employees would have more control over whether they would be willing to work for the reduced wage rate, so there would be less incentive for employers to reduce wages. Industrial democracy on the one hand could lead to fairer wages, and competition should compete away any excess profits. There would still be an important role for trades unions.

Unconditionality, coupled with a full BI, would mean that no individual could be forced into the labour market to carry out unfulfilling drudge-work on low wages, and parents could choose whether to take up paid work or to look after their families at home (Mason, 2015). 'The feminist version of the liberal egalitarian tradition that has as its foundation a universal, unconditional basic income at a level to meet basic needs... prioritises the emerging norm of combined care work and paid employment throughout adulthood' (Zelleke, 2011: 39).

Macroeconomic effects of a BI scheme

The main questions about the effects of a BI scheme on the macro-economy centre on the likely effect on GDP. While the introduction of a new system might bring about some temporary disruption, this is likely to be minimal if the scheme is implemented gradually. The larger concern is not proven. Would replacing the current social security system with an unconditional BI scheme necessarily lead to slower growth, especially if the levels of the BIS are indexed to mean income per head, which allows it to act as a self-stabilising mechanism?

A second concern is that of whether the introduction of a BI scheme would be inflationary. If the BI system is financed out of taxation, then a BI system merely transfers money from one part of the economy to another. If no new money is being introduced into the economy, then the BI scheme is not expected to be inflationary.

The continuing trend towards automation, with its shift away from labour income to income from investment in capital goods, is likely to have a greater impact on the economy than the introduction of a BI system. Every effort must be made to ensure that this source of income is taxed either through corporation tax, and/or as one of the components of personal income that is subject to income tax. International co-operation will be required to tax income from capital. Even with increased automation, there will still be demand for labour, both in hi-tech, high-paid innovative jobs and also in the caring professions, personal services where the personal touch is important, such as in the complementary therapies for example, and in the creative arts. It will take longer, if ever, to replace a whole range of practical jobs such as plumbers and electricians, police, fire and rescue services. There could be a risk of creating further income inequalities, splitting the working population into high and low wage earners. Education would be the long-term solution here. Wage protection would still be required.

Mincome program, Dauphin, Manitoba, Canada, 1974–79

There were four income maintenance experiments in the USA in the late 1960s and early 1970s, and a fifth one in Dauphin, Manitoba in Canada, which ran from 1974 to 1979. This Mincome (Minimum Income) program ended abruptly when centre-right governments at both provincial (1977) and federal (1979) levels came into office. The problems of the 1970s – inflation, rising oil prices, higher interest rates and unemployment – became urgent and overtook the commitment to address poverty issues. No final report was made. The records of the five-year experiment were hastily packed away in 1,800 boxes, stored and lost for 30 years, until tracked down by Professor Evelyn Forget (Forget, 2012) of Manitoba University. She was able to use a guest spot on a local radio station to invite participants to contact her, as a result of which several did so (Jourdan, 2013).

The conditions for the experiment were set up by Edward Schreyer, of the provincial government, and Prime Minister, Pierre Elliott Trudeau, of the Federal government. This led to a cost-sharing agreement where 75 per cent of the $17 million budget was paid by the Federal government (Lum, 2014). The objective was to help households whose income dropped below the poverty line, and to ask whether people would stop working or work fewer hours if they were guaranteed an income, would they be healthier, and would youngsters stay on at school for longer? The social assistance system in operation at that time had very strong work disincentives, with a 100 per cent withdrawal rate of benefits from earnings. As the National Council of Welfare (Lum, 2014) reported in 2010, the welfare rules trapped people in poverty. Those in need must first become virtually destitute before they qualify for temporary assistance. Those who are destitute tend to stay in that state. The social assistance scheme hands out paltry amounts of money (Lum, 2014).

Dauphin was then a city of about 10,000 people serving a farming community. The whole population was in the experiment, in the sense that they were promised help if their income dropped below the poverty level. One thousand families fell below the poverty line during the five-year experiment, comprising about one third of the population, and benefitted from a 'Mincome cheque'. This was not a true Basic Income in terms of the present day concept, but rather a Minimum Income Guarantee program. Nevertheless, it enables answers to be found for the questions posed. It was targeted on low-income people, including seniors and disabled people, who received income support with a 50 per cent withdrawal rate. It was based on the family rather than the individual, and the amount varied according to family size. However, it was unconditional. Either a researcher visited homes monthly to calculate their entitlement, or claimants appeared at the office each month, and filled out forms and produced pay stubs, while their identities were verified. The cheques topped up their incomes to the poverty line: 'everyone was given the same base amount: 60 per cent of Statistics Canada's low income cut-off. The cut-off varied depending on family size and where they lived. But in 1975, a single Canadian who was considered low-income earned $3,386 on average' (Lum, 2014). For a family of two it was $4,907, and the corresponding figures in 2014 were $16,094 and $20,443.

The results had not been analysed by the original team, and Evelyn

Forget's interest was mainly the health benefits of the experiment. Never-theless, it was established that few people had stopped working and hardly anyone with a full time job reduced the hours that they worked. The design of the program with its 50 per cent withdrawal rate had created incentives for people to work, and provided a much more effective method of supplementing the incomes of the working poor. Married women took longer maternity leave. Adolescents, mainly boys, reduced the hours that they worked. High school completion rates (grade 12) increased during the study. Many participants later expressed their grati-tude for their educational opportunities in school or in job training.

Poverty had been eliminated, aided by the financial predictability and stability of the Mincome support, keeping food on the table, bills paid, and the children in school. Researchers later said that they had not appreciated the depth of poverty experienced in Manitoba at that time. People were sick because they were poor. There were significant savings in health-care costs. Forget found that 'hospitalisation rates fell by 8.5 per cent among subjects in the experiment relative to the controls. The reasons for that are reductions in 'accidents and injuries', less domestic abuse, and reductions in hospitalisation for mental health issues' (Jourdan, 2013). In other words, there was a measurable positive impact on the health care system.

Despite the success of the experiment in eliminating poverty, and the fact that nearly 10 per cent of the population is living beneath the poverty line today, many people in Canada are still uncomfortable with the idea of a basic income, citing 'the best social policy is a job'. Now, low-income seniors receive a Guaranteed Income Supplement, and people with dependent children receive a National Child Benefit, but neither is adequate (Lum, 2014). Only the Federal Government could support a BI scheme, but social welfare is a provincial responsibility. Agreement between all the provinces would be needed for such a scheme.

Interest has risen recently, and Ontario announced in its 2016 budget that it will design and implement a Basic Income Pilot. On 24 June 2016, the Ministry of Community and Social Services announced that it has appointed Hugh Segal as Special Advisor and he will provide a discussion paper by the autumn. He will 'include advice about potential criteria for selecting target populations and/or locations, delivery models and advice about how the province could evaluate the results' (Ministry of Commu-nity and Social Services, 2016).

CHAPTER 8

Simplifying the administration system

Defining the population and criteria for eligibility

THE FIRST administrative task on implementing a BI system (as with any income maintenance system) is to define the population and establish eligibility criteria addressing specific residence requirements, and stipulating the conditions in which people are included.

De Wispelaere and Stirton (2007) examine the problems of establishing operational standards for eligibility that are clearly enough defined, so that they have universally acceptable meaning and are easy to apply in practice. Thus, in the UK context, there would be three criteria for evidence for eligibility for a 'universal' BI as discussed in chapter 5 above, paid as a right of citizenship:

- Proof of the legal right to permanent residence in the country;
- Proof of fulfilment of a minimum period of continuous legal residency in the country before becoming eligible to receiving the BI;
- Evidence of continuing residence (maintaining a physical presence) in the country for most of each subsequent year, while in receipt of a BI.

The problems associated with setting standards for eligibility for a BI then lead to the set of problems associated with identifying the beneficiaries. Any income maintenance system will involve:

> … producing and maintaining lists of individuals who satisfy the relevant criteria, as well as setting up a system to monitor whether they continue to fulfil these criteria.
>
> DE WISPELAERE *et al*, 2008: 5

This information is both difficult and expensive to obtain, and can involve intrusive and costly bureaucratic measures, for instance requiring regular visits from caseworkers:

> It is preferable that the sources of information against which such checking is done already exist, to avoid having to set up complicated and costly databases from scratch. Moreover, it would be crucial that the information

base itself only infrequently changes and is not susceptible to manipulation, to ensure reliability and stability of the assessment process.

DE WISPELAERE *et al*, 2008: 6

The design and administration of a *Participation Income* (PI) scheme
poses further problems: who decides what will be the approved forms of
education, training and voluntary work? While Atkinson's list may be
intuitively appealing, setting precise standards for eligibility for a PI is very
difficult (Atkinson, 2015: 218–223). De Wispelaere and Stirton (2008: 5)
correctly position PI between a 'universal' BI and workfare style policies
in terms of eligibility criteria, but with the criteria for BI being more
precise than for the PI, and workfare having very precise criteria. The
problems associated with setting standards for eligibility for a PI then lead
to those associated with identifying beneficiaries.

Alternative methods of assessment and delivery

While an income maintenance system is not usually defined by its admin-
istration method, it is nevertheless an important part of its structure.
There are two main delivery methods – the BI approach or the combined
Negative Income Tax (NIT) and Tax Credit (TC) method.

BI does not require a completely different administrative system, but
can build on the present one. The tax-exempt BIs can be paid automatically into the nominated bank account controlled solely by the recipient
or a parent with care. BIs should not be paid into a joint account, unless
authorised by a court of law, for instance, where necessary to enable the
BI to be administered on behalf of a person who is deemed as being
without the capacity to act. This delivery method ensures a regular,
predictable income, which is essential for those with no other source of
income. The frequency could be chosen by the recipient – weekly, fort-
nightly, or four-weekly. If the BI scheme is to be financed by the income
tax system, then the two systems are co-ordinated, but not integrated, and
the tax is levied separately from the BI scheme. The Pay-As-You-Earn (PAYE)
system already provides a good basis for collecting income tax from
employees at source throughout the year. The rest of the tax due is levied
after the end of the tax year in which the gross income was obtained. The
'sum of gross transfers' is the total of BIs paid out in a given time period
(a year). This sum together with any other cash transfer payments that
circulate around the economy and the administration costs of the system,
is relatively easy to calculate.

An alternative method could be provided by the NIT/TC system, in which the BI scheme and the income tax system are not just co-ordinated, but are integrated. A NIT is a net cash transfer payment to a recipient from which any lesser income tax due on gross income has been deducted from the BI. (NIT = BI – income tax, where BI > income tax). TCs in the context under discussion here, (in contrast to the means-tested Tax Credits paid to some working people in the UK today), is a net tax payment due on gross income, from which any lesser BI due has been deducted. (TC = income tax – BI, where BI < income tax) The 'sum of net transfers' of the scheme is defined as the sum of the TCs (the sum of the taxes paid minus the BIs received. paid by those are net tax payers, ie whose income tax is greater their BIs) and represents its real cost. The actual amount is difficult to calculate in advance because it depends directly on knowing the distribution of the gross income of all the individuals in the population.

The sum of the TCs would normally equal the sum of NITs, but the costs of administration, and various other items that have to be added to a margin in a hypothecated (ring-fenced) system, such as expenditure on disability benefits and other retained benefits and a social fund, have to be taken into account and added to the NITs (see chapter 11 below). The TC system, like the PAYE, could work relatively well for employees, but self-employed people would probably still have to make annual assessments for income tax after the end of the fiscal year.

Samuel Brittan (2006) commented: 'on the whole, basic income appeals to the left and negative income tax to the right. But analytically they are similar'.

If BIs are financed out of income tax, then government expenditure, which is spent on behalf of the population on services such as education, the NHS, social housing and infrastructure, would be financed out of indirect and other forms of taxation (see chapter 12 below).

The new Universal Credit (UC) system comes into the category of NIT/TC. However, its implementation has been delayed due to the computing problems that have arisen while trying to synchronise information about a worker from three different sources – (i) about the worker's current earnings from his or her employer, (ii) about his or her entitlement to benefit from the benefit agencies, and (iii) about tax liability from HMRC.

Three types of problems have arisen, due to:

- That of co-ordinating three different systems of different complexities: an employer has to give details of earnings for only a relatively small number of employees, but HMRC has details of millions of taxpayers, and the DWP has details of even more millions of people entitled to benefits.

- The frequency with which the units have to be assessed varies. Benefits have to be re-assessed whenever circumstances change. The new system tries to assess employees weekly for income tax and NICs, and adjust the benefit due accordingly.
- The current means-tested benefit system is based on the couple, while the income tax system is based on the individual.

The only difficulty likely to arise when combining the BI and tax systems is the different frequency with which individuals are usually assessed. Once eligibility has been established, a BI can been allocated on the basis of date of birth and, assuming that circumstances (a change of name or address, or a birth, adoption or death) do not change very often, reassessment will not occur frequently. The PAYE system deducts income tax from employees according to current earnings on a regular basis, and contributes regular revenue to the government throughout the year, while the assessment for income tax for the rest is usually made annually. The success of the system may depend on the frequency of re-assessment for BI status, and for income tax purposes.

Separating the systems into the delivery of the benefit, PAYE, and an annual income tax assessment system is by far the simpler administrative option.

Other effects of a BI on administration

Much of the social security system would be decriminalised. Claiming to be more than one person, or the care-giving parent claiming for more children than live with her, would be ways in which fraud could occur. Monitoring based on residence includes confirming that people live where they say that they do, and that they fulfil the residency conditions about the amount of time that must normally be spent in the country each year in order to remain eligible. Biometric records could have an important role to play here. Special arrangements would have to be made for some groups such as homeless people, travellers, and students studying abroad or taking a gap year. Monitoring also applies to the income tax system, to reduce illegal tax evasion. Nordic style transparency might help. In some Scandinavian countries, information about the gross income and taxes paid by every individual is available for any other citizen to view online. Many Scandinavians are proud of the amount that they contribute through taxation towards a good society.

One of the objectives for society listed in chapter 2 is to simplify the Social Security system, reducing the risk of errors and fraud, by either staff or recipient, leading to cheaper administration, (assessment, delivery, monitoring and compliance systems). This would make it more transparent and thus lead to increased accountability.

Administration includes defining the criteria for eligibility, identifying who meets the criteria, the monitoring of the population to ensure that everyone remains eligible, monitoring to ensure that they receive the appropriate amount. It involves delivering the BI, monitoring and dealing with those who would otherwise claim fraudulently, together with the administration of the income tax system or other taxes used to finance the BI scheme, including monitoring for tax evasion. The total cost of administration includes the cost of assessing and delivering the BI, monitoring the population, and bringing about compliance, together with the cost of error and fraud in terms of payments paid out unnecessarily and lost revenue.

Defining the population and establishing eligibility criteria would be necessary whatever system of income maintenance was in place. Choosing the individual rather than the couple as the tax/benefit unit will increase the number of units, but simplify the assessment and delivery of the BI. Universality will also increase the number of units. Reducing the number of means-tested benefits will simplify the system and reduce the inefficiency created by assessing an individual's means twice – once for income taxes and secondly again for the benefit.

Removing conditionality, and sanctions for its non-compliance, should also simplify the administration system. There will be no difference between out-of-work and in-work benefits. Selectivity will be reduced to a minimum, based on age, (date of birth), and being the primary care-giving parent, neither of which is likely to change very often.

However, a non-means-tested system of payments for disabled people will have to be retained and improved. Non-selectivity and removing conditionality will be less intrusive into people's lives than otherwise. But overall, monitoring for continued eligibility is likely still to be intrusive and costly, so the savings on administration might not be as substantial as many hope. Fewer social security staff are likely to be made redundant. Some could be redeployed, by offering them the opportunity to retrain for other professions, particularly as income tax inspectors, using their skills to help to prevent, or to recoup the gains from, illegal tax evasion. Their skills would also be useful for advising low-income people about retraining courses and job opportunities, and other related matters.

CHAPTER 9

Chronology of evidence from around the world

Overview

MUCH OF THE information for this chapter has been garnered from reports and articles in the Citizen's Income Newsletter, which can be read online or downloaded from www.citizensincome.org. The results of experiments and other projects over the decades and worldwide are also readily available. These can be explored through the website of the international Basic Income Earth Network (BIEN) (www.basicincome.org) by searching by country. This chapter serves as a chronology of BI projects around the world from the 1960s.

These projects include the Income Maintenance Experiments conducted in the USA in the late 1960s and early 1970s, and the Minimum Income (Mincome) experiment carried out in the town of Dauphin in Manitoba in Canada between 1974–79. The results of the Mincome project are only now being analysed by Professor Evelyn Forget of the University of Manitoba. Alaska has been able to distribute between $1,000 and $2,000 each year to every resident since 1982, from the income from a sovereign wealth fund based on its oil revenues. Brazil is the only country at present that has committed itself to transitioning from its current targeted, conditional cash payments to a BI in the future. Iran has virtually a BI *de facto* as a result of compensating its population for the loss of their subsidised fuel prices, which were contributing to pollution and increasing its carbon footprint. There are two recent well-documented pilot studies in a village in Namibia, and in India. The referendum on BI in Switzerland on 5 June 2016 rejected a change to the constitution. The proposal was popular with the population initially, but not with the government. The population is supportive of a BI experiment for Switzerland. The most ambitious proposal is the major experiment in Finland taking place over 2017–19. BI experiments have been mooted in Utrecht and other cities in the Netherlands and interest has been expressed in France and Germany. Scotland is the latest country to consider the possibility of a pilot project.

Few of these situations, with the exception of Alaska (discussed in Chapter 5), and the pilots in Namibia and India, involve a true BI, which is based on the individual, universal, and unconditional. The income maintenance experiments in the USA were minimum income guarantees (MIGs) targeted on poor people and were not based on the individual. The Mincome project (as discussed in Chapter 7) was also a MIG experiment. Brazil's *Bolsa Família* is targeted on children and is conditional on their attending school and health clinics. The Iranian experiment is almost a BI, being based on the individual, but it is delivered to the head of household (see chapter 6). Finland's initial announcement sounded as though it was going to conduct a *bona fide* BI pilot, but this has subsequently became watered down due to the cost involved and is now a MIG experiment. The same is true for the experiments in the Netherlands. Nevertheless, these projects provided benefits to their participants and much useful information can be gained from studying their effects on health, work incentives and the status of women, among other things.

Income maintenance experiments in the USA, 1968–80

Four income maintenance experiments (also known as negative income tax experiments) were carried out in the USA between 1968 and 1980:

- The New Jersey Graduated Work Incentive Experiment (NJ) of 1968–72;
- The Rural Income-Maintenance Experiment (RIME) of 1970–72 carried out in Iowa and North Carolina;
- The Seattle–Denver Income-Maintenance Experiments (SIME/DIME) of 1970–76 (or 1980) which was the largest; and
- The Gary, Indiana, Experiment (Gary) of 1971–74 (Widerquist, 2005a: 53).

Their purpose was to study the labour market effects of a negative income tax, but Widerquist finds their evidence inconclusive on this matter. However, they showed that NIT is financially feasible.

Mincome program, Dauphin, Manitoba, Canada, 1974–79 – Read about the Mincome Program at the end of chapter 7.

Alaska 1976 – Read about Alaska at the end of chapter 5.

It will be noted that these two incidences in North America occur early in the chronology of late 20th century Minimum Income Guarantee experiments and BI projects. Then not much happens for another two to three decades.

Brazil 2004 –

In 2001 Senator Eduardo Suplicy of the Brazilian Workers Party introduced a law for a conditional *Bolsa Família* cash transfer program. The Senate approved it in 2002 and the Chamber of Deputies in 2003. President Luiz Inácio Lula da Silva sanctioned it in Law 10.853/2004 on 8 January 2004. It was introduced to support those most in need, and then to transition over time into the unconditional Citizen's Basic Income, as a right of everyone to participate in the wealth of the nation (Citizen's Income Trust, 2010: 6).

Brazil was one of the most unequal countries in the world, with widespread poverty, due, among other things, to unexpected economic shocks and fickle labour markets. The poverty was unequally distributed, with greatest concentrations in the Northern and Northeast Regions (Illingworth, 2016: 6).

Luis Henrique Paiva, who worked on the *Bolsa Família* project for five years, described the program in an interview with Sarah Illingworth (Illingworth, 2016: 2–6). It provides small conditional cash transfer payments for those whose current income places them below the poverty line. These people tend to be in the informal economy and are not covered by the traditional social insurance and social assistance programs. They are able to work, and are working, but are not able to earn enough to raise themselves out of poverty. An earlier smaller program, *Bolsa Escola*, was conditional on children attending school and undergoing health checks, and it had the secondary outcome of poverty-stricken families reclaiming their children who had been abandoned on the streets, thus solving two problems at once. Children are disproportionately affected by poverty and the *Bolsa Família* program has a component addressed to improve the human capital of children to give them better prospects in the long term. The *Bolsa Família* payment is also conditional on children attending school and undergoing health checks.

The *Bolsa Família* (which translates as 'family purse') for the children is paid to the mother, wherever possible, thus helping to support families. There are four components. Currently, 170 reals (c. US$54) is paid on average to each family per month. If they are extremely poor, they receive 77 reals extra. They can also receive 35 reals for every child aged between

0–15, and 42 reals for each adolescent aged 16 and 17. If the family income is still below the poverty line, then they are topped up to this level. This is funded by less than 0.5 per cent of the country's GDP. An interesting feature is that there is no maximum period of entitlement, but instead, a family can continue to receive the *Bolsa Família* for a *minimum* period of two years after its earnings rise above the poverty line, to enable the family to stabilise its income in a fluctuating situation. By 2006, 11 million families were benefiting from the program. By 2015, it reached around 14 million families, comprising 50 million people – about a quarter of the population of Brazil – and the conditionality is being phased out.

The program has been evaluated frequently. It was found to have raised the income levels of the poorest, and improved their overall well-being. Poverty has been reduced and school attendance improved. It has been found that in spite of the design being the same all over Brazil, it works very well in the poor regions and, in fact, it works a little better there than in the more affluent municipalities.

In 2014 it was found that three-quarters of Brazilian voters supported this program to protect the poor population. However, it is recognised that economic growth can lead to an increase in jobs, providing a secure source of income, protected by social insurance, and reducing the informal economy as a percentage of the whole, with an attendant reduction in poverty. Economic growth also increases tax revenues from which transfers are made, which was also an important part of poverty reduction in Brazil. But, economic growth, while important, it is not the only solution to reducing poverty, and it can temporarily increase inequality. Rural-urban migration has meant that, with less than 15 per cent of the population living in rural areas, Brazil is no longer a rural economy, and while urban poverty has grown in incidence, its depth is less than for rural poverty. Brazil's *Bolsa Família* program is an important example of how a small conditional cash transfer, targeted at women and other poor people, can be a precursor to an unconditional basic income system.

Namibia 2008–9

The Namibian Basic Income Grant Coalition comprised several organisations including the Council of Churches, the Namibian Union of Namibian workers, the Namibian NGO Forum and the Namibian Network of AIDS Service Organisations. It started discussions with the Namibian government as early as 2004 to persuade it to set up a Basic Income Grant (BIG) scheme for all residents in Namibia, to address the severe poverty experienced by about half of its population. The government was unwilling to commit itself without some evidence about the effect of such a scheme. There were the usual prejudices predicting that it would encourage idleness, alcoholism and crime (Haarman, 2008). From 2004 the Namibian BIG Coalition campaigned to raise private donations from across Namibia and abroad, from both organisations and individuals, to finance an experiment.

The experiment took place in the two years from January 2008 to December 2009, in the small settlement of Otjivero-Omitara, a very low-income rural area in Namibia. Namibia is a low to middle income country, with average earnings per head of US$2,000 in 2009–10, but Namibia is one of the most unequal countries in the world, According to the CIA *World Factbook*, 34.9 per cent of the population lived on less than one Namibian Dollar, N$1, per day, and 55.8 per cent lived on less than N$2 per day (Wikipedia, 2016). Otjivero was at the lower income end, experiencing high levels of unemployment, poverty and frequent hunger. Every individual man, woman and child who was resident in Otjivero on 31 July 2007, and who was under 60 years of age, was registered for the experiment. For children under the age of 21, a primary care-giver was provided, who by default was the mother. A sample of 50 out of some 200 households, comprising 930 residents, were selected to receive an unconditional income of N$100 (about US$12, or £7) per month for the two years (Haarman *et al*, 2008). (The cost for 930 residents at N$100 per month for 24 months will have been N$2,232,000 or £156,240, together with the costs of the researchers). A smart card was used to deliver the BIG. This contained the name(s), ID numbers and a picture, together with a microchip containing the date of birth, fingerprints, and information about the amount of the BIG and the history of their receipt of the grant.

A four-part method was used to collect data for the experiment:

- A baseline survey of the residents took place in November 2007.
- This was followed by a panel survey every six months thereafter until November 2009.
- Further information was provided by key informants, including the local nurse, police chief, shopkeepers and other local leaders.
- Detailed case studies of individuals were recorded.

The objective of the experiment was to achieve several goals, such as the eradication of poverty, universal primary education, and to promote gender equality and empower women (Haarman, 2008: 96). Even after as little as six months, significant changes were obvious. The percentage of malnourished children dropped from 42 to 17. More children attended school, and the drop-out rates reduced from 30–40 to five per cent. The schools were able to improve their teaching materials out of increased school revenues. Women's economic status improved and women were empowered through gaining more choices, enabling them to escape from abusive relationships and avoid having to earn money through sexual services. Health benefits were noted. More people were able to afford to visit the health clinic, leading to a reduction in cases of diarrhoea. Better nutrition for pregnant women improved maternal health. Improved nutrition and access to the clinic complemented the government's efforts to provide anti-retroviral therapy drugs to combat AIDS and HIV.

The majority of the participants increased their work, whether their hours of work were for pay, for profit or family gain, or from self-employment. The income in the community increased more than the total value of the grants, indicating that they had engaged in productive activities. BIG fostered local economic growth and development, including several small local enterprises. The number of crimes due to poverty declined. The experiment also had positive environmental effects, when access to electricity replaced cooking over firewood (Haarman, 2008).

The experiment demonstrated the undeniable beneficial effects of a BIG program. However, the Namibian BIG Coalition was angry when the government failed to extend the Otjivero program or take steps to implement it elsewhere in Namibia. In a press release they stated:

> Despite the positive results, the Namibian government has still not committed itself to the introduction of a BIG (Basic Income Grant: Citizen's Income) in Namibia. Instead, senior government leaders have raised concerns that the grant would make people lazy and dependent on handouts. Such perceptions are rooted in prejudices rather than being based on the evidence provided by Otjivero! We wish to point out that the BIG coalition arranged for many Namibians, including Members of Parliament (MPs), to visit Otjivero and to witness the developments there firsthand. The honourable MPs were free to assess the impact of the BIG themselves and they were impressed with the results achieved in Otjivero. However, they preferred to express their views in private instead of speaking out publicly in support of a national BIG.

NAMIBIAN BIG COALITION, 2012

Further information about the Namibian BIG Coalition and the BI pilot project can be found via www.bignam.org.

Iran 2010 – Read about Iran
at the end of chapter 6

India 2011–13 Read about India
at the end of chapter 4

It is interesting to note that when Minimum Income Guarantee and BI projects resumed from 2004 onwards, it was not in the west, but they took place in developing countries. From 2012, attention switches to Europe.

European Citizens' Initiative on
Unconditional Basic Income, 2012–14

A long period followed after the implementation of the Mincome experiment in Canada (1974–79) and the APF Dividend (1982) before another four countries, all in the developing world, experienced a cash transfer program – Brazil (2004–), Namibia (2008–09), Iran (2010–) and India (2011–13) – of relatively small amounts, all with very positive results that had transformed the lives of the very poorest. The first move towards implementation of a BI in Europe resulted from the creation of a new procedure (2012) by the EU. Although that project failed, it has led to growing interest in the concept widely across Europe and has led to some new ventures, such as the Swiss Referendum (2016), a proposal for a pilot study in Finland in 2017–19, and other proposals and interest in the Netherlands, France and Germany. The BI proposals in Europe have been for higher levels of BI to replace current social security benefits.

In April 2012, the European Union (EU) created a new participatory procedure entitled the European Citizens' Initiative (ECI). This instrument enables citizens to register a petition before the European Commission, which will be discussed if the petitioners manage to attract one million signatures from the 500 million inhabitants across the 28 countries of the EU within a year of the date of registration. On 26–27 April 2012, more than 50 people of all ages met at the European Parliament in Brussels to agree the text for an ECI on 'Unconditional Basic Income (UBI) – Exploring a pathway towards emancipatory welfare conditions in the EU', that had been prepared by Klaus Sambor from Austria and Ronald Blaschke from Germany (Miller, 2012).

In the document, the emancipatory UBI is defined by the following four criteria: universal, individual, unconditional, and high enough to ensure a life of dignity and enabling participation in public life. There was some debate as to whether the definition should be relaxed in order to widen support for the ECI, but this was rejected. Some of this debate related to 'the wording of the 'universality' criterion, with respect to who should be eligible, whether the 'European citizen' (with its legal connotations), or a 'member', 'inhabitant', 'legal resident' or just 'resident' of the European Union. In the end those present voted to refer to the UBI as a human right, without specifying the population... leaving that battle for a later date' (Miller, 2012: 9). Similarly, no means of funding the UBI was specified. It would be up to each member state to work out the particular means of implementing its own scheme. The document set out the objectives of the UBI, and referred to Articles in various pieces of EU legislation, where the introduction of a UBI would help the Parliament to fulfil its obligations more satisfactorily.

The ECI asked the Commission to encourage cooperation between member states, aiming to explore the UBI as a tool to improve their respective social security systems. In the short run, the EU was asked to promote initiatives such as pilot schemes, and an examination of different models of UBI. In the long run, the objective is to offer to each person in the EU the unconditional right as an individual, to having his/her material needs met to ensure a life of dignity as stated by the EU treaties, and to empower participation in public life supported by the introduction of the UBI.

The ECI on UBI was registered by a group of some 50 people from 15 European countries on 14 January 2013. However, the real work of campaigning for the ECI–UBI and inviting people to sign up was slow to get off the ground. Partly it was due to unfamiliarity with the new procedure, and partly due to the fact that few of the countries had campaign groups already set up and available to spread the word. Developing those networks took up much of the valuable time. The rate of signings increased enormously in the final weeks. Unfortunately, the petition only raised 285,000 signatures during 2013 (www.basicincome2013.eu). This was not so much due to an antipathy to the idea, but to the enormous difficulty in educating the public, and the high bar of one million signatures that was set. However, it has raised the profile of UBI across the EU. The work of promoting the concept of a BI in Europe continues via UBI-Europe (www.basicincome-europe.org/ubie).

Switzerland 2012–16

During the year in which the ECI on UBI was trying to collect one million signatures, Switzerland, which is not in the EU, but which has a tradition of holding referenda, raised 126,406 valid signatures, (far more than the 100,000 necessary), to raise an 'initiative'. The organisers filed a petition to ask the Swiss Parliament for a referendum on Basic Income (Van Parijs, 2016). All Swiss citizens were asked to vote on the following proposition:

1 The Confederation introduces an unconditional basic income.

2 The basic income must enable the whole population to live a dignified life and to participate in public life.

3 The law will determine the funding and level of the basic income.

The referendum took place on Sunday 5 June 2016, and was rejected by 77% of the voters. Switzerland would seem an unlikely candidate for the introduction of a BI, since it has comparatively low levels of unemployment and poverty. However, the rejection may have had more to do with the fact that the figure of CHF 2,500 (Swiss Francs) per month for an adult and CHF 625 per month for a child had been mentioned on the campaign's website. At an exchange rate of 73 per cent, these figures are equivalent to £1,825 pm (£426 pw), for an adult and £456 pm (£106 pw) for a child. A BI of CHF 2,500 represents 38 per cent of Switzerland's GDP per capita. Yet Enno Schmidt, a co-initiator of the Swiss Referendum, on 1 October 2016 at the conference celebrating the 30th anniversary of the foundation of BIEN, at Louvain-La-Neuve, claimed that this was well within the ability of Switzerland to pay for it.

An equivalent for the UK would be 38 per cent of £550.68 pw in 2015, (see Appendix A), which is £209.26 pw, which in turn represents 51 per cent of mean income per head of £411.89 pw in 2015 (latest figures available). This would require a tax rate in a restructured income tax system in the UK of around 51 per cent plus a margin of 5–6 per cent to cover administration and retained benefits. While it is conceivable that such a high level could be demanded eventually by a population, and be sustainable, it may have been too large a leap in the dark for a nation where pilot experiments have not been carried out, and a suitable method of funding it has not been indicated. The introduction of lower levels of BI initially would seem advisable.

Despite the defeat, the Swiss referendum has had very positive outcomes in terms of educating the public both in Switzerland and further afield about basic incomes, but it has also revealed the challenges that face campaigners.

In Switzerland, it is fairly usual for another referendum on a particular subject to be put to the people a few years later.

Finland 2015–

The announcement in November 2015, that Finland will dedicate €20m towards a BI experiment over two years, starting in 2017, the first large-scale trial in Europe, was greeted with a flurry of excitement (Laterza, 2015). The Prime Minister, Juha Sipilä, of the newly elected, centre-right coalition, favours a BI, and is supported by most of the major political parties. Plans were being drawn up involving KELA, (The Social Insurance Institution of Finland that disburses benefits), four Finnish Universities, and three other institutions. KELA highlighted four objectives behind the trial:

- To overhaul the social security system taking account of changes in the labour market;
- To make it more effective in terms of providing incentives to work for pay and avoiding the poverty trap;
- To simplify the administration system, reducing bureaucracy and administration costs; and
- To evaluate the effects on members of different population groups.

The geographical areas to be covered by the experiment and the sample size had still to be decided. It was anticipated that the experiment will involve four different schemes – (i) a full BI, (ii) a partial BI, (iii) a BI delivered in the form of NIT and TCs, where the delivery is through the income tax system, and (iv) a Participation Income given to unemployed people. The full BI could involve €800 pm, or €187 pw, (£640 pm, £149 pw) paid to adults, but not to children. The partial BI would replace basic benefits, but leave intact almost all of the existing insurance–based benefits, and a level of €550 per month (£440 pm, or £103 pw) was mooted. 'In a recent survey carried out by KELA, nearly 70 per cent of respondents support the idea of a universal basic income, and most of them think that it should be set at around 1,000 euros per month' (ie about £800 pm, or £187 pw) (Laterza, 2015: 4).

On 30 March 2016, KELA released its preliminary report (Kangas, 2016). It concluded that a full basic income would be too expensive to implement, and that the negative income tax method would require access to a comprehensive registry of self-reported incomes that would not necessarily be reliable. The participation income would run into problems in defining the level of participation required by reciprocity and problems of supervision and control (McFarland, 2016). However, 'a partial basic income model would consolidate many of the existing benefits offering basic economic security, while earnings-related benefits would remain largely unaffected' (McFarland, 2016: 3).

The experiment started in January 2017:

> 2,000 unemployed people between the ages of 25 and 58 will receive a guaranteed sum… of €560 a month for two years. It replaces their unemployment benefit, but they will continue to receive it whether or not they find work. The government hopes it will encourage the unemployed to take on part-time work without worrying about losing their benefits.
>
> SODHA, 2017

Netherlands, France and Germany

Finland's announcement of its intention to carry out a basic income pilot project has stimulated interest elsewhere in Europe. The city of Utrecht responded first, announcing its intention of holding an experiment in the city. This was quickly followed by some 30 other cities expressing an interest in the idea (Jourdan, 2015). The Netherlands has a national minimum income system that is means-tested, conditional and household based. Utrecht's experiment is not strictly about a basic income, since it will be targeted at current welfare claimants, will not be based on the individual, and will still be means-tested. However, it will be less conditional with respect to work requirements and it aims to remove the poverty trap by allowing people to earn extra income. Figures of €900 and €1,300 per month per adult have been mentioned. In September 2015, the cities of Utrecht, Tilberg, Wageningen and Groningen were advised by the Dutch Ministry of Social Affairs that they should come up with a common plan, if they wanted official funding for their experiments.

BIEN (2016) reports on recent developments in France and Germany. In France, basic income activists organised a conference on BI in Paris on 2 February 2016, attended by 600 people. On 3 March a conference was organised at the Finnish Embassy in Paris to discuss the Finnish proposals. On 18 March, a report called 'Rethinking Social Minima' by Christophe Sirugue MP, commissioned by the government in October 2015, recommended a complete revamp of the French Welfare system. It included key measures demanded by the movement for BI in France, but did not go as far as recommending a BI. In early June, the French Senate rejected a motion calling on the government to introduce a BI, but decided to form a parliamentary commission to investigate the idea, and report back by the autumn.

A German paper calculated that a BI of €800 per month per adult (c. £640 pm, £150 pw) could be financed by a flat tax of 68.9 per cent. *Der Spiegel* published two articles on the idea on 25 December 2015 and 28 January 2016, reported in BIEN News (Joerimann, 2016). The first article compared a 'humanist' Swiss proposal of €1,500 per month each with the 'neoliberal' Finnish one of €664 per month and German supporters' proposal of €1,000 per month. These would cost a total of €1,200, €530 and €800 billions respectively, representing two thirds, a bare 30 per cent and about 45 per cent compared with the sum of all private incomes in Germany in 2011. The second article recounted an interview with Daniel Häni and Philip Kovce, authors of a book on BI in which 'one of the core motivations is the social transformation from alienated work into intrinsically motivated, freely chosen activities... No-one can seriously expect the return to full employment under the conditions and in the form we experienced in the 1970s' (Joerimann, 2016: 3). A campaign for a referendum on BI, called 'Omnibus for Direct Democracy' has been touring cities around Germany collecting more than 90,000 signatures to present to the German Parliament.

Update on BI projects in May 2017

Sadly, the initial aspiration of many BI pilot projects is not upheld in the final design. This has already been observed with the Finnish project. Similarly, the Dutch cities found themselves prevented by the Dutch Participation Act from making unconditional cash transfers. McFarland (2017) provides a useful update on these and four other current projects in Kenya, Ontario in Canada, Uganda and Oakland in the USA. These are summarised in Table 9.1. Now the focus is worldwide.

Not all of the pilot projects discussed earlier have come to fruition. Often the media flags up news of these as though they were much further along the process than is the case. Some proposed projects fail to raise the necessary finance.

To be regarded as a *bona fide* BI project, it must fulfil the following conditions of being:

- Based on the individual;
- Universal in the sense of including all age groups and all income ranges;

- Non-selective except by age;
- Unconditional and not means-tested; and
- Delivered regularly and automatically to all who qualify

It will be noted that only the projects in Kenya and Uganda in Table 9.1 fulfil these conditions. An authentic BI experiment would also include its potential source of finance endogenously, and the effects of both *a variety of levels of* BI and *a range of funding levels* would be examined.

Scotland

Growing interest has been expressed in a series of reports in the UK in which costed BI schemes have been proposed. These are discussed further in chapter 15. Trustees of the newly formed Citizen's Basic Income Network Scotland (CBINS) were invited to attend talks in Glasgow and Fife, together with Guy Standing, who had been heavily involved in the two pilot projects in Namibia and India. Glasgow, Fife and North Ayrshire Councils are keen to host BI pilot studies, and councillor, Matt Kerr, is pursuing the idea through Glasgow City Council (Brooks, 2017). The Glasgow City Council, in partnership with the Royal Society of Arts (RSA) in Scotland, has commissioned a feasibility study for its own basic income pilot (Sodha, 2017). Paul Vaughan, Head of Community and Corporate Development at Fife Council, is preparing a strategy document to lay out the procedures necessary to get such a project going. The initial phase is about getting the principal agencies on side – DWP, HMRC and HM Treasury – and the agreement of both Westminster and Holyrood governments. This is more likely to occur if citizens put pressure on all MSPs and Scottish MPs to insist that an authentic BI pilot experiment goes ahead. Much more planning is required, so a pilot study is unlikely to begin before 2019.

The Scottish Social Security Committee invited Donald Hirsch, Annie Miller, Siobhan Mathers, Anthony Painter and Howard Reed to give oral evidence on BI at Holyrood on 9 March 2017. The committee members were well briefed and asked pertinent questions, especially whether a BI scheme could be set up under the current devolved powers to Scotland. The limited powers devolved under the Scotland Act 2016 means that it would be difficult, but not impossible (Scottish Social Security Committee, 2017).

TABLE 9.1 SUMMARY OF SOME BI PILOT EXPERIMENTS OR PROJECTS

LOCATION; TEAM; LEADER(S).	Duration	SAMPLE SIZE; CONTROLS.	Sat/ RCT	Ind or HH?	Universal?	Un-conditional?	AMOUNT OF CASH PAYMENT	OBJECTIVES
FINLAND; KELA; Olli Kangas. http://www.kela.fi/web/en/basic-income-experiment-2017–2018.	01/01/17–31/12/18	2000 out of 175,000 eligible. The remainder comprise the control group.	RCT Man-dat-ory	Ind	No. Only subjects aged 25–58, receiving unemploy-ment benefit at end of 2016 are included.	Yes.	€560 per month: **NB**. No questionnaires or interviews will be used, to minimise influence on results – only data from administrative registers. No results until after end of project	Examine differences in: employment rates between those receiving BIs and those not receiving BIs; expenditure on medication; health care usage; and income variation.
KENYA; 'GiveDirectly' (US charity). www.givedirectly.org/basic-income.	First village, Oct 2016. Rest in Sept 2017;	300 villages randomly assigned to one of 4 groups; 200 villages (about 26,000 people) to 3 treatment groups. 100 villages in control group.	Sat	Ind	Yes	Yes	23 US$ (€21) per month: 40 villages for 12 years; 80 villages for 2 years; 80 villages receive lump sum equivalent to 24 months of regular BI.	How important is guarantee of future transfers, for risk-taking, eg starting a business? What difference does it make, having it as a lump sum rather than a regular payment? Will also investigate 'economic status', time use, risk-taking and gender relations.
CANADA, Ontario. Guaranteed Minimum Income Pilot. www.ontario.ca/page/ontario-basic-income-pilot	2017 late spring late spring autumn, – till 2020	4,000 potential participants from Hamilton, Brantford and Brant County; Thunder Bay & surrounding area; & City of Lindsay	RCT Vol	HH	No. Only subjects aged 18–64 on low incomes, who have lived there for at least one year	No, it is mean-tested with 50% with-drawal rate, but not work-	Single individuals: 16,989 CA$, (€11,340) pa. Couples: 24,027 CA$ (€16,038) pa. Disabled people: extra 500 CA$ (€334) per month.	Measure food security, stress and anxiety, mental health, health and healthcare usage, housing stability, education and training, and employment and labour market participation.

Study	Status / Dates	Sample	RCT	Unit	Randomised	Unconditional (tested)	Amount	Outcomes
NETHERLANDS: Municipal Social Assistance Experiments – under review by Ministry of Social Affairs	Start Sept 2017?	Cities: Grogingen; Tilburg; Wageningen. (Utrecht indefinitely delayed.)	Vol	HH, by law	No – sample randomly selected from a pool of current welfare recipients, assigned to either a treatment or a control group.	No, due to the Dutch Participation Act – claimants *must* search for work.		The effect of treatment groups (which are subject to workforce-reintegration requirements that are more intensive than current welfare programs), on: Employment (including part-time and temporary); Education; Health and well being.
UGANDA; 'Eight World' (Belgian charity).	01/01/17–31/12/18	All residents of village of Busibi: 56 adults, 88 children. More villages later. No control village.	Sat	Ind	Yes	Yes.	Adult: 18.25 US$ (€16.70) per month; Child: 9.13 US$ (€8.35) per month.	Compare data during and after the project with that from before, re: Girls' educational achievement, access to health care, entrepreneurship and economic development, and participation in democratic institutions.
USA, Oakland; Y Combinator; Sam Altman, Elizabeth Rhodes. Unconditional Cash Transfer Study	Pre-pilot, announced in May 2016, to help to design main pilot, ie now in design phase.	Stratified sample of 2–3,000 individuals from two states. 1,000 randomly assigned to receive BI for 3 years; a subset receives BI for 5 years. Remainder provides control group		Ind	No, aged 21–35, with household incomes less than the median in their area.	Yes.	1,000 US$ (€915) per month.	Holistic evaluation of individual-level outcomes such as: labour market participation, training and education, time spent with children, physical and psychological health and well being, risk-taking, financial health, and help given to friends and family.

Key for Table 9.1
- KELA = the Social Security Institution of Finland
- Sat = saturation sample, eg whole of one village.
- RCT = randomized control trials.
- Ind = individual.
- HH = household.

Ref: (McFarland, 2017)

PART III

Economic Viability – Facts and Figures

PART III

Economic Viability: Facts and Figures

AT A CONFERENCE on 1 October celebrating the 30th anniversary of the foundation of BIEN, sociologist Erik Olin Wright identified two elements that contribute to 'feasibility'. Viability refers to whether a scheme is economically sustainable once implemented, and achievability refers to the process of getting the scheme implemented in the first place. Economic viability is the subject matter of Part III, and achievability is discussed in Part IV, chapter 15.

In Part III, the information changes markedly. The emphasis is on facts and figures. While the concepts are not difficult, a lot of detail is provided to enable readers to follow the process, including the sources of the data. Some readers might prefer to skip straight to chapter 14, where a range of illustrative sample schemes is presented, from the cheapest entry-level scheme to more generous ones. The object of this exercise is to demonstrate that these schemes are economically viable, even if not necessarily considered to be politically achievable at the present time.

Chapter 10 puts forward two measures of prosperity for an economy and addresses the question of 'How much should the BI be?' by comparison with two poverty benchmarks. In chapter 11, an example of costing a scheme is presented. Chapter 12 addresses the question of 'How could it be financed?' and presents the pros and cons of different methods of financing a scheme, indicating the revenues that different taxes have yielded in recent years. The costs to the economy of various loopholes in the income tax system are examined. In chapter 13 a case is made for financing the more generous BI schemes via a hypothecated, restructured income tax system, and for estimating the cost of a scheme in terms of a flat rate income tax in order to obtain a single figure for comparisons between schemes. Obviously more progressive tax systems, alternative sources of funding and combinations of sources are feasible.

There is no single optimum scheme that can satisfy everyone. A variety of BI schemes is possible. Each scheme is determined by a set of prioritised objectives, assumptions and constraints, some with alternative sources of funding. When putting forward any BI scheme, it is essential that all of these starting points are made clear, together with the figures to back them up.

Some key figures for the UK 2011–15 and Scotland 2012–15 have been collated in Appendix A for easy reference.

CHAPTER 10

Deciding on the BI levels

HOUSING POLICY in the UK over recent decades has led to high prices and rents, making it increasingly difficult for poorer people to find affordable housing. However, the application of Local Housing Allowances to social housing as well as to private housing does seem to introduce a mechanism for rent controls once more. Substantial regional variation in housing costs across the UK makes it impossible to include an element for housing costs within the BI, without leaving many of the poorest in high rent areas with insufficient resources to cover their housing costs. In the meantime, until a housing policy is introduced that achieves greater affordability of housing costs, the BI system will have to rely on a separate, individualised, means-tested Housing Benefit and Council Tax Support, including water rates. The Housing Benefit would operate in the same way as for students sharing accommodation at present, and should cover both rent and mortgage interest up to a given level, but not repayment of capital. Given this assumption, the BI schemes discussed here have to be based on 'After Housing Costs have been deducted' (AHC) versions of poverty thresholds. This also implies that even those receiving a full BI based on AHC could effectively still be dependent on means-testing for housing costs, but to a lesser extent than now. Thus, the housing policy that has been implemented over the last four decades undermines the objective of ending MTBS completely and thus of obtaining labour market efficiency, but it is unavoidable under current housing policy.

Measures of prosperity in society

Gross Domestic Product (GDP) measures the value of all the output/income/expenditure of a country in a given year (Kishtainy, 2014: 182–4). Although widely cited, it is a flawed standard and the flaws are usually listed in any introductory economics textbook. The flaws include the fact that GDP excludes the value of the unpaid care and other domestic work contributed mainly by women, and the volunteer work given by all ages and both sexes, that underpins the whole monetary economy. Another flaw is that the GDP includes the cost of making good the bad outcomes of the economy, treating them as another good, rather than deducting them as a cost to society. However, GDP per person can be a useful measure of living standards.

In the examples developed here, in preference to GDP per person, BIS are compared with mean gross income per head as derived from the 'Income of Households and Non-Profit Institutions Serving Households (NPISH)' that measures the gross personal income that passes through wallets and purses of UK inhabitants each year (see Table 10.1 below). In economics, income is often given the symbol 'Y'. The symbol 'i' is used for an interest rate. In statistics, the average, or mean, of any variable is often indicated by writing a straight line above it, referred to as 'bar'. Thus, average or mean income is often referred to as 'Y-BAR' (pronounced 'why-bar'). Both GDP per person and mean gross income per head reflect the prosperity of society in different ways, while avoiding the issue of repatriated profits and transfer pricing inherent in measures based on Gross *National* Product (GNP).

Table 10.1 Measures of prosperity in UK and Scotland

	2014			2015		
£	UK	Scotland	Scot/UK %	UK	Scotland	Scot/UK %
GDP pc pa	28,120	26,141	92.96	28,714	27,284	95.02
pw	539.29	501.33		550.68	523.26	
Y-BAR pa	20,560	19,306	93.90	21,477	20,461	95.26
pw	394.30	370.25		411.89	392.40	
Y-BAR/GDP %	73.12	73.85		74.80	74.99	

Sources of Data
- For the UK, *United Kingdom National Accounts, The Blue Book*: 2015 and 2016 editions: tables 1.5 and 6.1.3;
- For Scotland, *Scottish National Accounts Project*, Tables A and 1.
- Mid-year estimates for population figures 2014 and 2015.

Reference will be made in chapter 14 to the weekly figures for Y-BAR given in Table 10.1 above.

The income measure, Y-BAR, is less than GDP. The difference between them is the income that is paid directly to the government without going through people's pockets or bank accounts, of which the largest component is 'Taxes on production and imports, less subsidies' (Compare *Blue Book* tables 1.2 and 6.1.3). Both GDP per head and mean gross income per head give an upper bound to what is possible in terms of a BI scheme in society at any given time. The income measure for the UK used to be about 80 per cent of GDP, but has slipped to around 74 per cent in recent years.

Y-BAR is the mean gross income for individuals and will be used as a reference throughout this work. It is:

- Claimed at the end of this chapter, that it is a better measure of the prosperity of society than median income;
- Easier to relate to one's own income than GDP per capita;
- Claimed at the end of this chapter that it is a preferable basis for allocating BIs than our official EU poverty benchmark based on current median equivalised net household income; and
- Also useful when relating the amounts of BI to income tax rates.

Scottish figures for Y-BAR are currently about 93–95 per cent of the UK figures, but this could improve if Scotland had more control over its fiscal and other economic instruments.

Poverty

We all know what we mean by poverty, but it is a very difficult concept to define. Preventing poverty could mean providing the inputs that would be necessary to combat it, or providing a share of a community's resources, whether in terms of a crop, or in terms of a money income, even though it may not actually achieve the aim of preventing poverty. Alternatively, one could aim to prevent poverty as the outcome.

Absolute poverty refers to a state in which the individual is unable to consume the necessary resources to maintain physical health, and his/her body starts to die, slowly at first. This concept has been applied in communities in dire poverty, where this is relevant. In advanced industrial societies, the term *relative poverty* is usually more appropriate, in which the individual does not have enough resources to maintain a dignified standard of living, and is unable to participate fully in society.

'Need' is often used to denote a drive or some inner state that initiates a drive' (Doyal *et al*, 1991: 35). There is a small number of universal, ahistoric, basic needs, (such as to maintain good health, provide protection and security, affection, leisure, etc), that can be satisfied by an infinite diversity of culturally determined satisfiers. It follows that an individual could be deprived in one or more needs. This implies that there could be different types of deprivation and different degrees of poverty. Recent research (Miller, 2015) predicts that an individual deprived in two dimensions of need experiences dysfunctional poverty, but if deprived in only one dimension, she/he may experience functional poverty, and thus be able to act as an economic agent and contribute to society.

For purposes of BI, we shall concentrate on income poverty, (an input measure).

Different methods of determining a poverty threshold have been developed. For absolute poverty, specialists in nutrition and heating have estimated how much is needed to sustain life, and then the cost of this is calculated. A second method applies some arbitrary amount that may, or may not, be underpinned by evidence (see, for example, the official EU poverty benchmark below). A third way is to ask focus groups belonging to a specific household configuration to estimate how much they would need to meet their basic needs. The Minimum Income Standard, discussed below, is an example of this. Fourthly, using statistical analysis and the relevant data, an appropriate economic model can estimate the minimum income required by a group of similar people, (pensioners, single parents, or married women, etc.), at a particular point in time.

A floor and two poverty benchmarks

a   Current UK means-tested benefit levels

The amounts of the UK government's own benefits are set arbitrarily, not necessarily bearing any relationship to a recognised method of measuring poverty. They are offered here, not as a benchmark or aspiration, but as a lower limit or floor for any proposed BI scheme. Some of the UK's current means-tested weekly Social Assistance benefits for 11 different household configurations for 2014–15 and 2017–18 are listed in Tables 10.4a and 10.4b respectively below. The tables list Pension Credit rates for those over pension-entitlement age, and Income Support (IS)/Jobseeker's Allowance (JSA)/Employment Support Allowance (ESA) entitlements, both for young adults aged 16–24 inclusive, and for working age adults aged 25 or over, without dependent children. The amounts for IS/JSA/ESA plus Child Benefit and Child Tax Credit are listed for families with dependent children aged 0–15.

b   The EU's official poverty threshold

The EU's official measure of poverty is defined as '0.6 of median equivalised household income' for a nation's population (DWP, 2015: 11, section 1.2). Median income divides the population into a half which has more income than the median income and a half which has less. Median income is always less than mean or average income in a skewed distribution such as the income distribution. The EU's official poverty measure is another example of an arbitrary measure, but it does bear some relationship to the prosperity of the nation, and has some authority having been agreed across the EU. It is an important benchmark, incorporated into UK legislation in the Child Poverty Act 2010 (DWP, 2015: 19).

Equivalisation is the process of adjusting household incomes according to the size and composition of a household, usually taking an adult couple without children as the reference point (DWP, 2015, 12–13). Weighting systems vary in both the differentiations that they make between members of the household, (first adult, spouse, other second adult, third adult, subsequent adults, children aged 14 years and over, and children aged under 14 years), and the weights that are applied (DWP, 2015: 13, Table 3). The distribution of weights among the members of the household reveal the different assumptions, perceptions or prescriptions made by those allocating them about the relative material living standards of the household members for the consumption of goods and services. In other words, no weighting system can be anything other than subjective. The weights for each individual in the household are aggregated. The intention of attaching weights is to enable comparisons to be made of the incomes of households of different composition. The actual household income is divided by the current weight to arrive at a comparable household income level for each size and composition of household.

> The process… increases relatively the income of single person households (since their incomes are divided by a value of less than one) and reduces relatively the incomes of households with three or more persons, which have an equivalence value of greater than one.
>
> DWP, 2015: 12

The official benchmark used to be 0.5 of *mean* income, and it is roughly equivalent to the 0.6 of *median* income benchmark, as illustrated below. The Department for Work and Pensions publishes figures for the EU's official poverty threshold for the UK in its '*Households Below Average Income*' (HBAI) publication, each year (DWP, 2015).

It gives both the mean and the median equivalised household income for the UK, using data for net disposable weekly household income from the Family Resources Survey. The current equivalisation process for households Before Housing Costs are deducted (BHC) uses a standard weighting of 0.67 for the first adult in the household, 0.33 for every additional adult and each child aged 14 years and over, and 0.20 for each child under 14 years. A different set of weights is used for After Housing Costs have been deducted (AHC), such that the first adult receives a weight of 0.58; it is 0.42 for all other individuals aged 14 years and over, and 0.20 for children aged under 14 years.

Table 10.2. EU official poverty benchmark
Income Before Housing Costs (BHC) and Income After Housing
Costs (AHC) for 2014–15

2014–15		Poverty benchmark	Proportion of household income		
£ pw		0.5 for couple	First adult	Second	Child < 14
Mean income BHC	£581	£290.50	£194.64	£95.87	£58.10
Proportions	1.00	0.5	0.5 x 0.67	0.5 x 0.33	0.5 x 0.2
Mean income AHC	£504	£252.00	£146.16	£105.84	£50.40
Proportions	1.00	0.5	0.5 x 0.58	0.5 x 0.42	0.5 x 0.2
		0.6 for couple			
Median income BHC	£473	£283.80	£190.15	£93.65	£56.76
Proportions	1.00	0.6	0.6 x 0.67	0.6 x 0.33	0.6 x 0.2
Median income AHC	£404	£242.40	£140.59	£101.81	£48.48
Proportions	1.00	0.6	0.6 x 0.58	0.6 x 0.42	0.6 x 0.2

Source: *Households Below Average Income* report: 2016 edition.

None of the measures is perfect, and this poverty benchmark has four obvious drawbacks. It is based on the median, net disposable income, for a household, and the figures are published relatively late in the UK for use as a benchmark for setting BI levels.

a) If the population was very markedly divided into a majority on very low incomes and a minority of very wealthy people, it could skew the outcome. A very contrived example will illustrate this. Suppose that 70 per cent of the population has an income of ten units each, and the other three deciles (30 per cent of the population) have average incomes of 80, 100 and 150 units each, giving a total income of a multiple of 400 units. In this example, the median income is ten units, and 0.6 of the median would be 6 units, therefore no one is in poverty. However, the mean is 40 units, and 0.5 of the mean is 20 units, and therefore 70 per cent of the country is in poverty. The income of the top three deciles could double, and while the median would remain the same, the mean would rise to 73 units. This suggests that the mean is the more appropriate measure of central tendency – unless use of the median is intended to mask the levels of poverty in extremely unequal societies.

b) The income measure used is weekly *net (disposable)* equivalised household income from all sources after income tax, national insurance and other deductions (DWP, 2015:141). Elsewhere it implies that benefit receipt has also been taken into account. The result indicates the prosperity of households after some redistributive measures have taken place. But sometimes it is important to know the distribution of *gross (pre-tax and benefits) income*, to be able to identify who is most at risk of poverty before taxes are levied and benefits are administered.

c) The EU poverty threshold is 0.6 of median *equivalised household* income for a couple without children, not that of an individual. That of an individual living on his/her own would be 0.6 x 0.58 = 0.348 of the AHC measure.

> HBAI assumes that all individuals in the household benefit equally from the combined income of the household. Thus, all members of any one household will appear at the same point in the income distribution.
>
> DWP, 2015:12

This is a heroic assumption that clearly is unsafe according to chapter 4 above. Household measures of income ignore and mask intra-household inequality. The distribution of the *gross income of the individual*, including all who have no source of gross income, would give a much more accurate picture of the actual distribution of income in the population. This information is not collected in the UK. Individual incomes are collected only for taxpayers, who by definition comprise the wealthier half of the population.

d) In the UK, the information is published (eg in June 2016) more than a year after the period to which the data refer (2014–15), and when used as a poverty benchmark, it will be applied nearly a year later (2017–18). Thus, there are considerable delays before it can be applied.

Note: the calculation of average *earnings* is even more difficult than for average *income*. We would need to know who comprises the population, whether earnings include overtime, and whether earnings include those of part-time workers, seasonal workers, unemployed workers, and domestic workers?

c   Minimum Income Standards

In 2006, the Family Budget Unit at York University combined forces with the Centre for Research in Social Policy at Loughborough University to produce a set of Minimum Income Standards (MIS) – comparable to the Family Budget Unit's Low Cost but Acceptable standard – funded by the Joseph Rowntree Foundation. Its first report was published in July 2008, with its MIS based on prices in April 2008. The figures were produced by 39 focus groups, involving more than 200 people, in combination with experts in heating and nutrition. Each group comprised people who were representative of the group for whom they were estimating the MIS. The figures have been updated each year, giving a series from 2008 to 2016, at the time of writing. MIS is the most generous of the three measures.

The Centre for Research in Social Policy publishes five sets of figures for 11 household configurations for each year. See Table 10.3 below.

For each household configuration, the MIS data gives a breakdown of their required expenditure on: food, alcohol, tobacco, clothing, household insurances, fuel, other housing costs, household goods, household services, personal goods and services, motoring, other travel costs, and social and cultural participation. Basic living costs comprise these items.

Given the distorting effects of current UK housing policy, it is not possible to include a component for housing costs in the BIs. The appropriate version to use as a poverty benchmark in the UK currently is in column 5, which corresponds to the *Housing Below Average Income*'s 'After Housing Costs have been excluded' figures. It excludes rent, council tax, water rates and childcare costs.

As one might expect, a poverty threshold will vary across countries, depending on the level of public services provided. For example, primary and secondary education and health-care are provided free at the point of use in the UK currently. In countries where this is not so, a higher proportion of income would be required to reach the same standard of living.

All of these measures contain an element of subjectivity. When samples

Table 10.3 Five measures of Minimum Income Standards for 11 household types, 2016

2016 £ pw	I*	2* BHC	3*	4*	5* AHC	Child-care	Rent	Cncl Tax	Water rates
single pens	264.87	248.92	186.77	170.82	165.15	0.00	78.10	15.96	5.67
couple pens	353.21	332.96	267.39	247.14	240.45	0.00	85.83	20.25	6.69
single w-age	286.53	271.34	198.85	183.66	177.99	0.00	87.68	15.19	5.67
couple w-age	426.80	406.55	330.17	309.92	304.25	0.00	96.63	20.25	5.67
LP + toddler	594.45	365.70	297.59	279.87	270.48	211.03	85.83	17.72	9.39
LP + pre + prim	692.58	446.45	372.21	354.49	344.62	228.41	91.97	17.72	9.87
LP + pre + prim + sec	800.94	554.81	480.57	462.85	452.98	228.41	91.97	17.72	9.87
Couple + toddler	678.53	443.87	381.67	358.05	348.66	211.03	85.83	23.62	9.39
Couple + pre + prim	776.28	524.25	455.90	432.28	422.41	228.41	91.97	23.62	9.87
Couple + pre + prim + sec	894.49	642.46	574.12	550.50	540.63	228.41	91.97	23.62	9.87
Couple + toddler + pre + prim + sec	1153.98	690.92	622.58	598.95	589.08	439.44	91.97	23.62	9.87

*Key to Table 10.3

- Col 1: Total costs.
- Col 2: HBAI BHC, Total excluding council tax and childcare;
- Col 3: Total excluding rent and childcare
- Col 4: Total excluding rent, council tax, childcare (comparable to out-of-work benefits)
- Col 5: HBAI AHC, Total excluding rent, council tax, childcare and water rates.

- Pens = pensioner, aged 65 or over;
- W-age = working-age, aged 16–64;
- LP = lone parent;
- Toddler = child aged 0–1;
- Pre = pre-school child aged 2–4;
- Prim = child at primary school;
- Sec = child at secondary school;
- Cncl Tax = Council Tax.

of people have been surveyed and questioned as to what they consider their necessary minimum income to be, it has been noted that the higher the income of the respondent, the higher s/he perceives her/his required minimum income to be. Even with the other methods, threshold drift (ie greater than inflation) can often be observed over time.

In Table 10.4a, the three measures for 2014–15 are relatively close for the pensioner rates, but diverge markedly for the working-age adults, and the differences are maintained in the households with children.

The task is to design BI schemes for pensioners, working-age adults and children that will meet the minimum conditions of current benefit rates, and other BI schemes that meet the poverty benchmarks.

The timing of availability of information

In order to be able to set the BI amounts for a given fiscal year, (eg 6 April 2017 to 5 April 2018), based on the GDP, Y-BAR, proposed Social Assistance benefit rates, HBAI or MIS figures, the timing of the publication of the information is critical. Wherever possible the figures quoted are the latest that were available at the time when they would have been required for decision-making, rather than the revised figures published later.

Table 10.4a A floor and two poverty benchmarks for the same time period, 2014–15

£ pw	Current system, as a floor		Official EU poverty benchmark	MIS
	MTBs*	MTBs 2014–15	0.6 of med income, AHC, 2014–15	AHC 2014
Single pensioner	Pension Credit	148.35	140.59	161.93
Couple pensioner		226.50	242.40	236.65
Single young adult (16–24)	JSA/ESA	57.20	140.59	175.06
Single older working-age		72.40	140.59	175.06
Couple working-age		113.70	242.40	295.06
Lone Parent + toddler	JSA/ESA CB, CTC.	156.09	189.07	264.85
Lone Parent + pre + prim		222.38	237.55	356.70
Lone Parent + pre + prim + secondary school child		288.67	339.36	458.24
Couple + toddler	JSA/ESA CB, CTC.	197.39	290.88	364.58
Couple + pre + prim		263.68	339.36	449.95
Couple + pre + prim + sec		329.97	441.17	557.82
Couple + toddler + pre + prim + secondary sch child		396.26	489.65	611.08

KEY: see Table 10.3 above for an explanation of the categories.

* Recipients of MTBs are usually also eligible for Housing Benefit and Council Tax Relief/Support in addition. The benefit levels quoted are for claimants aged 25 or over, unless otherwise indicated.

The figures for GDP, GDP per head, and Income for a given year in the UK are published in the UK *National Accounts, the Blue Book*, usually by July or August of the following year. That is, figures for 2012 were published in the 2013 edition in July 2013. However, the 2014 edition did not become available until 31 October 2014.

The Scottish figures for GDP, GDP per head and Y-BAR for a given year, eg 2015, published in the SNAP tables, are usually available in late spring of the following year, 2016. Mid year population estimates are also required and usually become available in late June or July of the following year.

Pension and Benefit Rates for a given fiscal year are usually published in the autumn of the previous year. The HBAI information for the official EU poverty threshold published in June 2016 gave the figures for fiscal year 2014–15, more than a year after the end of the period to which they relate. The latest figures for MIS, based on prices in April, are published in July of the same year, (eg July 2016, for use in 2017–18).

We notice from Table 10.4b, that the pension levels and benchmarks are relatively constant at £159.35, £140.59 and £165.15 pw, and even more so for pensioner couples. The single working-age benchmarks vary between £73.10, £140.59 and £177.99 pw. The child benchmarks vary between £48.48 / 66.87 / 84.29 / 94.40 / 101.81 pw. Rather than deciding on a weekly amount for a given year, which would have to change in the following time period, there are advantages in determining the amounts each year as proportions of either GDP per head, or Y-BAR, with the proportions indexed for at least the term of a Parliament.

Having chosen the floor or particular poverty benchmark, the task is to design a BI for a pensioner (aged 65 or over), a working-age adult (aged 16–64), and for a child (aged 0–15) that matches the requirements for the household. A premium BI for the Responsible Parent of a Dependent Child (the primary care giver) could also be considered, as discussed in chapters 4 and 6 above, in order to avoid family economies of scale and to reduce household economies of scale. Illustrative sample schemes are presented in chapter 14 and summarised in Tables 14.6.

A full BI for an adult can now be defined for practical purposes as a function of the chosen poverty benchmark for the given year, and the age of the recipient. It is suggested here that a full BI is one that is within two per cent of the poverty benchmark figure. Where a partial BI is chosen, it is recommended that it should be at least 75 per cent of the full BI amount, in order to minimise poverty among individuals living alone who are unable to obtain work or who are unable to work in the short run, for example, due to illness or caring responsibilities. Those with disabilities or chronic illness will, of course, receive their disability benefits in addition to their BI. A 'full' Child BI is one that meets the chosen poverty benchmark for each household configuration for all families with children, given that the BI for a working-age adult has already been determined.

There is no single optimum BI scheme that will satisfy everyone. Each scheme is the outcome of a particular set of prioritised objectives, assump-

**Table 10.4b A floor and two poverty benchmarks available
for a BI scheme for fiscal year 2017–18, based on information
available in 2016**

£ pw	Current system MTBS*	Current system MTBS 2017–18	0.6 of med income, AHC for 2014–15	MIS, AHC 2016
Single pensioner	Pension Credit	159.35	140.59	165.15
Couple pensioner		243.25	242.40	240.45
Young adult (aged 16–24)		57.90	140.59	177.99
Single older working-age	JSA/ESA	73.10	140.59	177.99
Couple working-age		114.85	242.40	304.25
Lone Parent + toddler		157.39	189.07	270.48
Lone Parent + pre + prim	JSA/ESA	224.26	237.55	344.62
Lone Parent + pre + prim + secondary school child	CB, CTC.	291.13	339.36	452.98
Couple + toddler		199.14	290.88	348.66
Couple + pre + prim	JSA/ESA,	266.01	339.36	422.41
Couple + pre + prim + sec	CB, CTC.	332.88	441.17	540.63
Couple + toddler + pre + prim + sec school child		399.75	489.65	589.08

KEY
See Table 10.3 for an explanation of the categories.

* Recipients of MTBs are usually also eligible for Housing Benefit and Council Tax Relief/Support in addition. The benefit levels quoted for working age adults are those for claimants aged 25 or over, unless otherwise indicated.

tions and constraints; the proposed levels of BI and the method of funding them will reflect this. A BI system is not a panacea for all ills, but it is a necessary, though not sufficient, condition for a better society.

An alternative poverty benchmark

The official EU poverty benchmark is defined as '0.6 of median equivalised household income'. As noted above, this benchmark has four drawbacks:

- It is based on the median rather than the mean.

- It uses net disposable weekly income, rather than gross income.
- It uses household income, rather than that of the individual.
- In the UK, two whole years elapse between the period to which the HBAI information applies, eg 2014–15, and the fiscal year for which it is required, 2017–18. This means that, by the time the information is available, it is already out of date for the purpose for which it is required. This is less of an issue when inflation is low and stable, but could be a problem if inflation is high and/or accelerating.

It was suggested above that the mean gross income of individuals, (ie BHC), might be a more appropriate basis for the benchmark, in which case one would use 0.5 of this measure, as was the case previously. This measure is already available in the form of Y-BAR. Thus, an alternative BHC poverty benchmark akin to the older version of the EU benchmark is '0.5 of mean gross income of individuals' that can be measured by 0.5 of Y-BAR.

How well do the mean income figures match up in Table 10.5, ie Y-BAR in row 2, and the mean income BHC for the first adult in row 5? The 0.5 figures are given in rows 3 and 6. The figures are relatively close, and are definitely of the same order of magnitude.

However, given the chaotic state of the UK housing market, it would not be possible to include a housing cost element in the BI. An AHC version is required.

The ratio of the AHC means to BHC means (rows 7 and 4) varies between 0.864 and 0.869 in Table 10.5. The ratio of AHC to BHC medians (rows 9 and 8) varies between 0.850 and 0.859. These figures imply that relatively small proportions of income are allocated for housing costs, compared with how these have become such a large element in people's budgets. It is proposed here that the ratio of AHC to BHC should be at 0.8. Thus the AHC poverty benchmark would be 0.4 of Y-BAR. This figure can be seen in row 3. It is slightly higher than the current AHC poverty threshold (row 11), although curiously, and quite spuriously, the figures in row 3 for 2010–12 appear to predict the figures in row 11 for 2012–13 to 2014–15 by 15 months.

The figure for Y-BAR for a given calendar year, eg 2015, that becomes available the following year, 2016, would provide the benchmark for the fiscal year starting in the next year, 2017–18. Thus another advantage of using Y-BAR as the benchmark is that there would be only a 15-month gap between the end of the calendar year to which it refers and the fiscal year to which it is applied, compared with two whole years for the HBAI data.

Table 10.5 Comparison of mean and median figures for the UK, 2010 to 2014

Row	UK £ pw	2010	2011	2012	2013	2014
1	GDP per person	451	464	471	513	539
2*	Mean gross income (BHC) of individuals, Y-BAR	332	337	348	379	394
3 § +	0.5 of Y-BAR	166	169	174	190	197
	0.4	133	135	139	152	158
	0.375	125	126	131	142	148
	0.32	106	108	111	121	126
	0.25	83	84	87	95	99
	0.16	53	54	56	61	63
		2010–11	2011–12	2012–13	2013–14	2014–15
4	*Mean* net disposable income of couple households, BHC	511	528	535	561	581
5*	1st adult allocated 0.67 of mean HH income, BHC	342	352	358	376	389
6 §	BHC poverty threshold = 0.5 x 0.67 of mean HH income.	171	176	179	188	195
7	Mean net disposable income of couple households, AHC	443	459	462	487	504
8	*Median* net disposable income of couple households, BHC	419	427	440	453	473
9	Median net disposable income of couple household AHC	359	367	374	386	404
10	1st adult allocated 0.58 of median HH income	208	213	217	224	234
11+	AHC poverty threshold = 0.6 x 0.58 of median HH income	125	128	130	134	141

KEY: HH = household

Sources of data: DWP, *Households Below Average Incomes*,
- editions 2012–2013, Chart 2.1;
- editions 2014–2015, Chart 1;
- edition 2016, Figure 2.1; 'Income distribution for the total population (BHC) and (AHC)', and Table 2.1 AHC.

Table 10.6 The proposed poverty benchmark for BI purposes

	Proportion of Y-BAR	
	BHC	AHC
Pension BI and full BI for working age, 16–64	0.50	0.40
Partial BI = 0.8 of full BI aged 16–64	0.40	0.32
Child BI, aged 0–15	0.20	0.16
Premium for boy or girl aged 14–15	0.10	0.08
Premium for Parent with Care of dependent child, 0–15	0.10	0.08

Three different BI schemes, based on this proposed poverty benchmark, are put forward in chapter 14, while ensuring that they compare well with the current EU benchmark:

- All working age adults could receive a partial BI. As the name implies, a single adult would not have quite enough to live on. Also, it may not fulfil the EU criterion for a lone parent with three children. In this case, a premium for boys and girls aged 14–15, in line with the higher weights used in the official EU poverty benchmark, would overcome that, but could lead to family economies of scale.

- All parents with care could receive a PWC premium in addition to their partial BI. This would meet the current EU benchmark for families with children.

- All working age adults could receive a full BI, but this increases the household economies of scale. It would meet the current EU benchmark.

CHAPTER 11

Costing a Basic Income Scheme

THE PURPOSE OF this chapter is to cost a sample BI scheme, but it begins by discussing different definitions of costs that could be applied to any BI scheme. Discussions about costs can be confusing and counter-productive if discussants use different concepts without realising it.

If the proposed BI scheme provides different amounts according to age, or any other criteria, then data about the population to which it will apply will be required. To simplify the calculations, a simple scheme is used below as an illustration, and the process will yield its 'sum of gross transfers', that is, the total amount that is paid out in a given time period.

A BI scheme usually implies that some current benefits will eventually be replaced, and others will be retained. The chapter ends by listing the current main social security benefits and suggests which could be replaced and which kept. It is also necessary to estimate the cost of the retained benefits and the administration costs of the benefit systems. These will constitute a margin that must be added to the sum of gross transfers.

A note about costs

There are many different concepts of costs, even associated with a simple BI scheme, and it is important to be clear as to which concept someone may be referring. When any new scheme is implemented, a set of changes will occur, and these can be assessed as gains or losses (costs). Some are overall costs that affect the whole economy; others refer to the experience of individuals. What is experienced as a gain for one person could be associated with a loss by another.

Economists use the concept of *opportunity cost*. Given a choice between, say, three options, of which one is chosen, then its opportunity cost is defined as the satisfaction that has been foregone associated with the next best option that was not chosen (Kishtainy, 2014: 16).

A BI scheme in which BIs are paid out automatically and regularly ensures that everyone has a regular predictable income, which is essential for poorer people. The most obvious measure of overall cost in this case is the sum of all of the BIs, or the *sum of gross transfers* in a given time period. This amount will be circulated in the economy on a regular basis.

An alternative administrative system may use a Negative Income Tax

(NIT), where a benefit payment is made after any lesser income tax has been deducted, (NIT = BI – income tax, where BI > income tax), and Tax Credits (TC), where a net tax payment is due after any lesser benefits have been deducted, (TC = income tax – BI, where BI < income tax). The *sum of net transfers* is the total that all net taxpayers pay to net benefit recipients. These two latter amounts would be equal, if there were no administration costs. The sum of net transfers is a measure of the true cost of a scheme. It depends on the initial distribution of gross incomes. If everyone had exactly the same gross income, and if an income tax of 50 per cent were levied and distributed as an equal BI to everyone, the sum of *gross* transfers would be 50 per cent of total income, but the sum of *net* transfers would be zero. (The sum of net transfers, like social mobility, is a concept that has relevance only in an unequal society).

Another set of costs is associated with *administration and fraud*. These comprise the administrative costs of assessment, delivery, monitoring and compliance, together with the costs of error or fraud, by either claimants or administration staff, in terms of lost revenue or excess benefits paid.

It is possible that a sudden *one-off reduction in GDP* associated with a major change in the economy could occur due to the implementation of a BI scheme. This would be concerning if it was followed by a *reduction in the growth rate of GDP*, or even worse, a slow decline in GDP, associated with a *negative rate of growth*. None of these is expected to occur but, when looking at the outcome of the implementation of a BI scheme, these are some of the questions that economists would wish to examine.

One might calculate the *indirect costs of poverty* under the current benefit system, such as where poverty impinges on the health service, personal social services, and on the justice system through increased crime. 'The relationship between low income and poor health is well established' (Marmot, 2010: 74). Similarly, the current benefit system, that penalises couples living together, can act as a barrier to the formation of two-person households (see chapter 4), and impose the indirect cost of increased demand for single-person housing.

Individuals could be losers, if their net incomes were less than they would have been under the current system. Using an alternative measure, the *Marginal Deduction Rate* (income tax rates and other deductions) facing some people could be higher with the BI system. It is probable that some poorer individuals could be better off in terms of increased net income, while facing higher MDRs than before.

Costing an illustrative sample BI scheme

These costs are more easily estimated using Excel software. Since age-related selectivity is accepted in BI schemes, it is necessary to have figures for the population by age. Tables 11.1 for Scotland and the UK also include figures for other financially vulnerable adults abstracted from the 2011 Census. In 2015, Scotland's population was 5,373,000, which was 0.0825 (roughly 1/12) of the UK population of 65,110,000 individuals. Tables 11.1 also give the figures as proportions, which will be useful later, in chapters 13 and 14.

The current qualifying age for the State Retirement Pension in the UK is different for men and women, with the qualifying age for women increasing from 60 in 2008 by one month of age every two months, until it will be equalised for both men and women at age 65 in November 2018. This is also the qualifying age for both men and women to receive Pension Credit and Winter Fuel Payment. Figures for men and women aged 63–64 are specified in Tables 11.1, because they were eligible for Pension Credit in 2015, which is the latest date for which figures were available at the time of writing.

Using the population data for Scotland and the UK, the cost of an illustrative BI scheme for 2017–18 is calculated in money terms in Tables 11.2 below. By 2017, only 64-year olds are eligible for Pension Credit. The BI scheme chosen is based on the proposed new AHC poverty benchmark specified in Table 10.6 above.

A margin must be added to the sum of gross transfers to cover administration costs, and retained benefits, etc. First of all, we have to decide which benefits are to be replaced by a BI and which are to be retained (Table 11.3). Then we have to find out what these will cost (Table 11.4). The costs of the components of this margin are justified and summarised in Table 11.5.

Which benefits to replace with a BI, and which to retain?

It is possible that the least generous BI schemes could be financed by replacing most of the current NI and means-tested benefits indicated in Table 11.3 below, together with reducing or removing the Personal Allowance, National Insurance Primary Threshold and some tax loopholes in the income tax system. BIs of similar or greater values will replace the benefits as they are eventually phased-out. However, there will

Table 11.1 SCOT Population of Scotland, mid-year estimates for 2015

AGE	SCOTLAND 2015	population	proportions	
All		5,373,000	1.00000	
Aged 65 or over	* with disabilities	245,952	0.04577	0.18295
	* unpaid carers	94,978	0.01768	
	Rest of 65 or over	642,070	0.11950	
	Total for 65 or over	**983,000**	**0.18295**	
Aged 25–64	men and women aged 64	61,736	0.01149	0.02288
	men and women aged 63	61,183	0.01139	
	* with disabilities	230,906	0.04297	0.10994
	* unpaid carers	359,842	0.06697	
	Rest of 25–62	2,148,933	0.39995	0.39995
	Total for 25–64	**2,862,600**	**0.53277**	
PwC 16–64	* Lone Parents, 16–64	170,760	0.03178	0.10314
	* Other responsible parents of dependent children	383,437	0.07136	
Aged 16–24	* with disabilities	13,521	0.00252	0.11448
	* unpaid carers	27,409	0.00510	
	Rest of 16–24	574,180	0.10686	
	Total for 16–24	**615,110**	**0.11448**	
Aged 0–15	* with disabilities	15,484	0.00288	0.16979
	* unpaid carers	10,002	0.00186	
	Boys and girls aged 14–15	111,782	0.02080	
	Rest of 0–13	775,022	0.14424	
	Total for 0–15	**912,290**	**0.16979**	

- from Census 2011.
- Some inaccuracies will have arisen since some of those aged 63–64 will also be people with disabilities or carers, etc.

Sources: 'Population estimates for UK, England and Wales, Scotland and Northern Ireland for 2015'. See Table 6 Scotland.

For further details, see Sources of Data section below.

Table 11.1 UK Population of the UK, mid-year estimates for 2015

AGE	UK 2015		population	proportions	
All			65,110,000	1.00000	
Aged 65 or over	* with disabilities	EW	2,518,702		
		SC	245,952	0.04392	
		NI	94,962		
	* unpaid carers	EW	1,279,890		0.17833
		SC	94,978	0.02161	
		NI	32,256		
	Rest of 65 or over		7,344,460	0.11280	
	Total for 65 or over		11,611,200	0.17833	
Aged 63–64	men and women aged 64		688,346	0.01057	0.02107
	men and women aged 63		683,633	0.01050	
Aged 25–64	* with disabilities	EW	1,953,199		
		SC	230,906	0.03516	
		NI	104,848		
	* unpaid carers	EW	4,077,422		0.10578
		SC	359,842	0.07062	
		NI	160,887		
	Rest of aged 25–62		25,590,317	0.39303	0.39303
	Total for 25–64		33,849,400	0.51988	
PwC 16–64	*Lone Parents 16–64	EW	1,716,000		
		SC	170,760	0.02981	
		NI	54,245		0.10527
	* Other responsible parents, of dependent children	EW	4,355,589		
		SC	383,437	0.07546	
		NI	174,304		
Aged 16–24	* with disabilities	EW	133,037		
		SC	13,521	0.00235	
		NI	6,703		
	* unpaid carers	EW	323,967		0.11352
		SC	27,409	0.00564	
		NI	15,745		
	Rest of aged 16–24		6,871,142	0.10553	
	Total for 16–24		7,391,524	0.11352	

AGE	UK 2015		population	proportions	
Aged 0–15	* with disabilities	EW SC NI	164,774 15,484 8,719	0.00290	0.18826
	* unpaid carers	EW SC NI	118,967 10,002 4,524	0.00205	
	Boys and girls aged 14–15		1,434,964	0.02204	
	Rest of ages 0–13		10,500,442	0.16127	
	Total for 0–15		12,257,876	0.18826	

KEY

EW = England and Wales;

SC = Scotland;

NI = Northern Ireland;

PWC = Parent with Care.

* from Census 2011.

* Some inaccuracies will have arisen, since some of those aged 63–64 will also be people with disabilities or carers, etc.

Sources of data

Population estimates for UK, England and Wales, Scotland and Northern Ireland for 2015.

For further details, see Sources of Data section below.

be some benefits that cannot, or should not, be replaced, and a margin to cover the cost of these retained benefits will have to be added to the BI costing tables above. Table 11.3 lists the main benefits paid in the UK in 2014, and indicates which could be replaced with a BI, and which are to be retained.

Council Tax Benefit/Support has been transferred to local authorities to control and administer. Thus it has continued, but has not come under central government finances since 31 March 2013.

A working-age claimant can normally receive at any one time a maximum of one 'key benefit', means-tested on the income of a couple or an individual. These include: Income Support, Jobseeker's Allowance, Employment and Support Allowance, Incapacity Benefit (up to Income Support rates), and Working Tax Credit (CIT, 2013: 9). These are in the process of being replaced by a new means-tested benefit – Universal Credit (Miller, 2011). In addition, an individual may receive other benefits based

Table 11.2 SCOT Costing a simple illustrative BI scheme for Scotland in 2017–18, in terms of £bn, based on data available in 2016

- Y-BAR Scotland 2015   =   £392.40 pw
- Pensioner BI   = 0.40 X Y-BAR = £157.00 pw
- Working-age adult BI   = 0.32 X Y-BAR = £125.60 pw
- Child BI   = 0.16 X Y-BAR = £62.80 pw
- Premium for Parent-with-Care   = 0.08 X Y-BAR = £31.40 pw

Column 1	Column 2	Column 3	Column 4	Column 5 = col. 3 x col. 4
Ages		population 2015	BI amounts	Totals paid pw for each group
			£ pw	£ pw
Aged 64 or over	* with disabilities, 65+	245,952	157.00	38,614,464
	* unpaid carers, 65+	94,978	157.00	14,911,546
	Rest of 65 or over	642,070	157.00	100,804,990
	Men and women aged 64	61,736	157.00	9,692,552
	Sub-total	1044,736		164,023,552
Aged 25–63	* with disabilities	230,906	125.60	29,001,793
	* unpaid carers	359,842	125.60	45,196,155
	Rest of 25–63	2,210,116	125.60	277,590,570
	Sub-total	2,800,864		351,788,518
Aged 16–64	* Lone parent premium	170,760	31.40	5,361,864
	* Other PWC premium	383,437	31.40	12,039,921
	Sub-total			17,401,785
Aged 16–24	* with disabilities	13,521	125.60	1,698,238
	* unpaid carers	27,409	125.60	3,442,570
	Rest of 16–24	574,180	125.60	72,117,008
	Sub-total	615,110		77,257,816
Aged 0–15	* with disabilities	15,484	62.80	972,395
	* carers	10,002	62.80	628,126
	Rest of 0–15	886,804	62.80	55,691,291
	Sub-total	912,290		57,291,812
	TOTALS	5,373,000		667,763,483
	Multiply by 365 / 7 to obtain total for year	Year: sum of gross transfers		34,819,095,185

Note: Total personal income (via wallets and purses) for Scotland 2015 was £109,936m, (see The Balance of Gross Primary Income from the Scottish National Accounts Project: www.gov.scot/Topics/Statistics/Browse/Economy/SNAP/QNAS2016Q2, Table I). Therefore the sum of gross transfers, (£34,819m), represents 31.67% of total personal income in Scotland.

Table 11.2 UK Costing a simple illustrative BI scheme for the UK in 2017–18, in terms of £bn, based on data available in 2016

- Y-BAR for UK 2015   =   £411.89 pw
- Pensioner BI   = 0.40 x Y-BAR = £165.00 pw
- Working-age adult BI   = 0.32 x Y-BAR = £132.00 pw
- Child BI   = 0.16 x Y-BAR =   £66.00 pw
- Premium for Parent-with-Care   = 0.08 x Y-BAR =   £33.00 pw

Column 1	Column 2	Column 3	Column 4	Column 5 = col. 3 x col. 4
Ages		population 2015	BI amounts	Totals paid pw for each group
			£ pw	£ pw
Aged 64 or over	* with disabilities, 65+	2,859,616	165.00	471,836,640
	* unpaid carers, 65+	1,407,124	165.00	232,175,460
	Rest of 65 or over	7,344,460	165.00	1,211,835,900
	Men and women aged 64	688,346	165.00	113,577,090
	Sub-total	12,299,546	165.00	2,029,425,090
Aged 25–63	* with disabilities	2,288,953	132.00	302,141,796
	* unpaid carers	4,598,151	132.00	606,955,932
	Rest of 25–63	26,273,950	132.00	3,468,161,400
	Sub-total	33,161,054		4,377,259,128
Aged 16–64	* Lone parent premium	1,941,005	33.00	64,053,165
	* Other PwC premium	4,913,330	33.00	162,139,890
	Sub-total			226,193,055
Aged 16–24	* with disabilities	153,261	132.00	20,230,452
	* unpaid carers	367,121	132.00	48,459,972
	Rest of 16–24	6,871,142	132.00	906,990,744
	Sub-total	7,391,524		975,681,168
Aged 0–15	* with disabilities	188,977	66.00	12,472,482
	* carers	133,493	66.00	8,810,538
	Rest of 0–15	11,935,406	66.00	787,736,796
	Sub-total	12,257,876		809,019,816
	TOTALS	65,110,000		8,417,578,257
	Multiply by 365 / 7 to obtain total for year	Year: sum of gross transfers		438,916,551,971

Note: Total personal income (via wallets and purses) for UK in 2015 was £1,398,377m (*Blue Book*, 2016, Table 6.1.3, item QWMF). Therefore the sum of gross transfers, (£438,917m), represents 31.39% of total personal income in the UK.

Table 11.3 **Which of these main UK benefits should be replaced by BIs?**

NI	SA	DB	via DWP	Replace by BI, or keep?
		X	Attendance Allowance	keep
		X	Disability Living Allowance	keep
		X	Industrial Injuries Disablement Benefit	keep
		X	Personal Independence Payment	keep
			Severe Disablement Allowance	Replace
X			Incapacity Benefit	Replace
			Carer's Allowance	Replace
	X		Pension Credit*	Replace
	X		Income Support – income replacement*	Replace
	X		Income-based Jobseeker's Allowance*	Replace
	X		Income-related Employment and Support Allowance*	Replace
	X		Universal Credit*	Replace
	X		Social Fund / Scottish Welfare Fund: cold weather payments: Sure Start Maternity Grant, funeral grant:	keep keep Replace***
X			State Retirement Pension and ST Pension	Replace
X			SERPS and S2P	keep
X			Contributory Employment and Support Allowance	Replace
X			Contributory Jobseeker's Allowance	Replace
X			Statutory Sick Pay – full salary	Paid by employers
X			Statutory Maternity Pay	Paid by employers
X			Statutory Paternity Pay	Paid by employers
X			Statutory Adoption Pay	Paid by employers
X			Guardian's Allowance	keep
X			Maternity Allowance (39 weeks, by DWP)	Replace***
X**			Widowed Parent's Allowance	Replace***
X**			Widow's Benefits (pre 2001...)	Replace***
X**			Bereavement Payment (lump sum), and Bereavement allowance for one year	Are being replaced
			Christmas Bonus	Replace
			Winter Fuel Payments	keep

NI	SA	DB	via DWP	Replace by BI, or keep?
			via HMRC:	
	X		Working Tax Credit	Replace
	X		Child Tax Credit	Replace
			Child Benefit	Replace
			via Local Authority:	
	X		Council Tax Benefit* / Support* / Reduction* (since 31/3/13)	keep
	X		Rent Rebates* = HB for LA tenancies.	keep
	X		Rent Allowances* = HB for private and housing association tenants	keep
			via the Student Loans company	
			Student loans – maintenance	Replace

KEY: NI = National Insurance benefits, paid to individuals.

SA = means-tested Social Assistance benefits.

DB = disability benefits.

* These benefits provide additional disability, housing cost, childcare cost and carer premiums to claimants who meet specified conditions (often relating to receipt of other benefits). New gateways will have to be provided for claimants to receive their 'packages covering the costs incurred by disabled people'. It would make sense to roll up all disability-related payments into a single scheme with a single set of criteria, but that reform is beyond the scope of this book. A case could also be made to reform the supply-side of childcare provision. Housing Benefit would be individualised (as currently for students sharing accommodation) and for it to cover mortgage interest payments up to a certain level and not just rents (see chapter 6 above). One might wish to reform the whole of the current housing policy, but that, too, is beyond the scope of this book and nor does it affect the operations, rates or impacts discussed here.

** These benefits are dependent on the claimant's age and the contribution record of his/her deceased spouse.

*** Bereavement grants and Maternity grants (apart from Statutory Maternity Pay) could be replaced by arranging for the BI to continue to be paid for six months after death into the estate of the deceased, and initiating the Child BI and parent-with-care BI for new mothers at, or be back-dated to, the 13th week of pregnancy, respectively.

Table 11.4 UK Social Security transfer payments, 2013, 2014 and 2015

REF		2013	2014	2015
	CENTRAL GOVERNMENT	£m	£m	£m
	NATIONAL INSURANCE BENEFITS			
L8LV*	Social security pension benefits in cash	82,350	85,701	88,464
CSDH	Widows' and guardians' allowances	590	572	573
CJTJ	Jobseeker's Allowance	563	407	314
CUNL	Incapacity benefit	4,880	4,319	4,454
CSDL	Maternity Benefit	401	411	435
CSDQ	Statutory Sick Pay	109	96	96
GTKZ	Statutory Maternity Pay	2,371	2,089	2,346
GTKN	Redundancy Fund Benefit	52	497	265
GTLQ	Social Fund Benefit	2,312	2,142	2,102
L8QP*	**Total social security benefits in cash**	93,628	96,234	99,049
QYJT*/ L8R9*	**Total unfunded social benefits, Other social insurance benefits**	32,377	34,529	35,948
	SOCIAL ASSISTANCE BENEFITS IN CASH			
CSDD	War pensions and allowances	1,000	887	807
CSDE	Income support	10,984	9,524	8,683
RYCQ	Income Tax Credits and Reliefs	27,037	29,577	28,978
EKY3	Child Benefit	11,671	11,511	11,640
EKY4	Non-contributory Jobseeker's Allowance	4,034	2,946	2,120
EKY5	Care allowances	8,526	8,681	8,576
EKY6	Disability benefits	14,681	14,728	14,455
EKY7	Other benefits	12,449	15,864	19,019
NZGO	**Total social assistance benefits in cash**	90,382	93,718	94,278
NMDR	**Total social benefits (Central Government)**	216,387	224,481	229,275
	LOCAL GOVERNMENT			
GCMO*/ L8RB*	Total unfunded employee social benefits Other social insurance benefits	5,006	5,439	5,907
	SOCIAL ASSISTANCE BENEFITS IN CASH			
GCSI	Student grants	2,583	2,977	3,407
CTML	Rent rebates	5,805	5,914	5,877
GCSR	Rent allowances	17,822	18,165	18,018
ADAL	Total social assistance benefits in cash	26,210	27,056	27,302
NSMN	**Total social benefits (Local Government)**	31,216	32,495	33,209
NNAD	**TOTAL SOCIAL BENEFITS, T 5.1.4**	247,603	256,976	262,484
	TOTAL AS % OF TOTAL GROSS INCOME	19.52%	19.35%	18.77%
	TOTAL AS % OF GDP	14.45%	14.15%	14.04%

Source: UK *National Accounts*, 2014, 2015 and 2016; Tables 5.1.4, 5.2.4S and 5.3.4S.

*The ONS allocates a four-letter reference code for each series in the *Blue Book*, which is helpful to trace continuity from year to year. The fact that some series are combined, or otherwise changed, from year to year can be very confusing.

Series CSDG used to be 'Retirement pensions', and FJVZ, 'Benefits paid to overseas residents', now seem to be combined as L8LV, 'Social security pension benefits in cash'.

QYRJ, 'Total social security benefits in cash' is now coded as L8QP.
QYJT, 'Total unfunded social benefits' is now L8R9, 'Other social insurance benefits'.
GCMO, 'Total unfunded employee social benefits', is now L8RB, 'Other social insurance benefits'.

on NI contributions or on personal circumstances, such as Incapacity Benefit, Statutory Maternity Pay, Statutory Sick Pay, Bereavement Benefits and Carer's Allowance. These count as income that reduces a household's entitlement to means-tested support.

Eventually, most of the NI and SA benefits will be replaced by BIS (or Disability Benefits) that fulfil the same function. Where entitlement to a NI benefit is greater than the BI that replaces it, the extra entitlement should be honoured, as with SERPS and the State Second Pension. If the income tax system is restructured, then self-employed and employees' people's NICs will be subsumed into it, and no new entitlements will be created. The Employers' NICs would become a payroll tax.

Table 11.4 lists the main types of Social Security transfer payments for the UK, and the expenditure on them in calendar years 2013–2015. It is important to distinguish the BIS and other cash payments transferred between members of the population, from Government Expenditure, which is the expenditure financed by a range of taxes to provide public services, such as health, education, defence, housing, transport, etc.

Table 11.5 estimates the costs of the components comprising the MARGIN, which must be added to the sum of gross transfers.

The added margin of £6,491m is approximately 5.90% of Scotland's income of £109,936m in 2015. This, added to the sum of gross transfers of £34,819m from Table 11.2 Scotland above, gives a grand total of £41,310m representing 37.57% of Scotland's income in 2015.

The added margin for the UK of £77,883m is approximately 5.57% of the UK's income of £1,398,377m in 2015. Added to the sum of gross transfers of £438,917m in Table 11.2 UK above, this gives a grand total of £516,800m representing 36.96% of the UK's income in 2015.

These calculations relating to data for 2015 indicate all of the antici-

Table 11.5 Components of an added margin

		2015 costs £m	
		UK	Scot
1	**Administration costs:** delivery, monitoring, compliance. The administration costs for non-means-tested benefits such as Child Benefit and the state pension has been estimated as 1% of the total disbursed (the sum of gross transfers), while the administration costs for Means-Tested-Benefits are about 6% of amount disbursed. (CIT, 2013: 8–10) Allow, say, 1.5% of the total amount disbursed in Tables 11.2 to cover both BIS and retained benefits.	6,001	500
2	**Disability benefits** (DBS), based on need, are in addition to, and separate from, the BI system. AA, DLA, IIDB, PIP (see Table 11.3 above) are not the sum total of DBS, since the main benefits, IS, JSA, ESA, PC, UC, HB & CTR also provide additional disability premiums, (series EKY6 in Table 11.4 above). Add another 50%. This sum will have to rise if DBS are to become adequate and cover the extra costs incurred by disabled people, (costs of care, mobility, special equipment, special diets, fuel, laundry). Entitlement to DBS may be on a mixture of bases – impairment and functionality.	14,455 7,228	1,205* 602*
3	**Social Fund, Scottish Welfare Fund,** for people facing urgent one-off situations, emergencies – eg fire or flood – and including Cold Weather Payments, (series GTLQ in Table 11.4 above).	2,102	175*
4	State Earnings-Related Pension Scheme (SERPS), set up in 1978, became State Second Pension (S2P) in 2002. This should be retained for all pensioners who have contributed to them because, when given the choice, workers had elected to contribute to these state NI schemes, rather than to occupational or private alternatives, and should not be penalised just because they trusted in, and opted for, state schemes. Similarly, pensioners would be 'topped up' to their previous accrued pension entitlements, if those were higher than their BIS. Estimate for 2015 (in 2013/14 prices) gained by interpolation.	17,800	1,483*
5	**A residual NI scheme** for those who are eligible for the UK State Retirement Pension, but who live abroad.	3,755	313*
6	**Guardians' Allowances** serve a useful function encouraging families and others to care for children who would otherwise have to be taken into the care system. They are currently added to Child Benefit, and could be added to the Child BI, (series CSDH).	573	48*

		2015 costs £m	
		UK	Scot
7	Winter Fuel Payments would be retained in spite of a perceived unduly generous treatment of senior citizens, merely to fulfil the commitment that those in households below average income should not be worse off under a BI system. (2015/16 forecast)	2,074	173*
8	**Council Tax Benefit; Water Rates (2012–13)** Council Tax Support has been devolved to Local Authorities from 1 April 2013, so will no longer be a central govt responsibility.	0	0
9	**Housing Benefit** for Local Auth tenancies (Rent rebates) (CTML)	5,877	490*
10	**Housing Benefit** for private rented and housing association tenancies (Rent allowances) (series GCSR in Table 10.4 above)	18,018	1,502*
	TOTALS	77,883	6,491

Most of the figures for the UK are taken from Table 11.4 above. Details of the sources for SERPS and S2P, Pensions paid to overseas residents and Winter Fuel Payments are given in the main 'Sources of Data' section, below.

* These estimates above for Scotland were based on one 12th of the cost for the UK in 2015, as printed in Table 11.4 'UK Social Security Transfer Payments' above.

pated costs of a relatively generous BI scheme, together with its administration costs and related cash transfers that could be applied to Scotland and to the UK in 2017–18. In the next chapter different sources of financing a BI schemes will be considered. A restructured income tax system fits the bill best in order to carry out the task fairly and efficiently and this is explored in chapter 13.

The BI schemes in this book are illustrative and all figures are necessarily approximations (ballpark figures). More accurate estimates would be necessary if/when a BI were to be implemented. A safety net will still be needed for those who are not eligible for a BI, but at this stage it is difficult to estimate what provision will be necessary. The added MARGIN might have to be increased or reduced, depending on how mean or generous are the BI schemes. The margin will also change over the years, as the demographic profiles of the nations change.

CHAPTER 12

How to finance a BI scheme?

Alternative sources for funding a BI scheme

SEVERAL POTENTIAL sources for funding a BI scheme have been proposed. There are pros and cons associated with each of them. Their suitability depends on their objectives, their propensity to raise revenue, and their other consequences. A BI scheme could be financed by a single tax or a combination of taxes. They include the following:

- Expenditure taxes, such as a sales tax, or an increased Value Added Tax. The difference between a sales tax and VAT is that the VAT that has been paid by VAT-registered businesses can be claimed back from HMRC. Thus, a sales tax of 20% would raise more revenue than VAT of 20%. Expenditure taxes tend to be regressive and a dampener on investment and jobs. However, a sales tax, as implemented in many states in the USA, could compensate for this disadvantage by taxing the products sold in the UK of many international companies that currently avoid paying UK Corporation Tax.

- Taxes on income, such as income tax, and National Insurance contributions. More is said about this below.

- Taxes on wealth. One can distinguish between the different concepts of: taxing the income from wealth (which is taxing income); taxing transactions in wealth, such as a Capital Gains Tax or Inheritance Tax; taxing the holding of wealth, a Land Value Tax for instance and other taxes on capital; and redistribution of wealth. The value of land in Scotland was estimated to be worth £120bn in 2009. It was proposed to levy a tax of 3.16p in the £, yielding £3.792bn to replace Council Tax (Wightman, 2009: 15). This is a far cry from the £35bn sum of gross transfers estimated as the cost of the BI scheme in Table 11.2 Scotland, based on figures available in 2016 for implementation in 2017–18. The UK has tended to follow the principle of taxing the income from the wealth, but not the wealth itself. However, the distribution of wealth in the UK, and especially in Scotland, is extremely unequal, and measures to redistribute it have been discussed.

- Taxing wealth is only part of that process. The other part concerns how to transfer wealth to the poorest in the population. In the first two or three decades after WWII, this was effected by the provision of pension pots, and the wider availability of mortgages to spread home ownership, starting with the professional classes and, as one assumed at the time, working downwards through the income spectrum. However, this and other measures had a limited impact to reduce inequality. Today income and wealth in particular are concentrated in the hands of a very small number of people. A modest start to wider redistribution could involve an Inheritance Tax with more bite, and the proceeds distributed to all 21-year-olds in the form of a capital grant. But, the current Inheritance Tax is seen as a voluntary tax by many, due to their ability to avoid it via the use of trusts. However, consideration of the taxation of wealth or, even further, the redistribution of wealth, while essential, is really beyond the scope of this book.

- Taxes on the use of scarce resource, or on pollutants, such as carbon taxes, are designed to change behaviour, and, when successful, should lead to a reduction in the tax base and a corresponding reduction in tax revenues! Thus, they are good for the purpose for which they are designed, but by themselves would not necessarily finance a BI scheme.

- The Tobin Financial Transactions Tax was first proposed by Professor James Tobin, winner in 1981 of the Nobel Prize for Economics. His original proposal was as a tax on currency deals, but it has since become widened to be 'chargeable upon the purchase and sale of financial instruments and upon speculation in money itself, including foreign exchange.' (Murphy, 2015: 187). It would tax international financial transactions, the high volume of which 'is, in itself a destabilising factor in the world economy' (Murphy, 2015: 188). But this would require international co-operation to implement it and so is more appropriate for European-wide or a broader implementation of a BI system.

- Sovereign wealth funds are based on the community-control of community-owned natural resources, such as land, water, clean air, minerals, forests, broadcast spectrum, real estate or beaches. These have already been set up in the 1970s in Alaska and Norway, both based on oil revenues. The oil revenues were invested in the international stock market, and have been subject to its vagaries. Sovereign wealth funds are potentially good community resources, and help to protect inter-generational equity. They could be long-term solutions to create the necessary levels to contribute to feasible BI schemes, for instance. If the UK had set up a sovereign wealth fund in the 1970s based on its oil revenues, which was worth the same now as Norway's £500bn fund, and if it had generated an average, steady 4% income stream, it would now provide £20bn pa. This would have been equivalent to 1% of UK GDP in 2015, but it could have contributed nearly 60% towards the sum of gross transfers required for the illustrative BI scheme for Scotland in Table 11.2 Scotland above. However, sovereign wealth funds could be created in other ways, for instance by taxing the use of energy and creating a fund to invest in the international financial markets. One question that arises is whether there is a limit to such investment if every nation adopted it. Maybe they could be invested in alternative public policy projects instead to generate a sufficient return? Widerquist (2010 and 2011) provides an easy introduction to the Alaskan Permanent Fund Dividend, and a thorough exploration can be found in (Widerquist *et al*, 2012a, 2012b).

- Seigniorage '…is usually defined as the profit made by government by issuing currency. Banking licences actively outsource this right to make profit: additional taxes on banks seek to recover the additional wealth that they have accumulated as a result.' (Murphy, 2015: 182), (Kishtainy, 2014: 102). In this case, it refers to paying for the BIs by printing money, as in Quantitative Easing (Kishtainy, 2014: 250). At the time of the Credit Crisis in 2008, if the UK government had paid a BI to every member of the UK population, on condition that they repaid their loans to the banks, instead of the government bailing out the banks directly, it could have saved the banks and also helped the population to avoid so much personal debt (Keen, 2011: 369–70). It would also work where the nation is facing the threat of deflation, as in 2016. However, on a regular annual basis it would be inflationary, unless the surplus money was extracted from the economy regularly via some form of taxation. Seigniorage can be justified at the rate of growth of the economy for the purposes of investment in infrastructure (eg 3 per cent), which adds to the wealth of, and therefore income for, the country, but not for consumption purposes (Anderson *et al*,

2014). This is how the Attlee administration financed growth in the immediate post WWII period, when the government's debt/ GDP ratio was 240% (Anderson, 2016: 68–70).

UK *taxes and their yields*

Table 12.1 lists the main UK taxes and their yields for 2013, 2014 and 2015. Income tax raises the most revenue, followed by VAT, employers' National Insurance Contributions, employees' National Insurance Contributions, and Corporation Tax.

It may be noted that the total expenditure on Social Security benefits, (cash transfer payments) as shown in Table 11.4 above, for all three years, 2013, 2014, and 2015, is greater than the total of Income Tax and National Insurance Contributions by both employees and self-employed people, in the same years, as shown in Table 12.1. It follows logically that, if all of the revenues from income tax and these NICs can be thought of as contributing to the social security expenditure, then it is not also available to finance Government Expenditure on services such as health and education. The difference between them (£48,762m in 2015 representing 3.49% of UK income) implies that the rest of the social security expenditure would have been financed by a broad base of indirect taxation and borrowing. Income tax and the NI contributions of employees and self-employed people could be hypothecated (ring-fenced) to finance a new BI scheme fully, without it affecting the use of the other tax revenues for financing public services in any adverse way. In fact, it could even reduce the pressure on indirect taxes and on the deficit as sources for financing Government Expenditure. There would also be other dynamic effects as more people enter the labour market and inequality decreases, such as reductions in other areas of Public Expenditure, and on VAT for instance.

The revenue from the current *Employers'* NI contributions (£66,169m in 2015, representing 4.73% of total personal income of £1,398,377m of the UK in that year) should continue to be levied as a 'payroll tax', and could be used to contribute towards a BI scheme in conjunction with revenues from income tax. This tax, which helps to protect employees, was hard fought for and many people would like to see employers continuing to contribute to their employees' well being, or instead, to the well being of society as a whole. Two points should be noted. First, it is not, and will not be, collected through the personal income tax system. Second, for the three years 2013–15, the total revenues from Income Tax and NICs by self-employed, employees *and employers* (£279,891m in 2015) were

Table 12.1 UK taxes and their yields, 2013, 2014 and 2015

REF	£ million	2013	2014	2015
	TAXES ON INCOME AND WEALTH			
DRWH	Household income taxes	152,409	158,876	166,291
NMDE	NI Self employed	2,580	2,672	3,122
GCSE	NI Employees	41,492	42,702	44,309
	TOTAL	196,481	204,250	213,722
CEAN	NI Employers	62,013	63,746	66,169
	OTHER TAXES ON INCOME AND WEALTH			
ACCD	Corporation tax	39,367	40,619	44,064
DBHA	Petroleum revenue tax	1,296	568	−552
BMNX	Other taxes on income	7,144	6,749	8,350
CDDZ	Motor vehicle duty (domestic)	5,124	5,029	4,787
BMNY	Nat non-domest rates paid by non-market	1,639	1,740	1,767
DH7A	Television licence fee	3,082	3,124	3,131
	Other current taxes	3,126	3,692	4,418
NMHM	Council tax, etc (local government)	27,057	27,781	28,723
NMGI	**CAPITAL TAXES** (mainly Inheritance Tax)	4,249	3,882	4,448
	TOTAL	92,084	93,184	99,136
	TAXES ON PRODUCTION AND IMPORTS			
NZGF	VAT to central government	118,296	124,260	128,816
QYRB	Taxes and duties on imports, excl VAT	2,914	2,949	3,077
GTAM	Beer	3,337	3,337	3,255
GTAN	Wines, etc	7,063	7,246	7,395
GTAO	Tobacco	9,479	9,436	9,190
GTAP	Hydrocarbon oils	26,698	27,095	27,416
CJQY	Betting, gaming and lottery	1,538	1,708	2,053
CWAA	Air passenger duty	2,960	3,154	3,119
CWAD	Insurance premium tax	3,018	2,964	3,294
LIYH	Camelot payments to nat lott distribn fund	1,644	1,721	1,713
EP89	Renewable energy obligations	2,388	2,931	3,691
GTBC	Stamp duties	11,542	14,069	13,791
	Other	7,669	8,529	9,365
CUKY	National non-domestic rates	24,445	24,837	25,268
NZGX	TOTAL	222,991	234,236	241,443
	TOTAL TAXES AND COMPULSORY SOCIAL CONTRIBUTIONS Paid:			
GCSS	to central government	543,066	564,146	587,865
GCST	to local government	27,577	28,310	29,518
FJWB	to the EU (VAT & Import duties)	2,926	2,960	3,087
GCSU	TOTAL	573,569	595,416	620,470
YBHA	GDP **at current market prices**, (T 1.2)	1,713,302	1,816,439	1,869,560
GDWM	**TOTAL AS % OF** GDP	33.48%	32.78%	33.19%

Sources: *UK National Accounts* (*The Blue Book*) 2014: Tables 1.2 and 11.1; 2015, 2016: Tables 1.2 and 10.1.

greater than the total cost of Social Security transfers (£262,484m in 2015). This implies that only part of the employers' NIC would have been used to finance the cash transfer program in years 2013–15, and the rest of it was used to fund Government Expenditure. The *Employers'* NICs could be hypothecated to contribute towards the BI scheme and thus could reduce the cost by 4.73 percentage points of income tax (in terms of a restructured income tax system developed in chapter 13). However, £17,407m (£66,169m – £48,762m, representing 1.24% of total income for the UK) would have been needed in 2015 to meet a shortfall in Government Expenditure on services. If the indirect costs of poverty, due to ill health for instance, fall as a result of the introduction of the BI scheme, then this may not be necessary.

The main purpose of Part III is to develop BI schemes that meet poverty benchmarks and are financially viable. Financing them by income tax provides a simple method of demonstrating this and of comparing the cost of each scheme with one summary figure. Although it would be possible and desirable to hypothecate the employers' NICs to contribute towards the funding of the BI schemes, this has not been taken into account for the costing of BI schemes in chapter 14, but it should be noted that it could shave 4–5% points off the required income tax rate to fund each BI scheme. Alternative sources and combinations of funding are, of course, also possible. Much depends on the objectives, priorities, assumptions and constraints of the particular scheme.

Why income tax is the best source

- Income tax, (together with National Insurance contributions paid by employees and self-employed workers) and cash transfer payments (benefits) are reverse sides of the same coin, the former garnering from income, and the latter transferring it. It is reasonable to regard them as a single system and co-ordinate the two branches, even if they are administered separately. Both the social security and income tax systems in the UK are in need of reform.

- Similarly, the benefits of the two systems, social security on the one hand and the benefits enjoyed by taxpayers (tax expenditures – see below) on the other, should also be considered as one benefit system.

- Financing a BI scheme from income tax is the most direct method by which income can be redistributed from rich to poor.

- When restructured, a progressive income tax would be a fair tax, taking from those who have most income, in order to give to those who have least. It is also fair that those who are net beneficiaries while poor should be net taxpayers if their fortunes improve. While a flat rate of income tax by itself may be regarded as unfair, when hypothecated (ring-fenced) and used for financing a BI, it can be shown to be very redistributive (see Appendix B).

- Income tax is the only tax that will raise the required amount of revenue on its own.

- A Laffer curve plots the potential revenues that can be raised from income tax against a range of income tax rates (Kishtainy, 2014: 264). When the tax rate is zero, revenue receipts are zero. As the income tax rate rises, revenues increase, but they reach a maximum and start to decrease as the rate of income tax increases further, so that by the time the tax rate is 100 per cent, tax revenues would be zero again, since no on-one would bother to work. The Laffer curve is roughly parabolic in shape, but is not symmetrical around the peak. The tax rate at which the maximum revenue occurs is not known and is likely to vary, for instance, according to the type of tax, and the culture of the country. My own personal estimate is that the upper limit for a standard rate of income tax that most taxpayers in the UK would accept is in the range of 50 to 60 per cent, (and may even be less), even if it were hypothecated to fund the entire cash transfer program, including administration costs, disability benefits and other retained benefits. However, it is unlikely that many high income people would leave the country even if income tax rates rose higher then 50 per cent, judging by the Nordic experience of high tax rates. These are empirical questions that need to be investigated.

- Hypothecation is a system of ring-fencing some sources of finance for particular purposes, in this case, ring-fencing income tax revenues for the purpose of financing the entire BI scheme and its associated administration costs and other cash transfer payments. This should impose discipline on the system, producing an equilibrium of sorts, where the upward pressure on benefits by weaker, but more numerous, net recipients is opposed by the downward pressure on the income tax rate by stronger, but fewer, net tax payers. It would be possible and viable to finance a BI scheme from a combination of taxes, including wealth taxes, but it loses the discipline of paying for the cash transfer program out of income tax revenue.

- This hypothecation implies that all Government Expenditure (as distinct from the cash transfer payments) must be paid for out of indirect taxes.

- There are already procedures in place for deducting income tax at source, including employee earnings through the PAYE system.

Financing a BI scheme through the benefit and income taxation systems

Paying for a BI scheme through the benefit and income tax systems involves several components:

- BI payments could replace most current contributory National Insurance and means-tested Social Assistance benefits, as indicated in Table 11.3.

- A BI scheme should lead naturally to a reduction in the errors and fraud associated with the current complex benefit system. Estimates by DWP put the cost of benefit fraud in GB at £1.2bn (just 0.7% of all benefits). A further £2.3bn was overpaid in 2012–13 as a result of error by both administrators and claimants without fraudulent intent, of which some £900m was subsequently reclaimed, (Hills, 2014: 263). Underpayments also occur that contribute to greater depth of poverty.

- The reduction or removal of the Personal Allowance (PA) and other tax reliefs, exemptions and allowances that comprise the tax loopholes in the income tax system, will increase the tax base and thus increase the revenue available to finance a BI scheme. Benefits to taxpayers through the non-collection of income tax or NI contributions are officially called 'tax expenditures'. These benefits for taxpayers are less visible in the UK National Accounts than benefits paid directly to claimants. Taking advantage of these loopholes is referred to as 'tax avoidance', which is legal. The cost of tax relief on pension contributions to registered pension schemes alone, of all the legal tax avoidance loop-holes in income tax and National Insurance together, based on official figures, was £50bn for the tax year 2012–13, (Murphy, blog,

2014/09/26; Murphy, 2015: 175). Table 12.2 below calculates total tax expenditures in 2013–14 and 2014–15 to be £225bn. and £236bn, of which the PA alone accounted for £81.2 and £86.9bn respectively. Which tax expenditures should be retained?

- An increased effort should be made to reduce the level of illegal tax evasion associated with the income tax system. Richard Murphy, of Tax Research, has estimated that the total taxes lost by illegal tax evasion amounted to £73.4bn in the tax year 2011–12, (Murphy, blog, 2014/09/22). Proposals to convert to a cash-less economy, where all transactions would be carried out and taxed electronically, could prevent tax evasion among the lowest income part of the population, but wealthy people could retain methods for evading tax. A cash-less society would not be without its problems. How does one give children their pocket money, or give them money to get some items of shopping at the local store? A cash-less society could increase incentives to be self-sufficient, go back to barter exchange or lead to a black economy.

- More generous BI schemes might require changes in the thresholds and rates of income tax and NI contributions by employees and self-employed people.

- The current higher and additional rates of income tax could be increased to 50 and 60 per cent respectively to make the system more progressive.

- The most generous BI schemes will almost certainly entail a restructuring of the income tax and employees' and self-employed people's NIC system, as described in chapter 13.

- Tackling poverty head-on should lead to savings by reducing the indirect costs of poverty on the health service, personal social services and the justice system.

Tax expenditures and structural reliefs

Some of the less generous schemes might be financed by the replacement of the current Social Assistance benefits by BIs, and by removing some of the tax loopholes – allowances, reliefs and exemptions – from the income tax system. The official term, used by economists and government officials alike for these tax allowances, reliefs and exemptions designed into the

Table 12.2 Estimated costs of the Principal Tax Expenditures and Structural Reliefs

	TAX EXPENDITURES	2014–15	2015–16
	Income Tax	£m	£m
Relief for	*Registered pension schemes	20,550	22,900
	Individual Savings Accounts	2,450	2,600
	Share Incentive Plan	220	220
	Save As You Earn	180	180
	Enterprise Management Incentives	70	70
	Approved Company Share Option Plans	70	70
	Venture Capital Trusts	125	110
	Enterprise Investment Scheme	385	395
	Seed Enterprise Investment Scheme	175	80
	Professional Subscriptions	120	130
	Employer Supported Childcare including workplace nurseries	460	480
	Seafarers' Earnings Deduction	260	280
	Rent a room	110	110
Exemption of	First £30,000 of payments on termination of employment	800	700
	Interest on National Savings Certificates, including index-linked certificates	250	250
	Premium Bond prizes	130	130
	Income of charities	1,790	1,890
	Foreign service allowance paid to Crown servants abroad	50	45
	Personal Tax Credits	2,700	0
	STRUCTURAL RELIEFS – Income Tax		
	Personal Allowance	86,900	93,800
	RELIEFS with Tax Expenditure & Structural Components		
	Income Tax		
	Age-related Personal allowances	440	20
	Married Couples Allowance	285	260
	Marriage Allowance	–	385
Exemption of	British Government securities where owner not ordinarily resident in UK	3,500	2,350
	Child Benefit	1,160	1,170
	Attendance allowance	495	495
	Disability living allowance	880	995
	War disablement benefits	65	45
	Income tax and corporation tax		
	Capital Allowances	25,000	23,545
	Double taxation relief and foreign dividends exemption/ Foreign Tax Credits and reliefs under Double Tax Agreement	15,000	1,600
	TOTAL re Income Tax	164,620	155,305

	TAX EXPENDITURES	2014–15	2015–16
	Income Tax	£m	£m
	TAX EXPENDITURES – National Insurance Contributions		
Relief for	Share Incentive Plan	165	165
	Save As You Earn	140	140
	Employer Supported Childcare including workplace nurseries	390	400
	Foreign service allowance paid to Crown servants abroad	40	35
	*Employer contributions to registered pension schemes	9,700	14,900
	Employment Allowance		1,500
	STRUCTURAL RELIEFS – National Ins. Contributions		
	Primary Threshold	22,800	23,700
	Secondary Threshold	27,400	27,700
	Lower Profits Limit	2,150	2,260
	Contracted-out rebate occupational schemes: *Rebates deducted at source by employers	5,400	5,690
	RELIEFS with Tax Expenditure & Structural Components		
	National Insurance Contributions		
	*Reduced contributions for self-employed not attributable to reduced pensions eligibility	2,800	3,200
	TOTAL for National Insurance Contributions	70,985	79,690
	Total tax expenditures on income tax & NI contributions	235,605	234,995
QWMF	Total income of households and NPISHs in 2015 and 2016	1,328,108	1,398,377
	Tax expenditures as a percentage of total income	17.74%	16.80%
	Total cost of tax and NI relief on contributions to occupational and private pension schemes as indicated * above.	38,450	46,690
L8LV	Social security pension benefits in cash, 2014–15, Table 11.4	85,701	88,464

KEY: * these are tax reliefs on pension contributions.

Source: HMRC, Table 1.5. December 2015 and 2016.

tax system, is 'Tax expenditures', or 'Tax welfare' or 'Fiscal welfare', since they are equivalent to subsidies, and are an expense to the country (Jones, 2014: chapter 6). The more generous the BI scheme, then the more tax loopholes that would have to be closed in order to finance it. For the most generous BI schemes, a restructured income tax would be necessary, in which all tax loopholes would be closed. Table 12.2 lists the most prominent of the tax expenditures in the income tax and National Insurance systems, indicating their cost to the UK in lost revenue.

The tax expenditures for 2014–15 and 2015–16 represent 17.74% and 16.80% respectively of the total income of Households and Non-Profit Institutions Serving Households in the UK, (the income that passes through wallets, purses, and personal bank accounts of individuals). This total income is the potential income tax base of the UK, and yet more than one sixth of it is being discounted. Tax expenditures subsidise taxpayers who comprise roughly half of the country's population and who are, by definition, the wealthier half of the population. The poorer half does not earn enough to pay income tax. The advantages accruing to those who are able to take advantage of the tax loopholes is often in proportion to their income. For instance, anyone may claim tax reliefs on pension contributions to registered pension schemes worth up to 100% of his/her annual earnings up to the annual allowance. This was £50,000 in each of the three tax years between 2011–14 and stands at £40,000 currently. Tax relief can be claimed at the highest rate of income tax that s/he pays. If a wealthy person puts £40,000 of earnings into a pension fund in 2016–17, then s/he would receive the full 45% additional tax relief of £18,000 as a free gift! Tax expenditures reduce the tax base and increase the tax burden on those who cannot avoid paying income tax and NI contributions.

The cost to the public of the tax expenditures on income tax and National Insurance contributions alone was estimated to be £236bn and £235bn for 2014–15 and 2015–16 respectively. (The scale of tax avoidance via Corporation Tax and other taxes is a separate subject that is not discussed here). Even excluding the Personal Allowance and the Primary Threshold of the NI contributions, which gives some advantage to those on low incomes, the subsidies to taxpayers amounted to £126bn and £117bn respectively. This compares with £248bn, £257bn and £262bn spent on total Social Security in 2013, 2014 and 2015 respectively. Comparison of the £257bn spent on Social Security in 2014 with £126bn on tax expenditures in 2014–15 indicates that the hidden subsidies for taxpayers are equivalent to approximately 49 per cent of the total bill for Social Security in 2014. It was 45 per cent in 2015. Rather than being outraged at the size of the Social Security budget, citizens should be apoplectic at the way, and to the extent, that wealthy people are subsidised. This table highlights the scale of subsidy for wealthy people paid for by those on lower incomes. Public concern would do well to focus more on this than the social security bill.

Even worse is the 'revolving door' phenomenon where:

... [accountancy firms] help to design the law in the first place, and then go off and advise their clients on how to get around it... But rather than simply providing objective, technical expertise, the big accountancy firms use the 'useful insight into the workings of central government' to find ways for their clients to negotiate tax law. It represents a manifest conflict of interest.

JONES, 2014: 212, 213

In his concluding chapter, Jones says:

The accountancy firms who have colonised the state need to be evicted from power, [rather than] being seconded to the Treasury to help draw up the tax laws.

JONES, 2014: 308

Sleights of hand with the Personal Allowance

Nearly half of the cost of tax expenditures arose from the Personal Allowance and the Primary Threshold of the NI contributions. These cost:

- £86,900m + £22,800m = £109,700m in 2014–15, and
- £93,800m + £23,700m = £117,500m in 2015–16.

These would no longer be required, if everyone received a sufficient BI instead. The *value* of the PA to the taxpayer is its amount multiplied by the income tax rate. It was worth:

- In 2014–15, £10,000 x 0.20 = £2,000;
- in 2015–16, £10.600 x 0.20 = £2,120; and
- in 2016–17, £11,000 x 0.20 = £2,200 to each taxpayer.

The value to non-tax payers is in proportion to their incomes.

Each of these amounts is less than a corresponding annual BI sufficient to replace Jobseeker's Allowance for a claimant aged 25 or over, worth £3,775 in 2014–15 and £3,812 in both 2015–16 and 2016–17 respectively. Thus, even the meanest BI would be worth more than the value of the Personal Allowance.

The Government claims that reducing the UK deficit is its number one objective. However, this claim is questionable since, at the same time, the Personal Allowance has increased from £10,000 to £10,600 in 2015–16, to £11,000 in 2016–17, and to £11,500 in 2017–18, leading to gains for nearly every taxpayer, as indicated in Table 12.3. There were further gains

**Table 12.3 The value of the increase in Personal Allowance
and changes to the threshold for the higher rate income tax**

	GROSS INCOMES, £		
	2015–16	2016–17	2017–18
Personal Allowance in previous tax year	10,000	10,600	11,000
Personal Allowance in current tax year	10,600	11,000	11,500
Increase	600	400	500
Current basic rate of income tax	0.20	0.20	0.20
Value of the increase to *every* income taxpayer	120	80	100
Higher rate threshold in previous tax year	41,866	42,386	43,001
Higher rate threshold in current tax year	42,386	43,001	45,001
Increase	520	615	2,000
Current higher tax rate less standard tax rate	0.20	0.20	0.20
Value of increase to every higher rate taxpayer	104	123	400
Combined value of increases in PA and higher rate threshold to higher rate tax payers	224	203	500

for higher rate taxpayers as a result of the increases in the higher rate threshold each year. This occurred while ignoring the fact that those who do not have enough income to pay tax get no benefit from this increase. The Government accepted a reduction in income tax revenue at a time when the annual deficit and the accumulating public debt are cited as major problems.

HMRC has an unusual way of presenting its tax rates and bands. It does not present them in a straightforward manner, as in Appendix A below. It states the 'Tax is paid on the amount of taxable income remaining after allowances have been deducted' (HMRC, 2016: 3). It then gives different tax rates for a series of bands of *taxable* income, (as opposed to *gross* income). The tax rates are given separately, as basic rate, higher rate and additional rate. The alternative would have been to specify the basic rate which would be payable on all taxable income, with an extra amount to be paid by those with income in the higher rate band, and an extra amount again for those with income in the additional rate band. This way of presenting tax rates and bands would change the basic rate of income tax, such that it would only affect the income falling in the first bracket. It would not change the tax due on the higher income bands. In contrast, in the current UK system, if the Personal Allowance is increased, the authorities tend to claim that it helps those taxpayers with incomes just at the bottom of the first band, (which is true). However, they omit to point out that it actually benefits nearly every taxpayer, its value to each being the increase in the Personal Allowance times the tax rate applicable at their top band of income for incomes up to £100,000. An increase in the Personal Allowance does not change the bands of 'taxable income', but they do change the bands of gross income. This is yet another means of obfuscation.

In 2013–14, the threshold for levying the higher rate was a 'taxable income' of £32,011, and in 2016–17 it was £32,001, which looks as though there had been a small decrease in the basic rate tax band. In fact the Personal Allowance has increased in the same time period from £9,440 to £11,000. Every taxpayer in 2016-17 will have paid less tax to the tune of £1,560 x 0.20 = £312 compared with what s/he would have paid in tax in 2013–14. However, the value of the increase to the basic rate and higher rate taxpayer is the increase multiplied by the highest tax rate that they pay. This can be demonstrated as follows for someone who has a gross income of £50,000 in each of these tax-years. Let us simplify the figures and make the threshold for the higher rate of income tax be 'taxable income' in each year of £32,000. In 2013–14, s/he would have paid

* (£32,000 x 0.20) + (£50,000 – 32,000 – 9,440) x 0.40 = £9,824 in tax; and

* (£32,000 x 0.20) + (£50,000 – 32,000 – 11,000) x 0.40 = £9,200 in tax in 2016-17, giving a saving of £624 compared with 2013–14. This just happens to be the same as (£11,000 – 9,440) x 0.40.

At earnings of £100,000, the Personal Allowance is withdrawn at the rate of 50 per cent until the whole Personal Allowance has been withdrawn. During this range of income, the taxpayer is also paying 0.40 on income, which means that s/he is effectively paying (0.50 x 0.40 = 0.20) on the reduction of the Personal Allowance. In addition, s/he pays 0.40 on income in this range, and a further 0.02 of employee NI Contributions. Thus, during the period when the Personal Allowance is being reduced, the effective Marginal Deduction Rate is 0.62. The upshot is that for those with incomes greater than £123,000 in 2017–18, an increase in the Personal Allowance does not affect their total tax due.

Table 12.4 National Insurance and income tax due on additional rate payers

2017–18	£	NIC rate + Tax Rate	NIC +Tax paid, £
Primary Threshold	8,164	0.00	0.00
PA	11,500	0.12	400.32
Higher rate Threshold (Upper Earnings Level)	11,501 – 45,000 (45,032)	0.12 + 0.20	10,720
	45,001 – 100,000	0.02 + 0.40	23,100
PA withdrawal	100,001 – 123,000	0.20 + 0.02 + 0.40	14,260
	123,001 – 150,000	0.02 + 0.40	11,340
Additional rate threshold	150,001 – 200,000	0.02 + 0.45	23,500
TOTAL TAX PAID on	£200,000	Average rate, 0.4166	£83,320.32

The cost of relief of income tax and of NI on pension contributions, as published in HMRC Table 1.5, was £38,450m and £46,690m for 2014–15 and 2015–16 respectively. However, it would seem that the cost could be even greater than this, given the official figure of £50bn published for 2012–13 (Murphy Blog: 2014/09/26). No explanation was given for these discrepancies. Some might not regard closing these particular tax loopholes as a valid way of financing a BI scheme. However, it would be appropriate as part of a pension policy, which ensures that everyone has an adequate pension, rather than subsidising taxpayers for increasing their private pension provision. Those who have the means to do so, would still be able to invest further for their own retirements, but would not be subsidised by the rest of the population. It would become similar to 'New Zealand's public pension system, the New Zealand Superannuation (NZS)… Its primary goal is to provide social protection rather than to replace earnings' (Pensionfundsonline, 2017). The flat-rate non-contributory pension is paid to all residents who fulfil the residence requirements at the age of 65. It is neither work nor means-tested.

Each tax expenditure should be examined:

- What is the objective behind its introduction?
- How does this objective contribute to the public good?
- Is this objective more important than that of operating a fair tax system?

- Did this tax loophole achieve its objective?
- Is this incentive still necessary?
- And, if so, is there a more visible alternative method that could be devised to bring this about, rather than that of using a tax loophole.

Just to give an example: many charities do much work for the public good that governments would like to encourage. Rather than offering Gift Aid of 25 per cent on donations made by taxpayers, a simpler administration method would be for the government to top up all of the donations received by each registered charity each year by 25 per cent. The increase in revenue to which this would lead could also compensate them for the loss of the charities' reduced Business Rate.

It is assumed that all of the BIS and all disability payments will be tax-exempt.

It may be that some of these tax loopholes will be retained, but until the examination process has been undergone, it will be assumed for the purpose of this exercise that all the tax loopholes can be closed and alternatives provided where essential.

CHAPTER 13

A restructured income tax system

A restructured income tax system

THE MORE generous BI schemes would probably have to be financed by a restructured income tax system:

- ...that merges the current income tax system and National Insurance contributions made by self-employed people and employees;

- Where all of the tax loopholes (personal allowances, tax reliefs, allowances and exemptions) that provide the means for legal tax avoidance have been closed. Table 12.2 above lists the Principal Tax Expenditures and Structural Reliefs in the UK's Income Tax and National Insurance systems for 2014–15 and 2015–16. Where the tax loopholes provide a public benefit, such as Gift-Aid on charitable donations, an alternative method may be devised, such that the benefit would appear as a cost in the public accounts, not as a hidden tax expenditure;

- Where everyone pays the same rate of tax on all sources of income;

- The structure of which is either proportionate (flat-tax) or progressive;

- Which is hypothecated; its sole use is to finance the BI system, the cost of its administration and other related cash transfers (disability benefits, a residual NI system – as listed for the required margin in Table 11.5).

Such a BI scheme and a restructured income tax system would be economically viable. Atkinson assumed the first three conditions in his examination of a BI and flat tax (1995: 2–3). Some have claimed that an income tax is a tax on labour. Income tax does not tax the number of hours worked, but only the earnings from that work, among other sources of income.

Once the National Insurance contributions have been subsumed into the restructured income tax system, the NI system as we know it would cease to exist and no new entitlements would be created. Existing entitlements, such as SERPS and S2P would be honoured. However, employers'

NI Contributions could be left in place as a payroll tax and hypothecated to contribute towards the BI scheme. This could reduce the required rates of income tax quoted in the tables below by 4–5% points.

Income sources will include:

- Earnings, wages, salaries, bonuses, (from full-time and part-time employment);
- Earnings from self-employment; part-time free-lance earnings;
- Share schemes and Options (free or cheaply from one's employer);
- Company perquisites (perks – such as a company car, private medical insurance, fringe benefits, commission);
- Pensions: occupational and personal;
- Royalties;
- Interest from banks and building societies;
- Dividends;
- Capital gains on the sale of shares and other assets, excluding owner-occupier homes. However, most of these capital gains on housing are free gifts due to inflation, rather than due to the efforts of the homeowners.
- Rental income from properties,
- Gifts and legacies – perhaps these should be taxed over the lifetime of the recipient, rather than on the estate of the deceased?

An alternative method for calculating the cost of a BI scheme

One objective of this book is to cost the sample BI schemes presented here to demonstrate that they are economically viable, and a flat rate of income tax presents the simplest method of obtaining a single summary figure for comparing different schemes. Table 13.1 for Scotland provides a different method for calculating the cost of the BI scheme from Table 11.2S. This method assumes that the restructured income tax system is used to finance it. The population in each age group is expressed as a proportion of the whole population, and the amounts of the BI paid are expressed as a proportion of the mean income per head of population, Y-BAR. The same margin as in Table 11.5 is added to cover the costs of administration, the costs incurred by disabled people, of Housing Benefit and of other retained benefits. The total cost is estimated in terms of a standard rate of income tax, (that is, a flat tax, or proportionate tax), that would be required to pay for it.

Table 13.1 SCOT Costing the same illustrative BI scheme for Scotland in 2017–18, in terms of a flat rate income tax, based on data available in 2016, as estimated in Table 11.2 Scot.

The BI of each group is expressed as a proportion of £392.40 pw, the mean income, Y-BAR, for Scotland in 2015. Note that the 16–24 and 25–62 groups have been combined for this calculation, since all of them will receive the same amount.

- BI for pensioner (64 or over)   = £157.00 pw = 0.4001 }
- BI for all working-age adults   = £125.60 pw = 0.3201 } of Y-BAR
- BI for a child (aged 0–15)   = £62.80 pw = 0.1600 }
- Premium for parent with care   = £31.40 pw = 0.0800 }

Col. 1	Column 2	Column 3	Column 4	Column 5	col 4 x col 5
Age group	Different groups of the population, by age	population 2015	population proportions	BI proportions	popn propns x BI propns
All		5,373,000			
64 or over	with disabilities, 65+	245,952	0.04577	0.4001	0.018312
	unpaid carers, 65+	94,978	0.01768	0.4001	0.007074
	rest of 65 or over	642,070	0.11950	0.4001	0.047812
	Men & women aged 64	61,736	0.01149	0.4001	0.004597
	Sub-total	1044,736	0.19444		0.077795
16–63	*with disabilities	244,427	0.04549	0.3201	0.014561
	*carers	387,251	0.07207	0.3201	0.023070
	*Rest of 16–63	2,784,296	0.51820	0.3201	0.165876
	Sub-total for 16–63	3,415,974	0.63576		0.203507
	*Lone Parent premium	170,760	0.03178	0.0800	0.002542
	*Other PwC premium	383,437	0.07136	0.0800	0.005709
	Sub-total				0.008251
0–15	with disabilities	15,484	0.00288	0.1600	0.000461
	carers	10,002	0.00186	0.1600	0.000298
	rest of 0–15	886,804	0.16505	0.1600	0.026408
	Sub-total	912,290	0.16979		0.027167
	To finance the sum of gross transfers, 2017–18, tax rate =				0.316720
	FOR SCOTLAND	ADD MARGIN			0.0590
	GRAND TOTAL FOR ALL SOCIAL SECURITY			tax rate =	0.3757

This gives exactly the same result, for the standard rate of income tax required to finance the sum of gross transfers, 31.67% in 2017–18, as was obtained for the sum of gross transfers as a proportion of total income, via the first method in Table 11.2 Scotland above, which was calculated in terms of £ millions.

Table 13.1 UK Costing the same illustrative BI scheme for the UK in 2017–18, in terms of a flat rate income tax, based on data available in 2016, as estimated in Table 11.2 UK

The BI of each group is expressed as a proportion of £411.89 pw, the mean income, Y-BAR, for the UK in 2015. Note that the 16–24 and 25–61 groups have been combined for this calculation, since they all receive the same amount.

- BI for pensioner (64 or over)   = £165.00 pw = 0.4006 }
- BI for all working-age adults   = £132.00 pw = 0.3205 } of Y-BAR
- BI for a child (aged 0–15)   = £66.00 pw = 0.1602 }
- Premium for parents with care   = £33.00 pw = 0.0801 }

Col. 1	Column 2	Column 3	Column 4	Column 5	col 4 x col 5
Age group	Different groups of the population, by age	population UK 2015	population proportions	BI proportions	popn propns x BI propns
All		65,110,000			
64 or over	*with disabilities, 65+	2,859,616	0.04392	0.4006	0.017594
	*unpaid carers, 65+	1,407,124	0.02161	0.4006	0.008657
	Rest of 65 or over	7,344,460	0.11280	0.4006	0.045188
	Men & women aged 64	688,346	0.01057	0.4006	0.004234
	Sub-total	12,299,546	0.18890		0.075673
16–63	*with disabilities	2,442,214	0.03751	0.3205	0.012022
	*unpaid carers	4,965,272	0.07626	0.3205	0.024441
	Rest of 16–63	33,145,092	0.50906	0.3205	0.163153
	Total for 16–63	40,552,578	0.62283		0.199616
	*Lone Parent premium	1,941,005	0.02981	0.0801	0.002388
	*Other PwC premium	4,913,330	0.07546	0.0801	0.006044
	Sub-total				0.008432
0–15	*with disabilities	188,977	0.00290	0.1602	0.000465
	*unpaid carers	133,493	0.00205	0.1602	0.000328
	Rest of 0–15	11,935,406	0.18331	0.1602	0.029366
	Sub-total for 0–15	12,257,876	0.18826		0.030159
	To finance the sum of gross transfers, 2017–18, tax rate =				0.313880
		ADD UK MARGIN			0.0557
	GRAND TOTAL FOR ALL SOCIAL SECURITY		tax rate =		0.3696

This gives exactly the same result, for the standard rate of income tax required to finance the sum of gross transfers, 31.39 per cent, in 2017–18, as was obtained for the sum of gross transfers as a proportion of total income via the first method in Table 11.2 UK above, which was calculated in terms of £ millions.

The fact that the method presented here calculates the cost of a BI scheme in terms of a flat rate of income tax, does not preclude future governments from introducing progression into the system, including introducing higher rates of income tax on people with higher incomes. This method can also be used to calculate the cost when an earnings or income disregard is introduced for working-age adults who receive only a partial BI. They would pay no tax on their first tranche of income until their net income tax schedule meets and merges with the income tax schedule that would have been in place, had they received a full BI according to the chosen poverty benchmark. This method of costing a scheme can be used even when it is not planned to finance the scheme from a restructured flat rate income tax. It provides a useful, simple method of summarising the cost of each BI scheme as a single tax rate, in order to compare the relative costs of different schemes, and it can demonstrate whether the schemes are economically viable.

One advantage of this method is that one can easily note how much is contributed to the final standard rate of income tax by any particular group. For instance, for the BI scheme for the UK scheme illustrated above, those aged 64 or over would contribute 0.0757 to the overall tax rate, while those aged 16–63 would cost 0.1996, and those aged 0–15, together with the Parent with Care premium, would require 0.0386, which adds up to 0.3139, which is the sum of gross transfers. Whereas pensioners' benefits comprise by far the largest single item on the current Social Security expenditure list, accounting for over a third of the total budget (see Table 11.4 above), it is the BIs for the working age group that contributes most to the total in this BI scheme, accounting for two-thirds.

Appendix C shows how a simple Excel program can be set up to calculate the cost of a BI scheme in this way.

These BI schemes for Scotland and the UK in Tables 13.1 are presented as sample schemes B(ii) in the sets of illustrative schemes in chapter 14.

Even though progressive taxes are more redistributive, a proportionate tax (flat tax), has some advantages

- It is simple to administer;
- It is simple to calculate a ballpark summary figure, to compare the cost of different schemes, without having to know the distribution of gross incomes in the population;
- While a flat tax on its own is not as redistributive compared with

progressive taxation, when coupled with a BI scheme, a flat tax is very redistributive in its own right. It is demonstrated in Appendix B that for a hypothetical population, using a restructured income tax system as described above, a flat tax of rate, t = β, where 0 ≤ β < 1, hypothecated for use as a BI that is the same proportion β of average income per head (Y-BAR), then this will reduce the Gini coefficient (a measure of inequality) by that same proportion β. 'Some… may regard a flat tax of, say 50 per cent, as a more redistributive device than a graduated rate structure' (Atkinson, 1995: 4).

- The more generous the level of the BI, the more difficult it is to introduce a graduated tax rate on lower incomes. This is also explored in Appendix B.

- In theory, the members of the population could vote for their preferred income tax rate, t = β, where 0 ≤ β < 1 is the proportion of Y-BAR that will determine the level of the BIs in a simple hypothecated BI / flat rate income tax system, and the resultant mean figure could be adopted.

- A proportionate tax might be more feasible politically, since higher income people might support it, and they could not claim that they were being taxed more than the rest of the population, and;

- It could add to the feeling of 'all being in it together on the same terms', in addition to the greater harmony resulting from the redistribution brought about by the BI scheme.

In practice, during the transition period if/when a BI were to be implemented, those on higher incomes should not on principle pay a lower rate of income tax than the combined income tax and NIC rates that they would have paid under the current or last such system operated. Otherwise they would profit unduly from the introduction of a BI scheme. The potential yield from raising income tax rates is given in Table 13.2.

An increase of the higher rate tax from 40 per cent to 45 per cent in 2017–18 should raise £3,750m, and increasing the additional rate of income tax from 45 per cent to 50 per cent should yield £300m. However, this would be unlikely in practice, since the outcome of larger changes in the income tax rates are unlikely to be proportionate, as individuals adapt their behaviour to the new circumstances.

Table 13.2 Direct effects of illustrative changes in income tax rates

	2017–18	2018–19	2019–20
Forecasts of the yields due to:	£ m	£ m	£ m
A change in the basic rate of income tax by 1p	3,900	4,450	4,500
A change in the higher rate of income tax by 1p	750	1,050	1,000
A change in the additional rate of income tax by 1p: Increase (yield) Decrease (cost)	60 75	105 135	95 125

Source: www.gov.uk, 'Direct effects of illustrative changes in income tax rates'.

An income/earnings disregard (EDR)

Calculating the cost of a BI scheme in terms of a flat tax does not preclude some future government from introducing progressivity into the income tax system. This could take the form on the one hand of higher rates of

Figure 13.1 Basic Income schedules without an earnings disregard compared with 2017–18 UK income tax schedule:
Mean gross income (2015) Y-BAR = £21,477;
Income tax rate for BIS = 40%
Full BI = 0.50 Y-BAR; Partial BI = 0.30 Y-BAR

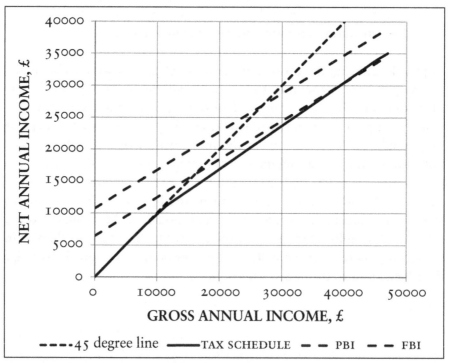

tax on those with higher incomes, or, on the other, introducing an income / earnings disregard (EDR) for working-age adults who receive only a partial BI (PBI). These latter would pay no tax on their first tranche of income until their net income schedule meets and merges with the income tax schedule that would have been in place had they received a full BI (FBI) according to the chosen poverty benchmark.

With different levels of BI being paid for different age groups, and with maybe some on FBI and some on a PBI, all paying the same flat rate of income tax, the graphs of their net incomes plotted against their gross incomes would be a set of parallel lines (see Figure 13.1). This would imply that the differences in the levels of BI, deemed necessary for those with no other sources of gross income, are still valid at higher levels of gross income. The merged schedules lead to a single standard rate of income tax, t, for all who receive a FBI, even those with modest gross incomes (see Figure 13.2).

However, an EDR is more expensive to finance, since the government

Figure 13.2 Basic Income schedules with and without an earnings disregard compared with 2017–18 UK income tax schedule: Mean gross income (2015) Y-BAR = £21,477; New income tax rate for BIS = 50% Full BI = 0.50 Y-BAR; Partial BI = 0.30 Y-BAR

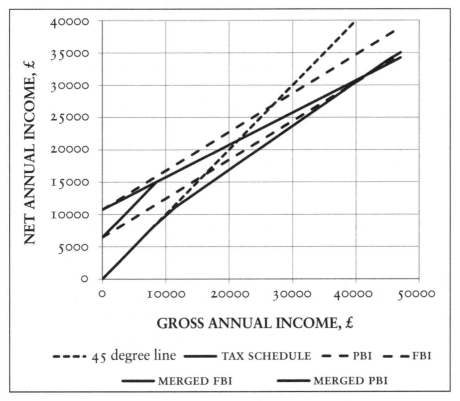

foregoes all the tax revenue on the first tranche of income, and so a higher rate of income tax would be required to finance the BI scheme if an EDR were introduced. The concept of an EDR in the context of a BI scheme has been explored (Miller, 2013). The paper concluded that introducing an EDR will cost no more (and is likely to be less) than if those receiving the PBI and eligible for the EDR had received a FBI instead. Thus, the relevant maximum standard rate of income tax, t, which would have been necessary to finance this, can easily be calculated, by assuming that everyone actually receiving a PBI had received a FBI instead. Then the gross income, Yo, at which the FBI and PBI schedules merge, is given by:

$$Yo = (FBI - PBI) / t.$$

And the net income, Ys, at which the two schedules merge, is given by:

$$Ys = PBI + Yo = (FBI - (1 - t). PBI) / t.$$

An EDR has administrative advantages since it will reduce the number of tax returns that HMRC will have to process. Individuals whose gross income is less than Yo, in addition to his/her PBI, will not have to submit one. It means that someone earning only, say, £3,000 from a part-time cleaning job, for instance, would not have to become a taxpayer. It also has the added advantage of maximising the incentive to work-for-pay for low-wage earners.

The structure of the income tax schedule

The next stage is to decide on the structure of the income tax system that could be introduced to finance the scheme. The choices are of:

- A flat tax, or
- A progressive system, made by allowing an income/earnings disregard (EDR) on the first tranche of gross income for those who receive only a PBI, and/or
- A progressive system, made by adding higher rate(s) of income tax for those with higher gross incomes.

This is summarised in Table 13.3.

Each column in Table 13.3 represents a political option, with pros and cons. Readers can identify their preferences. The effect of different progressive tax schedules on a hypothetical population is explored in Appendix B.

Table 13.3 Pros and cons of the structure of the income tax schedule

Proportional income tax, (standard flat rate), for all.	Progressive for those receiving a PBI via an income or earnings disregard (EDR), (zero tax rate on first tranche of gross income until PBI and FBI schedules meet and merge)	Progressive: higher rates for those with higher incomes
It is simple to administer, and reduces the opportunities for tax evasion, but it leads to a large caseload, since all are liable to tax on the first £ of gross income.	Simpler to administer, since some low incomes can be ignored for tax purposes, – therefore leads to a lower case load.	More complex to administer.
It is simple to calculate and predict a ballpark standard rate of income tax as a summary figure.	Relatively easy to calculate and predict a ballpark figure for the standard rate of income tax.	Very difficult to calculate a summary without knowing the distribution of gross incomes, – a function of net wage rates and unearned income.
Hypothecated with a BI, it is still very redistributive. (See Appendix B)	Even more redistributive.	Even more redistributive. Incentives to redistribute to family members – good, if real, but not if just nominal.
In theory, the adult population could vote directly for the rate of income tax (and the proportion of mean income per head) for the related BI in a hypothecated system.		
It could appeal to people with higher gross incomes – political support for BI.	It could appeal to people with higher gross incomes – political support for BI.	Wealthy sector could (threaten to) leave the country on grounds of discrimination.
Harmony, as all pay the same rate of income tax.	Fairly harmonious.	
There is nothing to prevent a future government from introducing an EDR, or higher rates of income tax on higher incomes, on implementation of a BI.		

A flat tax leads to parallel tax schedules, for those receiving FBI or PBI, over the whole range of gross income.	FBI and PBI schedules can meet and be merged. The EDR will cost nearly as much as giving a full BI to all those with PBIs.	
	**Evidence from economic theory of labour supply suggests upward-sloping, very elastic labour supply curves for those on low incomes. A zero tax rate for those receiving partial BIs and with an EDR increases incentives to work-for-pay.	**Evidence from economic theory of labour supply suggests backward-sloping, inelastic labour supply curves for those on higher wage rates. Higher tax rates will reduce net wage rates, providing incentives for wealthy people to work more hours for pay, for any given level of BI.
**Suggested further reading on labour supply theory in Borgas (2009). (See also Miller, 2015).		

Will it cost too much? Can we afford it?

The question 'Will it cost too much?' depends on the generosity of the particular BI scheme. It is possible to choose from a range of different schemes.

The UK has the fifth or sixth largest economy in the world. How rich does the UK have to be before it can afford to treat its most vulnerable citizens compassionately and fairly? Or, to put it more bluntly, of how many years of life is a rich society entitled to deprive a poor person? How much would wealthier people be prepared to pay in income tax, if they and members of their families could benefit, and if it contributed to a fairer society? While the population seems to have voted for a neoliberal regime at the General Election in May 2017, there are plenty of taxpayers who are alarmed at the way that poor and vulnerable people in society are being treated. They do not wish their comfortable life-styles to be bought at the expense of making poor people suffer. Their concern is both for the sake of the poorer people, and for fear of the possible revolution that might break out when the strains get to breaking point and the comfortably-off themselves could be targeted by the oppressed. There are also many middle-class, middle-aged people today who are worried about their offspring, who are not necessarily guaranteed to occupy the privileged jobs of the past, and might need some independent financial security. A neoliberal, low-level BI scheme, where the rest of the welfare state has been dismantled, would not be the solution.

Let us assume that 50 per cent is the maximum standard rate of income tax that Britons would be prepared to pay, although it could be less. Can we devise a satisfactory scheme where the standard rate of income tax required to finance it is no greater than 50 per cent? Would poorer people be willing to accept a tax rate of up to 50 per cent if it meant that they could be better off financially? Many claimants and unemployed people already face a Marginal Deduction Rate much greater than this. What progressive models of taxation could contribute to financial gains for the poorest while sustaining levels of revenue? These are questions that need to be answered empirically.

CHAPTER 14

Sample BI schemes for Scotland and the UK

No single optimum BI scheme

A BASIC INCOME is defined as being 'universal, individual, and unconditional', and in addition it is neither means-tested nor selective except by age, and is delivered automatically and regularly. However, more than this is needed for designing a particular scheme. An infinite number of schemes is possible, each being the outcome of the specific prioritised objectives, assumptions and constraints of those who devise them, and these starting points should be clearly stated. Thus, each is essentially subjective. As stated before, as long as two people want different outcomes, a *single optimum* BI scheme that satisfies everyone cannot exist. The only thing that can be guaranteed is that few will be satisfied with the details of particular schemes that s/he reads about. Thus, it is important that those wishing to design their own versions should state clearly at the start of the process, their objectives, priorities, assumptions and constraints in addition to prioritising the broad objectives listed in chapter 2.

One of the aims behind presenting these last few chapters of facts and figures, together with their sources, is to indicate what should be taken into account when trying to devise a BI scheme, and to enable readers to try out ideas for themselves. Then they can set up the simple Excel program laid out in Appendix C to cost it for themselves using the method presented in chapter 13. Or readers can devise other BI schemes, using both alternative and multiple sources to finance them, each with their own advantages and problems, and cost these in their own way.

The focus of this chapter is that of providing some illustrative sample BI schemes and to show that they are economically viable, with a summary figure for each scheme with which to compare their costs. It is for this latter reason that I have chosen to cost the schemes in terms of a restructured income tax system using a flat tax.

Graduated income tax schedules should also be considered, and a comparison of progressive income tax systems using a hypothetical income distribution is explored in Appendix B. Some difficulties arise:

- Data for the distribution of gross incomes for individuals, apart from taxpayers, in the UK is not available;

- The scope for introducing realistic progression into the tax rates on lower-income groups is more limited as the BI becomes more generous.

  Although it would be quite possible to combine the basic income with a graduated rate schedule, the initial tax rate necessary to finance an adequate basic income is likely to be close to the present higher rate of tax in Britain (40 per cent in 1989), so that the scope for graduation would in practice be limited;

  ATKINSON, 1995: 2

- If the tax-benefit schedule awarded a net income that was greater than Y-BAR, to an individual who had a gross income equal to Y-BAR, then the system would be unsustainable. Y-BAR provides a natural constraint on the system;

- And as with all of the analysis presented here, it would not necessarily predict the effect of people changing their behaviour as a result of the implementation of different benefits and tax rates.

Table 13.2 above gives HMRC's forecasts for the yields from increases of one penny in the pound for different income tax bands. The yield from increasing tax rates by more than one penny in the pound is not proportionate, because people will adjust their behaviour in response to changes in benefits and tax rates. Future governments with access to accurate data on the distribution of gross incomes of individuals could estimate more accurately the revenues from levying higher rates of income tax on those with higher incomes. Higher rates are not included as part of the illustrative schemes presented here, because of this lack of data.

While a flat tax has traditionally been regarded as unfair, because it favours wealthier people compared with progressive tax schedules, a flat tax in conjunction with a BI can be a very different proposition. In Appendix B it is demonstrated that a flat tax that is hypothecated for use on the BI scheme can be redistributive in its own right. It also has other qualities, as indicated in Table 13.3, including administrative advantages and it provides a unitary summary of the cost of each scheme for easy comparison. The costing of the sample schemes presented here is based on a flat tax with the option of an income / earnings disregard for those receiving only a PBI, to make it slightly more progressive. This also has administrative advantages – casual earnings and children's pocket money would not have to be taxed. The use of a flat tax for illustrative purposes should not be taken as indicative of libertarian-type proclivities (Murphy, 2015: 68–80).

I note some other caveats here:

- The very unequal wealth in Scotland, and the UK as a whole, should be redistributed, and a land value tax would have an important role in this, but that is a whole other topic which is outwith the remit of this book about *income-based* schemes.

- Corporations should be made to pay their fair share of tax, but that too is outwith the scope of a book on Basic Income (Murphy, 2015: 233–4).

- More should be invested into detecting and prosecuting illegal tax evasion. Economic theory suggests that it would be profitable for HMRC to invest in this to the extent that the marginal cost outlaid is equal to the marginal revenue obtained by recouping the spoils of tax evasion, or even until marginal revenue is zero.

- Wage-protection, such as a realistic National Living Wage, will still be required.

Clearly-stated prioritised objectives, assumptions and constraints

As stated above, it is important that the specific objectives, priorities, assumptions and constraints that guide the illustrative sample schemes in this chapter should be declared and they are laid out in Table 14.1. The overall objectives are to provide sample schemes that meet the poverty benchmarks and to demonstrate that these BI schemes are economically viable. It should be emphasised that the estimated costs are merely ballpark figures.

As described in chapter 10 above, a floor and two poverty benchmarks are presented. The current benefit system provides a lower limit for any BI scheme. The first poverty benchmark is the EU's 0.6 of median equivalised household income, details of which are published in the DWP's *Households Below Average Income* (HBAI), and the second is the *Minimum Income Standards*, produced at Loughborough University. Three sets of schemes, each set relating to a different measure, are put forward below and costs estimated using the method illustrated in Tables 13.1 above.

For each scheme, at least three, and sometimes five, different levels of BI are given: for those over pension-entitlement age; either a full or a partial BI for working-age adults (aged 25–64); for young adults (aged 16–24);

Table 14.1 Objectives and solutions for the design of the sample BI schemes

OBJECTIVE	SOLUTION – BI SCHEME
Emancipation	Not paid into a joint account unless sanctioned by a court
Choice	Recipient can choose frequency of payment of BI, (weekly, fortnightly or 4-weekly), paid in advance of the period to which it applies.
No person / household on low incomes should be worse off in real terms by the introduction of a BI scheme.	This acts as a constraint on the system introduced. No one should receive a BI less than the means-tested or NI benefit that the BI was replacing. No one should receive less in BI than that to which s/he would have been entitled in State Retirement Pension, etc.
Prevent / reduce income poverty	BI schemes should be more generous to working-age people than in the recent social security system, ensuring that the poorest working-age individuals are better off financially, and preferably BI schemes should aspire at least to the official EU poverty benchmark.
Ameliorate the problem of regional variation in rents and house prices, created by the current housing policy, which preclude a housing-cost element being included in the BI.	Retain an individualised, means-tested Housing Benefit scheme, such as that used for students or other adults sharing accommodation, but which covers either rent or mortgage interest up to a certain limit (and with less than the current 65% withdrawal rate), and Council Tax Support. Choose a poverty benchmark using 'After Housing Costs have been deducted' (AHC) version. This acknowledges that some individuals, even when receiving a full BI, may still need means-tested benefits.
Reflect the prosperity of society. Provide a self-stabilising mechanism, and prevent a downward spiral of the economy	Index the BIS as proportions of the mean income per head of man, woman and child (Y-BAR), the proportions being fixed for the term of a government administration. This indicates what is economically viable and is especially relevant when financing a BI scheme from a hypothecated restructured income tax system.
Define a full BI for an adult; and for a family with children	A full BI is one that is within 0.02 of the chosen poverty benchmark for a single adult of the relevant age. A full BI for a child is such that the sum of BIS for all within the household is within 0.02 of the chosen poverty benchmark for the relevant household configuration.
Protect financially-vulnerable adults and families with children	These are disadvantaged in the labour market and a compassionate society would not compel them to top up a partial BI from earnings. They include those over pension-entitlement age, dependent children (aged 0–15), the primary care-giving parent, and people with disabilities. These adults should receive a full BI, or have a partial BI topped up through their disability benefit package.

OBJECTIVE	SOLUTION – BI SCHEME
Protect people with disabilities, chronic illnesses and those who are deemed as incapable of working–for-pay	Retain / improve all current disability benefits as a parallel but separate system and devise new Gateways to enable them to access these benefits, where necessary.
Protect other single, working-age adults, and enable those adults who wish to do so, to afford to volunteer as unpaid carers for family and friends*.	Since there is no guarantee that every adult will be able to access a full-time, well-paid job, partial BIs should be equal to at least 75 per cent of their full BI equivalent.
Simplify maternity and death benefits.	Initiate Child BI and BIs for new Parents with Care at, or backdated to, 13th week of pregnancy, and extend BI for six months after death into the estate of the deceased to help with funeral costs.
	SOLUTION – INCOME TAX SYSTEM
Redistribute income to reduce income inequalities...	Restructure the income tax system, such that income tax and employees' NI contributions are subsumed into it; no tax loopholes, (except that the BIs and all disability benefits are tax-exempt); everyone pays the same rate of income tax on all sources of income.
... and ensure that the system is viable.	Hypothecate the restructured income tax system such that it is used entirely for the BI scheme, retained benefits, associated cash transfer payments and administration. Thus there will be equal upward pressure to increase the amount of the BIs and downward pressure to reduce the income tax rate. Constrain a flat rate of income tax, or the standard rate, to be no greater than 50 per cent.
Ensure that wealthy people do not profit unduly from the introduction of a BI system.	Introduce higher and additional rates of income tax for all higher income people on principle, so that they would pay at least as much income tax on equivalent gross income levels as they were paying pre BI, and thus they will not become net beneficiaries by its introduction.
Provide an incentive for those receiving only a partial BI to increase their income, and thereby also reduce the number of income tax returns necessary.	For those eligible for only partial BIs, set up an income / earnings disregard (EDR) on their gross income until their tax schedule meets and merges with their corresponding full BI tax schedule. This untaxed tranche of income is likely to be relatively small, but will cost more. It will give an increased incentive to work-for-pay, even if only part-time. Both earnings and other income, including royalties, interest and dividends, capital gains, rental income and gifts could be included in the disregard because it has administrative advantages in reducing the number of income tax returns necessary.

OBJECTIVE	SOLUTION – INCOME TAX SYSTEM
Redeployment of redundant civil servants	Offer retraining in areas of their choice, including as income tax inspectors using their experience to increase the pool of people preventing and prosecuting tax evasion and as advisors to low-income people about returning to work, retraining and job opportunities, for instance, and about disability, housing and other retained benefits.

* Even a partial BI, if sufficiently generous, and being unconditional, will enable people to be able to afford to volunteer to care for relatives and friends without making themselves destitute. A full-time carer of a disabled person, for instance, would have to be registered as a carer for that person, and any extra emoluments would be organised through the separate Disability Benefits system. Other paid carers would receive their remuneration from local authorities that would provide care packages for those who need them.

for a dependent child (aged 0–15 inclusive). In some schemes a premium for a working-age Parent with Care (the primary care-giving parent) and in others a premium for boys and girls aged 14–15, matching them up with the categories used in the EU poverty benchmark. In the more generous schemes, young adults receive the same BI as other working-age adults, as in the EU poverty benchmarks. An increased amount for the Parent with Care (PWC) is equivalent to giving an extra amount to the oldest dependent child in a family in the current social security system. However, it will be slightly simpler administratively, since the identity of the parent with care is likely to change less frequently than the identity of the oldest dependent child.

In the sample schemes that follow, the BI for those over pension entitlement age is of the same order of magnitude for all three sets. In the first set, it is the level of Pension Credit. In the third set it is the amount that the MIS focus groups thought necessary as a Minimum Income. In the middle group it is 0.4 of Y-BAR. In the first set, the BI for the working-age adult is less than for the older adult. For the second set, the full BI is the same for all adults. In the third set, the focus groups found that the working age adult needed a higher income than an older adult. In the first two sets of sample schemes the BIs for the dependent child are very similar, but it is much higher in the third set in order to meet the Minimum Income Standard for dependent children.

The costing figures take into account the fact that individuals aged 64 are eligible for Pension Credit in 2017–18, and thus would also have been eligible for a pensioner BI, but this group will change over time. Each BI level is expressed in money terms for 2017–18, and also as a proportion of the average income per head, Y-BAR, in Scotland and in UK for 2015 and published in 2016, (the latest available figures at the time when a decision would have been required re 2017–18).

The cost was calculated in the same way as for the scheme in Tables 13.1, as though financed by a restructured income tax system. It entails expressing the population in each group as a proportion of total population in Scotland, or in the UK, and multiplying this figure by the corresponding BI expressed as a proportion of the appropriate Y-BAR. (These proportions are noted to seven places of decimals, because these are relevant for the Appendix C, if costing your own schemes). The products are added up and a margin of 0.0590 in Scotland, or of 0.0557 for the UK scheme, is added to cover administration costs, disability and other retained benefits, social fund, and a residual safety net, etc. This gives the cost (in terms of the flat-rate of standard income tax in a restructured income tax system) necessary to finance the whole social security system, and is a useful method for gauging the relative costs of different schemes.

The first set of sample BI schemes, compared with current means-tested benefits

The first set comprises entry-level schemes that are designed so that they at least match the floor provided by the current benefit system. The amounts and proportions are laid out in Table 14.2a. Table 14.2b then compares these illustrative schemes with the current benefit system for 11 different household configurations, and indicates the standard rate of income tax required.

The BIS are expressed as proportions of Y-BAR for Scotland or the UK in Table 14.2a.

Scheme A(i) is designed to replace Pension Credit, IS/JSA/ ESA (aged 25 or over rates), Child Tax Credit and Child Benefit with a BI of the same amount to which a single person was entitled. Both Child Benefit and Child Tax Credit give a greater amount for the first child, and the extra is credited here as a premium to the PWC, over and above the amount of BI that s/he would receive as a working-age adult. Thus, a PWC would receive her/his own working-age BIS, and a PWC premium, together with the Child BIS to administer on behalf of the children. The BIS for single adult households match up with the current MTBS, but household economies of scale are evident in households with couples compared with the current benefit system.

A(ii) is more generous to working-age adults than scheme A(i), and to

Table 14.2a Money values for BIS for entry-level BI schemes for 2017–18, and as proportions of Y-BAR for Scotland and the UK 2015

	£ pw	Proportion of Y-BAR Scot	Proportion of Y-BAR UK
Y-BAR Scotland 2015	£392.40	1.0000	
Y-BAR UK 2015	£411.89		1.0000
BI Scheme A(i)			
Pensioner	£159.35	0.4060909	0.3868752
Working-age adult (25–64)	£73.10	0.1862896	0.1774760
Parent with care (16–64) premium	£17.42	0.0443935	0.0422929
Young adult (16–24)	£57.90	0.1475536	0.1405716
Child (0–15)	£66.87	0.1704129	0.1623492
BI Scheme A(ii)			
Pensioner	£160.00	0.4077472	0.3884533
Working-age adult (25–64)	£100.00	0.2548420	0.2427833
Young Adult (16–24)	£100.00	0.2548420	0.2427833
Child (0–15)	£65.00	0.1656473	0.1578092

most families with dependent children. This adds an extra four per cent to the income tax rate necessary to finance the scheme in each case, compared with scheme A(i). These are designed as entry-level schemes during a phase of transition towards a more authoritative poverty benchmark, and the terms partial and full BIS, as defined above, are not relevant for these schemes.

The second set of sample BI schemes, compared with the official EU poverty benchmark (AHC version)

The second set of sample schemes is designed to meet, for most cases, the EU poverty standard for the UK, AHC version. The latest available figures in 2016, at the time when decisions would have to be made for 2017–18, refer to 2014–15 and so there is a two year gap between the period from which the data were gathered and when they will be used.

The proposed alternative poverty benchmark for BI purposes (see Table 10.6) was adopted, to see whether it would at least meet the criteria for the official EU benchmark.

Table 14.2b Money values for BIS for entry-level BI schemes for
2017–18, and as proportions of Y-BAR for Scotland and the UK 2015

2017–18		Current benefit system £ pw, 2017–18, FLOOR		BI Scheme A(i), £ pw	BI Scheme A(ii), £ pw
		MTBS	MTBS		
Pensioner (65 and over)			£159.35	£159.35	£160.00
Working age (25–64)			£73.10	£73.10	£100.00
PWC premium (16–64)			£0.00	£17.42	£0.00
Young Adult (16–24)			£57.90	£57.90	£100.00
Child (0–15)			£84.29, 1st £66.87, rest	£66.87	£65.00
single pensioner	Pension	159.35		= 159.35	= 160.00
couple pensioner	Credit	243.25		318.70	320.00
single working-age (25+)	JSA/ (25+)	73.10		= 73.10	100.00
couple working-age (25+)	ESA (25+)	114.85		146.20	200.00
Young adult (16–24)	JSA/ESA	57.90		= 57.90	100.00
Lone Parent + toddler	JSA/ (25+)	157.39		= 157.39	165.00
Lone Parent + pre + prim	ESA (25+)	224.26		= 224.26	230.00
Lone Parent + pre + prim + secondary school child	CB, CTC	291.13		= 291.13	= 295.00
Couple + toddler	JSA/ (25+)	199.14		230.49	265.00
Couple + pre + primary	ESA (25+)	266.01		297.36	330.00
Couple + pre + prim + sec	CB,	332.88		364.23	395.00
Couple + toddler + pre + prim + sec school child	CTC.	399.75		431.10	460.00
SCOTLAND					
Cost (in terms of tax rate)				0.2265	0.2694
Current margin				0.0590	0.0590
Income tax rate for all Social Security transfers				0.2855	0.3284
UK					
Cost (in terms of tax rate)				0.2144	0.2543
Current margin				0.0557	0.0557
Income tax rate for all Social Security transfers				0.2701	0.3100

KEY
Pre = pre-school child, aged 2-4;   ESA = Employment and Support Allowance;
Prim = primary school child;   CB   = Child Benefit;
Sec = secondary school child;   CTC = Child Tax Credit.
JSA = Jobseeker's Allowance;

> The BI levels preceded by an '=' sign show that the BI is within two per cent of the current benefit system.
>
> The *figures in italics* show that the BIS are higher than the current benefit system by more than two per cent.
>
> The 'current margin', to cover the costs of administration and of retained benefits, is as derived in Table 11.5 above.

Table 14.3a Money values of BIS for EU benchmark schemes for 2017–18, and as proportions of Y-BAR for Scotland and the UK 2015

Column 1	Column 2 £ pw	Column 3 Proportion of Y-BAR Scotland	Column 4 £ pw	Column 5 Proportion of Y-BAR UK
Y-BAR Scot 2015	£392.40	1.000		
Y-BAR UK 2015			£411.89	1.0000
EU Benchmark				
Pensioner	£140.59/£101.81	0.35828/0.25945		0.34133/0.2472
Working age	£140.59/£101.81	0.35828/0.25945		0.34133/0.2472
Child aged 14 +	£101.81	0.25945		0.24718
Child 0–13	£48.48	0.12355		0.11770
Scheme B(i)	SCOTLAND		UK	
Pensioner BI	£157.00	0.4001020	£165.00	0.4005924
Working-age BI	£125.60	0.3200816	£132.00	0.3204740
Premium 14–15	£31.40	0.0800204	£33.00	0.0801185
Child BI 0–15	£62.80	0.1600408	£66.00	0.1602370
Scheme B(ii)				
Pensioner BI	£157.00	0.4001020	£165.00	0.4005924
Working-age BI	£125.60	0.3200816	£132.00	0.3204740
Premium PWC	£31.40	0.0800204	£33.00	0.0801185
Child BI 0–15	£62.80	0.1600408	£66.00	0.1602370
Scheme B(iii)				
Pensioner BI	£157.00	0.4001020	£165.00	0.4005924
Working-age BI	£157.00	0.4001020	£165.00	0.4005924
Child BI 0–15	£62.80	0.1600408	£66.00	0.1602370

Table 14.3 SCOT BI sample schemes for Scotland, 2017–18, compared with the 2014–15 EU median income poverty benchmark (AHC)

2015 SCOTLAND Y-BAR = £392.40 pw	BI Scheme B(i) 2017–18 £ pw	BI Scheme B(ii) 2017–18 £ pw	BI Scheme B(iii) 2017–18 £ pw	Benchmark 0.6 of med income, AHC, 2014–15, £ pw
Pensioner BI	£157.00	£157.00	£157.00	£140.59/£101.81
Working-age BI	£125.60	£125.60	£157.00	£140.59/£101.81
PWC premium	£0.00	£31.40	£0.00	
Child 14–15 premium	£31.40	£0.00	£0.00	£53.33
Child BI (0–15)	£62.80	£62.80	£62.80	£48.48
single pensioner	157.00	157.00	157.00	140.59
couple pensioner	314.00	314.00	314.00	242.40
single working-age	125.60	125.60	157.00	140.59
couple working-age	251.20	251.20	314.00	242.40
Lone P + toddler	= 188.40	219.80	219.80	189.07
Lone P + pre+ prim	251.20	282.60	282.60	237.55
Lone P + pre + prim + secondary school child	= 345.40	= 345.40	= 345.40	339.36
Couple + toddler	314.00	345.40	376.80	290.88
Couple + pre + primary	376.80	408.20	439.60	339.36
Couple + pre + prim + secondary school child	471.00	471.00	502.40	441.17
Couple + toddler + pre + prim + sec school child	533.80	533.80	565.20	489.65
SCOTLAND				
Cost (in terms of tax rate)	0.3101	0.3167	0.3593	
Current margin	0.0590	0.0590	0.0590	
Income tax rate for all Social Security transfers	0.3691	0.3757	0.4183	
Cost (in terms of EDR rate)	0.3610	0.3593	-------	
Income tax rate for all Social Security transfers, with an EDR	0.4200	0.4183	-------	
Tax-free gross income, Yo	£74.76 pw	£75.07 pw	-------	
Tax-free net income, Ys	£200.42 pw	£200.67 pw	-------	
KEY as for Table 14.3 UK				

Table 14.3 UK BI sample schemes for the UK, 2017–18, compared with the 2014–15 EU median income poverty benchmark (AHC)

2015 UK Y-BAR = £411.89 pw	Scheme B(i) 2017–18 £ pw	Scheme B(ii) 2017–18 £ pw	Scheme B(iii) 2017–18 £ pw	Benchmark 0.6 of med income, AHC, 2014–15
Pensioner BI	£165.00	£165.00	£165.00	£140.59/£101.81
Working-age BI	£132.00	£132.00	£165.00	£140.59/£101.81
PWC premium	£0.00	£33.00	£0.00	
Child 14–15 premium	£33.00	£0.00	£0.00	£53.33
Child BI (0–15)	£66.00	£66.00	£66.00	£48.48
single pensioner	165.00	165.00	165.00	140.59
couple pensioner	330.00	330.00	330.00	242.40
single working-age	132.00	132.00	165.00	140.59
couple working-age	264.00	264.00	330.00	242.40
Lone P + toddler	198.00	231.00	231.00	189.07
Lone P + pre+ prim	264.00	297.00	297.00	237.55
Lone P + pre + prim + secondary school child	363.00	363.00	363.00	339.36
Couple + toddler	330.00	363.00	396.00	290.88
Couple + pre + primary	396.00	429.00	462.00	339.36
Couple + pre + prim + secondary school child	495.00	495.00	528.00	441.17
Couple + toddler + pre + prim + sec school child	561.00	561.00	594.00	489.65
UK				
Cost (in terms of tax rate)	0.3072	0.3139	0.3553	
Current margin	0.0557	0.0557	0.0557	
Income tax rate for all Social Security transfers	0.3629	0.3696	0.4110	
Cost (in terms of EDR rate)	0.3571	0.3553	-------	
Income tax rate for all Social Security transfers, with an EDR	0.4128	0.4110	-------	
Tax-free gross income, Yo	£79.94 pw	£80.29 pw	-------	
Tax-free net income, Ys	£211.94 pw	£212.29 pw	-------	

KEY

Pre = pre-school child, aged 2–4;   Prim = primary school child;   Sec = secondary school child.

The **figures in bold** indicate that the BIS are less than the relevant poverty benchmark by more than two per cent, being a partial BI.

Figures preceded by the '=' sign show that the BI is within two per cent of the relevant poverty benchmark.

The *figures in italics* show that the BIS are higher than the relevant poverty benchmark by more than two per cent.

The process used in Tables 14.3a, 14.3 Scot and 14.3 UK is as follows:

- A pensioner BI was set to equal 0.4 of Y-BAR (£156.96 for Scotland and £164.76 for the UK). These were rounded up to the nearest 50 pence. This would also be the level for a full BI for a working-age adult. The other levels were determined as proportions of the rounded up full BI.

- The partial BI for working-age adults is 0.8 of the full BI;

- There is no distinction between the amounts received by young adults and other working-age adults;

- The child BI is 0.4 of the full BI.

- Where the child BI does not meet the EU poverty benchmark, a premium is granted for 14–15 year olds at 0.2 of the full BI. If this is insufficient it is increased until it fulfils the full BI for the relevant household.

- The premium for a PWC was 0.2 of the full BI and it tops up her/ his partial BI entitlement to the full BI.

- The cost was calculated using the method laid out in Tables 13.1 above.

A similar process was carried out for Tables 14.5a and 14.5b

The money amounts in the rows relating to the 'EU benchmark' above are the values recommended for first and subsequent adults, and for older and younger children, according to the definition of 0.6 of median equivalised household income for 2014–15. The figures in columns 3 and 5 are the proportions of Y-BAR for Scotland and the UK that these money amounts represent.

Tables 14.3 Scot and 14.3 UK show that the BIS, which are determined according to the proposed alternative poverty benchmark, also meet the criteria of being at least as great as the EU poverty benchmark, (except for a working-age single adult who is not a PWC in schemes B(i) and B(ii) and who receives only a partial BI). It will be interesting to observe whether this pattern of proportions of the mean income for Scotland continues to meet the EU poverty benchmark over the next few years.

The BI levels are derived as proportions of Y-BAR for Scotland or the UK in Table 14.3.

The 'current margin', to cover the costs of administration and of retained benefits, is as derived in Table 11.5 above.

For Scotland, 0.4 of £392.40 pw is actually £156.96. This figure was rounded up to £157.00 and used as the full BI. In order to calculate the relevant income tax rate, the actual proportion of £392.40 must be used, which is 0.400102.

The levels of the BIS for the UK according to the alternative benchmark that was proposed in Table 10.6 above may seem very generous compared with the EU official poverty benchmark, in Table 14.3 UK. This will partly be due to the relatively low levels of the out-of-date official figures. The figures yielded by the alternative benchmark when based on Y-BAR for 2014 also fulfilled this same EU poverty benchmark that is applied to 2017–18 benefit schemes.

Any scheme in which working-age adults receive a partial BI (PBI), offers the opportunity to introduce an income / earnings disregard (EDR). This is a true tax-free allowance for those receiving a PBI, such that those recipients pay no income tax on their first tranche of income, until their tax schedule meets and merges with that of those receiving a full BI (FBI). This is more expensive to finance, because the tax revenues from the first tranche of income is foregone, but it has been shown that the cost will not be more than if all working-age adults had received a FBI, (Miller, 2013). This increased tax rate, t, (i.e. the tax rate before the margin is added), can be calculated via the costing method in Tables 13.1, while assuming that all working-age adults receive a FBI. Although the cost is the same for scheme B(iii) and scheme B(ii) with an EDR, the latter has administrative and incentive advantages over scheme B(iii), as expressed in Table 13.3.

In 2017–18, the higher income tax rate and employees' NI contribution together is 42 per cent, and the additional tax rate and NI on incomes over £150,000 is 47 per cent. Rates of restructured income tax at least as high as these should be levied on those in higher income groups on principle, or even higher at 45 and 50 per cent, if they are not to profit unduly from the BI scheme, even if it detracts from the harmony of everyone receiving the same BI, and paying at the same rate of income tax. This is more relevant for the B(i) – (iii) schemes than for the C(i) – (iii) schemes. These higher rates of income tax have not been taken into account in the costing method above.

The value of gross income, Yo, where the FBI and PBI schedules merge, is calculated from Yo = (FBI – PBI) / t, where t is the higher rate calculated for the merged schedules, after the margin has been added. For the Scottish schemes:

* Yo for scheme B(i) is (£157.00 – £125.60) / 0.4200 = £74.76 pw (£3,898.20 pa).

* Yo for scheme B(ii) is (£157.00 – £125.60) / 0.4183 = £75.07 pw, (£3,914.36 pa).

Added to their partial BIS, this means that individuals will be able to receive and earn a total of Ys before they have to start paying any income tax:

* Ys for scheme B(i) is £125.60 + £74.76 = £200.36 pw (£10,447.34 pa).

* Ys for scheme B(ii) is £125.60 + £75.07 = £200.67 pw (£10,463.51 pa).

Thus, individuals could benefit from tax-free incomes up to levels that compare well with the Personal Allowance of £10,600 in 2015–16.

These three Scottish BI schemes, the details of which are laid out in Table 14.3a, and Table 14.3 Scot, are variations on the same idea. All give a full BI to those over pension-entitlement age. B(i) and B(ii) provide only a partial BI equal to 80 per cent of the full BI to working-age adults. Partial BIS on their own would fail to reach the standard of the EU poverty benchmark for some families with older children. Scheme B(i) solves this problem by adding a premium for 14–15 year olds, in line with the weighting used in creating the EU poverty benchmark. Scheme B(ii) solves the problem by adding a PWC premium to the working age adult BI to create the full BI for the PWC, which is better for lone parents and other families with dependent children. Scheme B(iii) grants all adults a full BI, but it shows signs of Household Economies of Scale (HES). This set was designed to show how Scheme B(ii) helps to maintain a better balance between increased household economies of scale while still protecting families with children. The set of three schemes for the UK follows the same pattern.

Comparison of a set of three BI schemes

In the table that follows, the three schemes are compared for the following factors: poverty prevention, household economies of scale, family economies of scale, fairness within the household, (if all receive the same BI, then those without caring responsibilities can choose between more

Table 14.4 Comparison of sample BI schemes B(i), B(ii) and B(iii)

	B(i)	B(ii)	B(iii)
Prevents poverty?	Not for a single w-a adult – partial BI only.	Not for a single w-a adult – partial BI only.	Yes.
Housing cost element?	An individualised, means-tested HB and CTR/CTS would still be required.	An individualised, means-tested HB and CTR/CTS would still be required.	An individualised, means-tested HB and CTR/CTS would still be required.
Household economies of scale (HES), for couples.	Moderate HES, based on added partial BI for a couple.	Least marked HES, based on a Parent-with-Care Premium.	Greatest HES, based on full BI for both working-age adults, but provides incentive for adults to share accommodation.
Harmony re BI?	Yes, all working-age adults receive the same PBI.	No, w-a adults without dependent children receive only PBIS.	Yes, all working-age adults receive the same FBI.
Fairness within the household?	Same PBI for a non-parent, and for a parent with caring responsibilities. The care free can choose between more leisure and more earnings.	Greater equity between parent-with-care and the care free.	Same FBI for a non-parent, and for a parent-with caring responsibilities. The care free can choose between more leisure and more earnings.
Standard rate of income tax	Scotland: t = 0.3691 UK: t = 0.3629	Scotland: t = 0.3757 UK: t = 0.3696	Scotland: t = 0.4183 UK: t = 0.4110
Redistributes income?	Yes, redistributive.	Even more redistributive.	The most redistributive.
Incentives to work for pay?	Yes, for all working-age adults receiving a partial BI.	Yes, for working-age adults receiving a PBI, but less so for PWC.	Less so. Basic needs are met, but incentive to earn for luxuries remains.
Potential for EDR, and fewer units to assess?	Yes, with added incentive to work for all w-a adults; costs: Scotland: t = 0.4200 UK: t = 0.4128	Yes, with added incentive to work for those receiving a PBI: Scotland: t = 0.4183 UK: t = 0.4110	No

Note: The BIS do not cover housing costs, disablement benefits, or childcare costs, all of which have to be supplied via separate but parallel systems, in addition to their BIS.

leisure or more income), incentive to work-for-pay, and the potential for an income / earnings disregard.

Each reader will have his/her own favourite version from these three schemes. In terms of cost, it is a choice between B(i) and B(ii), each financed by a 37 or 37.5 per cent (Scotland), or 36.5 or 37 per cent (UK), income tax rate, or a choice between B(i) with EDR and B(ii) with EDR (which has the same cost as B(iii)), each financed by a 42 per cent (Scotland) or 41 or 41.5 per cent (UK) standard tax rate respectively.

All three schemes are economically viable – well below the 50 per cent constraint, and could even allow for more generous disability benefits to be introduced.

A Child BI is paid to the PWC, the primary care-giving parent or guardian, to be administered on behalf of the child, as now. However, a BI system cannot solve every problem. A means of allocating a child BI between separated parents who share childcare has not yet been devised.

The third set of sample BI schemes, compared with the MIS poverty benchmark (AHC version)

The third set of sample schemes is compared with the Minimum Income Standards, AHC version. These three schemes have similar characteristics as the schemes B(i), B(ii), and B(iii), but the differences between them are not as marked. The proportions were chosen and the amounts rounded to the nearest £.

The process used in Tables 14.5a and b is as follows:

- A pensioner BI was set in order to be within 0.02 of the level of the chosen poverty benchmark for a single pensioner, or of the level of Pension Credit, whichever was greater;

- Young adults and other working-age adults receive the same amounts as each other;

- The working-age full BI was set to be within 0.02 of the level of the chosen poverty benchmark for a single working-age person;

- A working-age partial BI was **chosen** as a proportion of the full BI;

- Where a PWC premium was granted, it topped up the working-age partial BI to the full BI for a single working-age adult from the chosen poverty benchmark;

- A Child BI was calculated so that the total of BIs for any lone parent's household, (a working-age BI, with or without a PWC premium, plus the appropriate number of Child BIs), was at least equal to the poverty benchmark for the relevant lone parent household;

- The cost was calculated using the method laid out in Tables 13.1 above.

In practice, the only real variable to be chosen is the working-age partial BI, and everything else follows from this choice. Of course, other procedures could be adopted depending on different prioritised objectives, assumptions and constraints.

Table 14.5a Money values of BIS for MIS benchmark schemes 2017–18, and as proportions of Y-BAR for Scotland and the UK 2015

Column 1	Column 2 £ pw	Column 3 Prop of Y-BAR Scot	Column 4 Prop of Y-BAR UK
Y-BAR Scot 2015	£392.40	1.00000	
Y-BAR UK 2015	£411.89		1.00000
Scheme C(i)			
Pensioner BI	£165.00	0.4204893	0.4005924
Working-age BI	£150.00	0.3822630	0.3641750
Child BI	£120.00	0.3058104	0.2913400
Scheme C(ii)			
Pensioner BI	£165.00	0.4204893	0.4005924
Working-age BI	£150.00	0.3822630	0.3641750
PwC premium	£30.00	0.0764526	0.0728350
Child BI	£90.00	0.2293578	0.2185050
Scheme C(iii)			
Pensioner BI	£165.00	0.4204893	0.4005924
Working-age BI	£180.00	0.4587156	0.4370099
Child BI	£90.00	0.2293578	0.2185050

Table 14.5b BI sample schemes for Scotland and the UK, 2017–18, compared with 2016 MIS benchmark

	Scheme C(i), £ pw 2017–18	Scheme C(ii), £ pw 2017–18	Scheme C(iii), £ pw 2017–18	MIS AHC, £ pw 2016
Pensioner BI	£165.00	£165.00	£165.00	
Working age BI	£150.00	£150.00	£180.00	
Parent with care premium	£0.00	£30.00	£0.00	
Child BI	£120.00	£90.00	£90.00	
single pensioner	= 165.00	= 165.00	= 165.00	165.15
couple pensioner	330.00	330.00	330.00	240.45
single working-age,	150.00	150.00	= 180.00	177.99
couple working-age	= 300.00	= 300.00	360.00	304.25
Lone P + toddler	= 270.00	= 270.00	= 270.00	270.48
Lone P + pre + prim	390.00	360.00	360.00	344.62
Lone P + pre + prim + secondary school child	510.00	= 450.00	= 450.00	452.98
Couple + toddler	420.00	420.00	450.00	348.66
Couple + pre + primary	540.00	510.00	540.00	422.41
Couple + pre + prim + secondary school child	660.00	600.00	630.00	540.63
Couple + toddler + pre + prim + secondary school child	780.00	690.00	720.00	589.08
SCOTLAND				
Cost in terms of tax rate	0.3767	0.3716	0.4123	
Current margin	0.0590	0.0590	0.0590	
Cost in terms of tax rate for all Social Security Transfers	0.4357	0.4306	0.4713	
Cost in terms of EDR tax rate	0.4253	0.4123	-------	
Income tax rate for all social Security Transfers, with EDR	0.4843	0.4713	-------	
Tax-free gross income, Yo	£61.95 pw	£63.65 pw	-------	
Tax-free net income, Ys	£211.95 pw	£213.65 pw	-------	

	Scheme C(i), £ pw 2017–18	Scheme C(ii), £ pw 2017–18	Scheme C(iii), £ pw 2017–18	MIS AHC, £ pw 2016
UK				
Cost in terms of tax rate	0.3573	0.3513	0.3890	
Current margin	0.0557	0.0557	0.0557	
Cost in terms of tax rate for all Social Security Transfers	0.4130	0.4070	0.4447	
Cost in terms of EDR tax rate	0.4027	0.3890	--------	
Income tax rate for all Social Security Transfers, with EDR	0.4584	0.4447	--------	
Tax-free gross income, Yo	£65.45 pw	£67.46 pw	--------	
Tax-free net income, Ys	£215.45 pw	£217.46 pw	--------	

KEY:

Pre = pre-school child, aged 2–4; Prim = primary school child.

The BIS are expressed as proportions of Y-BAR for Scotland or the UK in Table 14.5a above.

The **figures in bold** imply that the BI is less than the relevant poverty benchmark by more than two per cent.

Figures preceded by the '=' sign indicate that the BI is within two per cent of the relevant poverty benchmark.

The *figures in italics* show that the BIS are higher than the relevant poverty benchmark by more than two per cent.

The 'current margin', to cover the costs of administration and of retained benefits, is as derived in Table 11.5 above.

Schemes C(i) and C(ii) provide only a partial BI, equal to 83.3 per cent of the full BI for working-age adults. Scheme C(i) requires a large BI for children, while scheme C(ii) adds a parent-with-care premium to the working-age adult BI instead, in order to protect families with children. In scheme C(iii), all adults receive a full BI. The schemes are economically viable, and could even allow for more generous disability benefits to be introduced without breaking the 50 per cent income tax barrier.

Schemes C(i) and C(ii), in which some working-age adults receive a partial BI, offer the opportunity to introduce an income / earnings disregard, and the increased rates of income tax required to finance the schemes is below the 50 per cent income tax constraint.

All of these illustrative BI schemes are viable, and the estimated restructured income tax rates required to finance them should be compared with the current basic rate of income tax in the UK of 20 per cent together with the NI Contributions of 12 per cent (current t = 0.32).

The value of gross income, Yo, where the FBI and PBI schedules merge, is calculated from Yo = (FBI − PBI) / t, where t is the higher rate calculated for the merging schedules, after the margin is added. The values for the UK schemes are as follows:

* Yo for scheme C(i) is (£180.00 − £150.00) / 0.4584 = £65.45 pw (£3,412.94 pa).

* Yo for scheme C(ii) is (£180.00 − £150.00) / 0.4447 = £67.46 pw, (£3,517.62 pa).

Added to their partial BIs, this means that individuals will be able to receive and earn a total of Ys before they have to start to pay any income tax.

* Ys for scheme C(i) is £150.00 + £65.45 = £215.45 pw (£11,234.18 pa).

* Ys for scheme C(ii) is £150.00 + £67.46 = £217.46 pw (£11,338.99 pa).

Summary of the illustrative sample BI schemes

Tables 14.6 below lay out the eight sample schemes for Scotland and the UK separately. They follow the same pattern. The first set of two schemes is designed to be at least as great as the current main income-replacement means-tested benefit levels. Each starts with an entry-level scheme A(i) that provides BIs of the same value as the key means-tested benefits that they will replace. The second scheme, A(ii), is more generous to the working-age adult. The development of these schemes is shown in Tables 14.2a and 14.2b.

The second set, comprising three BI schemes B(i), B(ii) and B(iii), is designed to meet the EU's official poverty benchmark of 0.6 median equivalised household income (AHC version), as discussed in chapter 10. A set of BI schemes based on an alternative benchmark (see Table 10.6) was adopted to see how it matched up with the EU's official poverty benchmark. The third set, comprising schemes C(i), C(ii) and C(iii), aims to meet the Minimum Income Standard (AHC) benchmark. The sample schemes in the second and third sets follow the same pattern: the first scheme offers only partial BIs to working-age adults, but these are insufficient to meet the poverty standards for families with dependent children. Increasing an aspect of child BI solves this problem in the first BI scheme of the set. In the second BI scheme of each set, a Parent with Care premium was granted. This better protects families with children. The third BI scheme of this set provided a full BI to all working-age adults. It met the poverty benchmark, but there was evidence of Household Economies of Scale, the disadvantages of which may be offset by its incentive for adults to share accommodation and decrease the demand for single-adult households.

The tables below summarise the amounts of the BIs in terms of money and also gives them as proportions of mean gross income per head, Y-BAR. It will be noted that the amounts for the pensioner BI is very constant over the eight schemes. The child BI is very similar for the first two sets, but is much increased for the third set. The main differences are provided by the

Table 14.6 SCOT A summary of the eight sample BI schemes for Scotland 2017–18

Y-BAR 2015 = £392.40 pw	A(i)	A(ii)	B(i)	B(ii)	B(iii)	C(i)	C(ii)	C(iii)
Proportions of Y-BAR								
Pensioner	0.4061	0.4077	0.4001	0.4001	0.4001	0.4205	0.4205	0.4205
W-age	0.1863	0.2548	0.3201	0.3201	0.4001	0.3823	0.3823	0.4587
Young Adult	0.1476	0.2548	0.3201	0.3201	0.4001	0.3823	0.3823	0.4587
PwC premium	0.0444	0.00	0.00	0.0800	0.00	0.00	0.0765	0.00
Premium 14–15	0.00	0.00	0.0800	0.00	0.00	0.00	0.00	0.00
Child BI	0.1704	0.1656	0.1600	0.1600	0.1600	0.3058	0.2294	0.2294
£ pw								
Pensioner	159.35	160.00	157.00	157.00	157.00	165.00	165.00	165.00
W-age BI	73.10	100.00	125.60	125.60	157.00	150.00	150.00	180.00
Young Adult	57.90	100.00	125.60	125.60	157.00	150.00	150.00	180.00
PwC premium	17.42	0.00	0.00	31.40	0.00	0.00	30.00	0.00
Premium 14–15	0.00	0.00	31.40	0.00	0.00	0.00	0.00	0.00
Child BI	66.87	65.00	62.80	62.80	62.80	120.00	90.00	90.00
Total income tax rate to finance whole Soc Sec	0.2855	0.3284	0.3691	0.3757	0.4183	0.4357	0.4306	0.4713
Total income tax with EDR	------	------	0.4200	0.4183	-----	0.4843	0.4713	-----

increasing amounts for the working-age adult, which is what largely contributes to the differences in cost of the schemes. The cost, which is summarised in a single figure, is given in terms of a flat rate of restructured income tax, in the penultimate line of each table. For the four schemes based on partial BIS, the tax rates for the versions with income / earnings disregards are given in the last row of the tables.

The generosity of the BIS increases with each new sample scheme, as does the cost, ranging from 29 to 33 per cent respectively for the entry level schemes, and 37 to 42 per cent for the schemes based on the EU poverty benchmark, and 43 to 48.5 per cent for those based on the MIS. Correspondingly, the redistributive power of successive schemes also increases.

Table 14.6 UK A summary of the eight sample BI schemes for the UK 2017–18

Y-BAR 2015 = £411.89 pw	A(i)	A(ii)	B(i)	B(ii)	B(iii)	C(i)	C(ii)	C(iii)
Proportions of Y-BAR								
Pensioner	0.3869	0.3885	0.4006	0.4006	0.4006	0.4006	0.4006	0.4006
W-age	0.1775	0.2428	0.3205	0.3205	0.4006	0.3642	0.3642	0.4370
Young Adult	0.1406	0.2428	0.3205	0.3205	0.4006	0.3642	0.3642	0.4370
PWC premium	0.0423	0.00	0.00	0.0801	0.00	0.00	0.0728	0.00
Premium 14–15	0.00	0.00	0.0801	0.00	0.00	0.00	0.00	0.00
Child BI	0.1623	0.1578	0.1602	0.1602	0.1602	0.2913	0.2185	0.2185
£ pw								
Pensioner	159.35	160.00	165.00	165.00	165.00	165.00	165.00	165.00
W-age BI	73.10	100.00	132.00	132.00	165.00	150.00	150.00	180.00
Young Adult	57.90	100.00	132.00	132.00	165.00	150.00	150.00	180.00
PWC premium	17.42	0.00	0.00	33.00	0.00	0.00	30.00	0.00
Premium 14–15	0.00	0.00	33.00	0.00	0.00	0.00	0.00	0.00
Child BI	66.87	65.00	66.00	66.00	66.00	120.00	90.00	90.00
Total income tax rate to finance whole Soc Sec	0.2701	0.3100	0.3629	0.3696	0.4110	0.4130	0.4070	0.4447
Total income tax with EDR	------	------	0.4128	0.4110	-----	0.4584	0.4447	-----

The generosity of the UK-based BIs increases with each new sample scheme, as does the cost, ranging from 27 to 31 per cent for the entry level schemes, and 36.5 to 41.5 per cent for the schemes based on the EU poverty benchmark, and 41 to 46 per cent for those based on the MIS. Correspondingly, the redistributive power of successive schemes also increases, and there could also be secondary effects and impacts to be considered which are beyond the scope of this book.

As previously pointed out, there is no single optimum BI scheme that will satisfy everyone who supports the idea of a BI, because so much depends on one's objectives, priorities, assumptions and constraints, all of which lead to different outcomes. Three sets of illustrative schemes for Scotland and for the UK have been presented above, based on Table 14.1 as the starting point. Now readers can repeat the exercise, starting from their own objectives and assumptions, and devise their own schemes and compare them with those of their friends. Appendix C will help those experimenting with their own ideas to cost BI schemes financed by a restructured income tax system. The process presented here is not the only way of devising a scheme, nor of financing it. Those wanting to use different methods of funding their proposed scheme will, of course, need to provide the relevant figures.

The BI schemes proposed here are economically viable but would not necessarily be politically achievable at the present time. A campaign to inform the public about the advantages of BI schemes would be necessary, followed by the implementation of a modest BI scheme. Then the gradual restructuring of the income tax system as suggested above, accompanied by gradual increases in both BI levels and income tax rates over ten years, could be feasible.

PART IV

How Do We Get From Here To There?

CHAPTER 15

How do we get from here to there?

Although the high cost of an experiment, along with its ethics, may constitute an obstacle to launching an experiment, the cost of policy-making based on unreliable evidence and beliefs may be many times higher. To implement a policy, without conducting a small-scale experiment beforehand, amounts to putting the whole population into an experiment.

GROOT, 2005: 4–5

Implementation

CERTAINLY, A well-planned pilot project could provide answers to many questions and also give the administrative authorities the opportunity to iron out any problems associated with the transition towards a BI. Logically, the political process precedes implementation, but part of the former is that of anticipating future events in order to smooth their path. By the time of implementation, the main decisions will have been made, including the initial amounts of the BIS and how they will be funded.

The next decision is whether to implement a new BI scheme all at once – which could be feasible for modest schemes – or whether the transition should take place in stages. If in stages, transition divides into a) a sector approach, where the BI is introduced to different sectors of the population in turn over time; and b) a gradual approach, where a modest BI scheme is introduced first and then the amounts are gradually augmented over time. They have different advantages and disadvantages. In fact, a scheme could be implemented using a combination of the two, by introducing the BIs by sector and then gradually increasing the BI for each sector in turn.

As noted in chapter 8 above, any income maintenance system will involve 'producing and maintaining lists of individuals who satisfy the relevant criteria, as well as setting up a system to monitor whether they continue to fulfil these criteria' (De Wispelaere *et al*, 2008: 5). There are advantages if monitoring can make use of existing sources of information, particularly where the base changes only infrequently, and is not susceptible to manipulation via discretionary decisions. Further, it is easier for a country to implement a BI scheme if it already has the following in place:

- A system for the collection of National Accounts data
- A database of records of individuals maintained for the assessment and distribution of benefits or BIS

- A benefit delivery structure;
- A reliable banking system for the receipt of the BIS, where every adult has his/her own bank account, or similar, that enables cash transfers to be made efficiently;
- A tax-collection system;
- A database of records of individuals maintained for the assessment and collection of income tax
- A system of deduction of taxes at source, such as PAYE;
- A culture where the inhabitants are accustomed to paying taxes, however reluctantly;
- A monitoring system for compliance (biometric identity cards, for example, might be useful for this).
- A monetary economy with an economic surplus would be an advantage.

Even without having this infrastructure already in existence, the pilot studies and experiments that have been carried out in developing countries demonstrate that it is possible to set this up in a relatively short time and that even modest levels of BIS can make a major difference in poorer countries (see chapter 9 above).

The sector approach

The sector approach, based on introducing the proposed changes to different demographic groups in the population in turn over time, usually starts by putting forward a BI scheme for people of pension-entitlement age or over and for children. In the UK, these two groups are regarded as 'deserving' and there is little opposition to their being given 'something for nothing', and so starting with them is likely to be more popular. These two cohorts, currently aged 64 or over and children aged 0–15, accounted for nearly 38 per cent of the UK population in 2015. The main problem with the sector approach occurs when trying to match the introduction of the BIS to different sectors at different times with the set of increases in taxation that are required to finance the scheme.

Only UK-wide BI schemes, rather than Scottish-based ones, will be used to illustrate the process in the rest of this chapter. Let us use scheme A(i) for the UK for 2017–18 from chapter 14 (tables 14.2a, and 14.2b) to illustrate this, except that it will be financed by changes to benefits and current taxes, rather than by the full restructuring of the income tax system suggested in chapters 13 and 14. The sum of gross transfer costs are summarised in Table 15.1 below. It aims to replace the current main income-replacement, means-tested benefits with BIs of the same magnitude, and it leaves the rest of the social security system in place. The scheme will cost £300bn, or 21.45 per cent of total income in the UK.

Table 15.1 The cost of scheme A(i) for the UK in 2017–18

Column 1	Column 2	Column 3		Col 4	Col 5 = Col 2 x Col 4
UK 2015	Population	Mean income, Y-BAR, 2015			INCOME
Age groups		£ pw		£ pa	£m
Total population	65,110,000	411.89		21,447	1,398,377
		BI levels 2017–18			COST
		£ pw		£ pa	£m
64 or over	12,299,546	159.35		8,309	102,197
Parents with Care premium, aged 16–64	(6,854,335)	17.42		908	6,224
Children, aged 0–15	12,257,876	66.87		3,487	42,743
Young Adults aged 16–24	7,391,524	57.90		3,019	22,315
Working-age adults aged 25–63	33,161,405	73.10		3,812	126,411
TOTAL = Sum of gross transfers					299,890
This can be shown to be equal to 21.45% of total income					
Sources of data: Population: table 11.2 UK above; BI scheme A(i): table 14.2a above.					

The replacement of the current means-tested benefits represents a saving to the state, which contributes to the funding of the scheme. The estimates of the savings are based on information that would have been available in 2016 at the time of decision-making for 2017–18. However, the cost of the BIs is greater than the saving from the benefits that they replace and so extra funding has to come from somewhere else. Since these BI amounts are greater than the value of the income tax Personal Allowance, it can be reduced or removed and similarly the National Insurance Primary Threshold set to zero. In addition, the employees' NI contribution, (which is a regressive tax, because lower-income employees pay it at the higher rate of 12 per cent, compared with the lower rate of two per cent paid by higher-income employees), could be charged at 12 per cent over the whole range of earnings. However, these may still not be sufficient to pay for the scheme. Other changes may also have to be made.

Even without going into the specific figures, imagine the following. The BI can be introduced for those aged 64 or over, replacing the basic level of the State Retirement Pension, Pension Credit, (but not SERPS or S2P), and withdrawing the Personal Allowance. This will still not cover the cost. However, ending income tax relief for registered pension schemes will do so. Providing an adequate universal Pensioner BI is a key part of a pensions policy based on the principle that it is far more important to ensure that all senior citizens receive the necessary minimum amount, (that is, the level of the current Pension Credit to which they would have otherwise been entitled), rather than to subsidise investment by some of the wealthier members of the population into occupational or private pensions. This latter group will be able to continue to contribute to these schemes, but without the tax relief provided by other taxpayers. The pensioner BI is likely to be popular with senior citizens, but the cost of removing this concession on pension contributions falls on a younger cohort of people, who might nevertheless welcome the future security that they themselves would experience in their declining years. The alternative would be to raise a similar amount through raising the basic rate of income tax.

Although the population tends to agree that (deserving) children should be supported, they are often reluctant to do this by helping the (presumed undeserving) parents. Child Benefit, which is targeted by age, and is selective since the amount varies according to position in the family, is still the closest to a BI that we have in the UK, and is very popular. The administration for this is already set up, and it would be very easy to increase the CB appropriately and for it to be a Child BI for all children aged 0–15. The savings from replacing Child Tax Credit are insufficient to cover the increased cost.

Working-age people (aged 16–63) account for more than 60 per cent of the total population. The cost of providing BIs of £73.10 pw for older adults and £57.90 pw for young adults would amount to £148,726m in 2017–18. This is just under half of the cost of the BI scheme. Even with the changes already suggested, it will not be sufficient to finance the scheme without increasing income tax rates or changing thresholds. Making these changes in one step for the working-age cohort is feasible.

It would be possible to use a sector approach for the above three different age groups, (seniors, children and then working-age population), but if the working-age group were to be divided further into three different cohorts, for instance starting with the young adults aged 16–24, followed by the cohort closest to retirement, aged 50–63, and lastly those aged 25–49, the problem becomes more complex. The question is when, and for whom, should the rise in income tax take place. Should the cohort for whom the BI scheme has just been implemented have a separate tax system from the rest of the working-age group? Or should the income tax rate be increased gradually for everyone, (including the pensioners), as new groups are included in the scheme, even though other groups will not have benefitted yet from the BI scheme? It could be very messy trying to match up the funding to the costs and might increase the risk of poverty in the short term among those paying more tax but gaining less from the BI using this method. This 25–49 age group is a key group for family formation, and risk of poverty has greater consequences even than the sufferings of individuals.

How long will the sector process take? It would involve the introduction of the BI scheme to between three and five different age groups. It could take five years or, if spaced out to every two years, it would take ten years to introduce it to everyone, and this is just for one introductory scheme. It might be more suitable to use this method of implementation for introducing a more generous scheme in one go.

Conclusion:

- This method of implementation could take several years.
- It might work for a simple disaggregation into three distinct cohorts of seniors, children and working-age adults.
- Greater disaggregation increases the problems of trying to match the funding to the groups for whom the BI scheme is implemented.
- This method of implementation might be suitable for introducing a relatively generous scheme in one go.

The gradual approach, increasing the amounts of the BIs over time

It might be possible to implement some of the less ambitious schemes in one go. The more familiar that the population is with the idea and the more research and pilot studies that have been carried out, the easier it is likely to be. However, for more ambitious schemes, it might be easier to adopt a transition process involving gradual augmentation of the BI amounts over time, rather than to adopt the sector approach.

Torry (2017) has devised and examined an introductory Citizen's Income scheme for the UK, using data for 2015–16. A pensioner would receive £30 pw, each working-age adult (aged 25–64) receives a BI of £60, a Young Adult (aged 16–24) receives £50 pw, and each dependent child (aged 0–15) has a Child Benefit augmented by £20 pw. All the current benefits are kept in place, (including the State Retirement Pension). This BI scheme is 'embedded' in the current social security system. In this type of implementation there are administrative advantages if the BIS of the adults are equal to, or exceed, the value of the Personal Allowance plus the value of the NI Primary Threshold. In 2015–16, the BI for all working age adults would have amounted to (£10,600 x 0.20) pa + (£155 x 52 x 0.12) pa = (£2,120 + £967.20) pa = £3,087.20 pa. This is equivalent to £60 pw. (Note: those over pension retirement age do not pay NICs on their earnings, so the Primary Threshold does not apply).

The Personal Allowance is removed from the income tax system, and the threshold for higher rate of income tax is reduced by that amount, making all income taxable. In addition, setting the NI Primary Threshold to zero, and removing the Upper Earnings Level, means that employees' National Insurance Contributions will be paid at 12 per cent throughout the earned income range.

Claimants' MTBS are adjusted to take account of their BIS, which are deducted from their entitlements, thus reducing the amount to be withdrawn if their gross incomes increase. Where an individual is not in receipt of MTBS, or the MTBS are less than the BI, then each person receives a net monetary increase. Torry (2017) calculated that this scheme could be financed by adding three per cent to the income tax rate at every level of income. A small BI will neither prevent poverty nor get rid of means-testing. However, even a very small BI should help those who are currently financial dependents and others who are currently excluded from MTBS, who for the first time would be eligible for a universal benefit in their own right. It would give them financial security and more choices than currently. It should also lessen the stigma, low take-up and disincentive effects of MTBS.

This system will be easy to implement, because it changes very little of the underlying social security system. It ensures that relatively few individuals are worse off on account of the introduction of the BI scheme. Torry notes that very few households would suffer losses of over ten per cent, and the vast majority of these would be among people with the highest disposable incomes. It should not involve a major upheaval in the economy, and any initial problems can be ironed out. It gives the population an opportunity to gauge the effects of even a small BI scheme on their lives, and anticipate a more generous version being rolled out.

A second stage might be to introduce the A(i) type scheme from chapter 14, *again keeping the main social security benefits in place*, and with some further restructuring of the income tax system, as described in the sector approach above. The BIS should raise most of the population above the level at which they would be eligible for MTBS (apart from Housing Benefit, etc) and therefore claims on the current MTB system should decline dramatically. Any needs that are not being met by the BIS would become identifiable. This stage could be funded with a further small increase in the basic rate of income tax. When this BI system has become established, then the third stage could involve more restructuring of the income tax system, which should increase the tax base, thereby reducing the basic rate of income tax necessary to finance scheme A(i) as indicated in chapter 14.

These three stages might take up to five years. If they have been implemented smoothly and the scheme was popular, then plans could be made to roll out one of the more ambitious schemes. While the current levels of MTBS for elders and children will meet the official EU poverty benchmark, those for working-age adults are far below it, and their BIS must be increased markedly. A gradual approach, starting with a small BI, sounds sensible, but it runs the risk of being corrupted before the more generous levels can be adopted. The kettle might have come off the boil and the more ambitious schemes been put on the back burner. However, if cross party parliamentary agreement as to its desirability can be achieved, then each political party could put forward its own BI scheme in its manifesto for the following elections.

The implementation processes explored above assume the continued existence of the Housing Benefit and Council Tax Support systems, current disability benefits, state-funded childcare services and wage-protection legislation. It should be emphasised that the implementation of these BI schemes cannot, and should not, replace the free health, education and other welfare services provided around the UK. An urgent strategy to ensure sufficient affordable housing is also required.

The political process

Professor Joseph P Overton, a former vice president of the Mackinac Centre for Public Policy in the USA, put forward a model of policy change. He identified a sequence of six stages, the Overton window, that any new political idea usually has to go through before it is finally adopted and completely accepted (Bregman, 2017: 254–5). These stages are Unthinkable, Radical, Acceptable, Sensible, Popular and Policy.

The current interest in the UK goes back to the Liberal Party's adoption of a Social Dividend policy in 1974, when the idea was largely Unthinkable. The concept was regarded as Radical in the 1980s, when the Basic Income Research Group (BIRG) was often laughed out of court as being too utopian. In the 1990s it became more Acceptable, and in the 2000s was Sensible enough, so that the topic of BI had to be on the agenda for income maintenance discussions, even though it was usually put on the back burner for the time being. Wilkinson and Pickett, and Dorling, examined current social problems and, in passing, proposed BI as part of the solution (Wilkinson *et al*, 2009: 264; Dorling, 2011: 267).

Now in the late 2010s, we are probably in the middle of the fifth stage, with it having become more Popular, as evidenced by the explosion in the number of articles and books that refer to the idea as part of the solution to many current problems (Skidelsky *et al*, 2012:197–202; Atkinson, 2015: chapter 8; Srnicek *et al*, 2015: chapter 6; Mason, 2015: 284–6; Murphy, 2015: 192–5; Story, 2015; Sayer, 2016: 361; Harrop, 2016; Cooper, 2016: chapters 4, 7, 10, 11). In addition, there have been seven reports recommending BI schemes in the last three years (Scottish Green Party, 2014; Duffy *et al*, 2014; Painter *et al*, 2015; Mackenzie *et al*, 2016; Reed *et al*, 2016; Ross-Tatum, 2017; and Torry, 2017).

A BI scheme could be implemented widely as Policy in the 2020s, while in the 2030s it could be recognised as so beneficial and natural that it would become part of the nation's identity. If the recent proliferation of books and reports on the subject are not enough evidence of interest in the concept of a BI, then the fact that it was the subject of a question on BBC TWO's television program *University Challenge* on Monday 17 October, and answered correctly, must surely be evidence of it having arrived in the mainstream.

The question is, how do we get there from here?

De Wispelaere and Noguera (2012) suggest four key aspects of political feasibility:

- Strategic (the search for a robust coalition of advocates);
- Psychological (legitimation of the policy via a broad social acceptance);
- Institutional (state capacity for implementation); and
- Behavioural (policy sustainability in the face of possible behavioural change in line with incentives) (McLean, 2016: 184).

Torry identifies six feasibility tests that must be fulfilled before a BI scheme could be launched successfully (Torry, 2016b: xiii):

- Political (Would the idea cohere with existing political ideologies?)
- Policy process (Would the CI idea be able to travel through the policy process from the proposal to implementation?)
- Psychological (Is the idea readily understood, and understood to be beneficial?)
- Administrative (Would a government be able to administer a CI? Would it be possible to manage the transition?)
- Financial (Would it be possible to finance a Citizen's Income? Would implementation impose substantial financial losses on any households?)
- Behavioural (Would a CI deliver the expected advantages?).

The orders in which the feasibilities are listed above roughly correspond to the chronological order in which the tests would have to be fulfilled. The psychological and the behavioural tests cover the same sort of ground in each system, and the 'institutional' aspect in the first system covers roughly the same area of interest as 'administrative' in the second. The 'strategic' aspect from the first system would fit in after the 'political' test in the second. In Erik Olin Wright's terms, where feasibility can be divided into achievability and viability, the tests from 'political' to 'psychological' are about achievability – getting the BI to be accepted politically and to be implemented – and the latter three are about viability (will it work?) once the system is in place.

The Westminster political parties are very aware that the current Social Security system is past its sell-by date, but none of them – except for the Green Party – appears to be prepared to stick its neck out and promote a radical alternative to the existing flawed system unless it has first been made safe to do so. Safety comprises two aspects. First of all, a well-informed public must clamour for it and thoroughly-briefed politicians must be able to speak in favour of it confidently, and secondly, some of the questions about the short- and long-run effects of BI schemes must be answered. A well-designed BI scheme could redistribute from rich to poor, leading to a more inclusive, harmonious society and helping to heal some of the enormous divisions in UK society as revealed in the debate surrounding the EU Referendum of 23 June 2016. It could also have an important role in helping many ethnic minority communities to feel included in British society, rather than feeling alienated from it. This should raise it higher up the agendas of several political parties.

The Citizen's Income Trust and the newly formed Citizen's Basic Income Network Scotland, along with their partner organisations, have important educational roles to play. A two-pronged approach is required, on the one hand seeking to inform the opinion-formers and policy-makers and on the other encouraging a grassroots swell of interest. Enthusiasm is contagious. It is vital to ensure in both cases that the advocates are well schooled in the subtleties of the debate. It is important that a large proportion of the population – converts, open-minded and sceptics alike – should become familiar with the concept, its definition, desirability, feasibility, the criticisms made against it and the counter-arguments. Training workshops for *cognoscenti* who would be willing to write and speak as ambassadors at public meetings could be an important way forward. Mobilise the converts to convince the electorate, who will convince the politicians. Conferences and debates will also help the public to clarify their own ideas.

While sharing one's enthusiasm for the idea of a BI scheme, it is useful to emphasise the following:

- Of how many years of life is a rich society entitled to deprive poor people?
- Everyone should have the right not to be destitute and to have access to the means of meeting one's basic needs and to be able to participate in public life and to flourish. This is an ethical standpoint, and takes priority over any arguments about cost.
- Discuss the broad objectives and ask whether people agree with them. What would be their orders of priority?
- Point out that illustrative BI schemes that meet approved poverty benchmarks are economically viable.
- Discuss further specific objectives that they would like social security systems to meet. What levels of income taxation would they be prepared to pay for a BI scheme?

At the same time, further research is needed to estimate the cost of some illustrative schemes more accurately, and identify potential gainers and losers – who they are, how many, and how much better or worse off they might be. We need to find other answers, too. How much does poverty and insecurity cost the NHS and other key public services, and so what might be the savings if a BI were implemented that reduced poverty and insecurity? Some research would need funding from government resources, as called for under Early Day Motion 164 in June 2016, such as for a Commission on Basic Income, or for a Pilot Project (Parliament, 2016).

Petitions can be put to both Westminster and Holyrood Parliaments asking for more research to be conducted, or for pilot projects to be set up.

Political support would need to be built up in the parties. Few MPs or MSPs have felt confident about conducting a debate about the details of the present, complex Social Security system, but it is to be hoped that many more will be able to contribute in a knowledgeable way to a debate about BI.

While the Westminster Parliament has the powers to introduce a Basic Income Bill, even after the implementation of the Scotland Act 2016, it would be difficult, but not impossible, for the Scottish Parliament to implement a BI scheme. Scotland would need to be more fiscally devolved (or independent) to implement a generous scheme that met the official EU poverty benchmark. While the then Prime Minister, David Cameron, claimed that Scotland would be the most devolved country in the world, Spicker points out that the 'Scottish Parliament has fewer powers than an English local authority' (2016: 3). Similarly, the tax-raising powers devolved under the Scotland Act 2016 will not give Scotland complete control over income tax, since it will only cover earnings, and not other sources of income. Similarly, Scotland has no power to make changes to the tax allowances or exemptions that comprise tax expenditures. Control over these will be necessary to bring about a fairer system. The prospect of a BI scheme could provide a major incentive for Scotland to insist on further devolved powers.

One of the criticisms against BI schemes is that powerful interests will prevent their implementation. Even though both ends of the political spectrum might favour the idea of a BI, one end could criticise the levels as too mean and the other that they are too generous and might be tempted to try to erode their real value over time, as has been the fate of National Insurance benefits, Child Benefit and the State Retirement Pension. Is it possible to prevent the system from being corrupted in the long run? Once implemented, how should the right to a universal, individual, unconditional, non-means-tested basic income be safeguarded in law for the future? Might it be incorporated in a cross-party Bill of Human Rights? Bills of Parliament can be overturned. Would a written constitution and Bill of Rights be more likely to give protection than an unwritten one?

How might the scheme to be implemented be chosen?

Let us look further ahead to a time when an All Party Parliamentary Group agrees that a BI scheme would be the best way forward and a Parliament is ready to introduce a Basic Income Bill. After the initial phase of implementing entry-level schemes, to what scheme might they aspire? Three possibilities are put forward here:

- Each political party would include its favoured scheme in its manifesto for the next General Election or Scottish Election, and the party that is elected would implement its scheme, or a coalition would negotiate a compromise between their two schemes. If the amounts in the scheme to be implemented were indexed by being expressed as a proportion of mean gross income per head, Y-BAR, then the scheme could be adopted for the five-year administration period of the government, thus reflecting the prosperity of society.

- Adoption of the proposed new official poverty benchmark for BIS, as explored in chapter 10, where the amounts are specified as proportions of the latest available figure for Y-BAR, the *mean gross income per head* of the population, with the proportions as presented in Table 10.6 above.

- The last suggestion is that the adult population could be invited to vote for the flat-rate income tax in a restructured income tax system that they would be prepared to pay. This would be conditional on all of the tax raised being ring-fenced to be used for a BI scheme, but knowing that an extra 5–6 per cent would have to be added to cover the margin of costs of administration and retained benefits. For instance, if the mean of the tax rates for which the population voted turned out to be 30 per cent, then it could be used for a working-age BI of 0.30 of Y-BAR. Slightly more could be allocated to pensioners and parents with care, and slightly less for children, but the actual income tax that would be levied would be 30 + 6 = 36 per cent.

CHAPTER 16

Conclusion

Recap: features of income maintenance systems – definition of a BI – broad objectives

THIS FINAL CHAPTER is a good place to summarise the material covered in earlier chapters and bring all the strands together.

Each income maintenance system has an internal structure, comprising features based on:

- The unit chosen for assessment and delivery of benefits;
- Who is eligible;
- Whether entitlement is selective; and
- Whether behavioural conditions are imposed before the recipient can receive that to which s/he is otherwise entitled.

The options chosen for each feature of the structure help to determine the nature of the society in which we live.

A basic income is defined as follows:

- It is based on the individual rather than on the married, civil partnership, or other cohabiting, couple;
- Is 'universal' rather than targeted on specific groups in society;
- Is non-selective except by age, and is therefore not means-tested; and
- Is unconditional.

Even a small BI can provide advantages that accrue from changing the structure of the social security system. The benefit unit being the individual rather than a cohabiting couple can grant some financial autonomy to each partner. Universality provides essential financial security to working-age adults for whom there is no universal provision in the UK at present. Universality also avoids the stigma and humiliation experienced by those claiming targeted benefits, and take-up is expected to increase. Less means-testing should reduce the disincentives to work-for-pay inherent in the current social assistance system, and can make work pay for more people. Finally, unconditionality frees the poorest from the oppression of conditionality and sanctions associated with the current means-tested benefit system. A BI is less intrusive into people's lives and has the potential to transform society.

A BI scheme can contribute towards the broad objectives of:

- Valuing all individuals and emancipating adults, giving them more control over, and choice in, their lives;
- Preventing income poverty, and providing financial security;
- Reducing income inequality and creating a more united and inclusive society;
- Restoring the incentive to work-for-pay provided by the wage-rate, and increasing labour market efficiency; and
- Simplifying the social security system.

An examination of the internal structure helps to relate the BI option for each feature to the broad objectives, as in Tables 3.2 and 3.3 above, and thus confirm the desirability of BI schemes.

Current problems that BI schemes could help to solve – criticisms of BI schemes addressed

BI schemes could address some current problems. These include:

- The widespread feeling of financial insecurity;
- The increasing proportion of the population living in poverty;
- The increasing gap between rich and poor;
- The complexity of the social security system and the increasingly punitive manner in which it is delivered.

In addition, today's rapidly changing labour market is a persistent source of problems, including low wages, and part-time, seasonal or other short-term, precarious jobs, some with zero hours contracts. These lead to fear of losing one's job, long-term unemployment, experiencing greater poverty, increase in real-life personal debt, losing one's home, marriage break-up and home-lessness, all of which contribute to greater stress and health problems.

BI schemes can provide several advantages for women. The benefit unit being the individual ends the status of 'financial dependent' that traps many women in unequal power relationships, and instead offers them financial autonomy and security. The individual basis, together with universality and unconditionality, helps to emancipate and empower women, giving them more life choices and control over their lives. The prevention or reduction in poverty, and the reduction in income inequality, leading to the creation of a united and inclusive society, could also transform women's lives. Non-selectivity and unconditionality together will end the cohabitation rule that intrudes into the lives of many lone mothers and other single women claimants.

The most frequently posed criticisms of BI schemes have been addressed, and either unsupported assumptions have been exposed or aspects that appear to be counter-intuitive have been put into a clearer context.

- **Having the individual as the unit of assessment and delivery would lead to household economies of scale.** These are accepted currently for other adults sharing accommodation, but couples are discriminated against. Acceptance that economies of scale will be an integral part of BI schemes could, at the same time, acknowledge that living with other people can be difficult and that compromises are needed. The availability of economies of scale could provide an incentive for adults to live together and reduce the demand for single person housing.

- **Why give a BI to rich people who don't need it?** Giving a BI to rich people would not necessarily make them better off, if they were taxed more progressively than at present. It is more efficient to assess people once only for income tax. Targeting does not protect poor people but segregates them and makes them more vulnerable. A universal system from which both rich and poor can benefit is more likely to be protected by rich people.

- **People's lives and needs are too complex to be met by a single simple system.** This is true. Separate but parallel systems will have to be retained to meet housing costs, the costs usually incurred by disabled people, and childcare facilities.

- **Why give 'something for nothing'?** Most of the value of our economy is built on the contributions of all our forebears. The amount of the BI will never provide for more than people's basic needs. Everyone should be entitled to his/her necessities. An unconditional BI values all citizens. The current social security system brings out the worst in people. A BI system will bring out the best. A feeling of inclusion could induce a reciprocal desire to contribute to society through, for example, care or community work. The number of free riders is likely to be a very small proportion of the population.

- **Will everyone give up working?** Luxuries will still have to be earned. Most people want to work, not only for the earnings, but also for the many social and health advantages that it provides. Since the BIS are not means-tested, they will restore the incentive to work-for-pay contained in the net wage rate. Some may choose to work less in order to achieve a better work-life balance. There could be a redistribution of an individual's hours between paid and unpaid work. Wage rates are likely to adjust. If the BI is indexed as a proportion of mean income per head, then it will act as a self-stabilising mechanism in the economy.

- **Can we afford it?** Yes we can! An introductory BI scheme embedded in the current social security system could easily be afforded. In chapter 14 it is demonstrated that moderate schemes that fulfil the EU official poverty benchmark can be financed by a restructured income tax system with flat tax rates of 36.5 to 41.5 per cent for the UK, or of 37 to 42 per cent for Scotland. Additional sources of funding to finance the cash transfer program could reduce these rates.

- **Will rich people (threaten to) emigrate?** Rich people enjoy living in the UK with its political stability, temperate climate, English language, and cultural diversity. It is not obvious where they would go, since the UK has one of the lowest levels of taxation in the western world. How many left when the additional rate of income tax was introduced in the fiscal year 2010–11 at 50 per cent? 'And actually the threats to leave are exaggerated' (Sayer, 2016: 128).

Illustrative BI schemes

In Part III, three sets of illustrative sample schemes have been devised, of different levels of generosity, the least generous set aims to match current means-tested benefit levels as a floor. The other two sets aim to meet specified poverty benchmarks. The underlying objective of Part III is to demonstrate that these schemes are economically viable. A ballpark figure for the cost of each BI scheme was calculated based on its being financed by a flat rate tax in a restructured income tax system, providing a single summary figure for comparison. This does not preclude the adoption of more progressive income tax systems by a government, or of other sources of taxation being used to supplement or replace the income tax system. More accurate estimates would have to be calculated by government departments eventually, when it is decided to implement a scheme.

Readers can use the method illustrated here to devise and cost their own preferred BI schemes. The exploration of more progressive income tax schedules and other sources of funding, either on their own or in combination, to finance BI schemes, would be welcome.

Certain caveats apply. These BI schemes are expected to cover basic necessities, such as food, clothing, utilities, some leisure activities, some travel and other costs, and are unlikely to provide a life of luxury for anyone. A BI scheme is too simple to cover all the complexities of life, and a parallel but separate system will be required to provide benefits to cover the extra costs incurred by disabled people. Similarly, given the current state of the housing market, a separate system of individualised Housing Benefit with less fierce withdrawal rates will be required, until the current situation has been made more equitable through the implementation of a different housing policy that makes homes accessible to everyone – renters and owners alike. A separate system for providing help with childcare costs is needed, and the most efficient method is likely to be by state provision of high quality nurseries and childcare facilities. A full BI for parents with care gives them a more realistic choice of caring for their children themselves, and similarly, a sufficiently generous BI enables individuals to volunteer to care for family members and friends, without making themselves destitute.

A BI is not a panacea for all ills. It can reform many aspects of the Social Security system, but it would not, and should not, replace the rest of the welfare state. There still remain important roles for the state in the public provision of an adequate health service, social care, education, infrastructure for transport, flood defences, communications, energy and other utilities, personal social services, the justice system and an urgent and intensive home-building program for both private and social housing. Wage-protection will still be needed. Wealth redistribution is essential, including land reform, where a land value tax would be likely to have a prominent role, especially in Scotland.

Hope for the future

The UK and its constituent nations are now in a time of great flux. The General Election on 8 June has led to a hung Parliament. The recent referendum on whether to remain in or leave the EU has led to a vote for 'Brexit', and, in the process, has revealed the enormous divisions in prosperity in UK society. The neoliberal policies over four decades in the UK have led to increasing inequality, contributed towards the financial crisis of 2008 and to the recession that followed. The subsequent austerity programmes have hit the poorest sections of society hardest and delayed recovery. Cuts in welfare benefits have increased financial insecurity and personal debt. The resultant stress is one of the factors that has led to an increase in demand for health services.

Globalisation has been a policy that has increased the dominance and profits of large corporations, but has lowered wage rates for low and unskilled workers. The labour market has been changing quickly, again adversely for low-waged and unskilled workers, with insecure, part-time jobs. A BI scheme could help to increase financial security and reverse the trend towards greater inequality in the UK. It has great potential at a global level. An international BI scheme could help to invest in the people of poorer nations, giving them the opportunity to develop creative lives for themselves in their own countries, as demonstrated in the experiments in Namibia and India.

One purpose of this book has been to explore the ways in which changing the features of the current social security system into those defining a BI can enable it to fulfil a set of broad objectives. These would underpin the type of society that many people would like to create for themselves and future generations. A second purpose has been to demonstrate that economically viable BI schemes can be devised to meet the poverty benchmarks put forward by reputable institutions, even if some people regard the proposed methods of financing them as not politically feasible at the present time. Another purpose has been to encourage people to inform themselves about BI schemes and discuss it with family and friends and within their other spheres of influence. Governments are more likely to listen to a groundswell of informed opinion demanding a change to this new system, than to a few disparate voices.

There will be times of great uncertainty ahead. A basic income is not a sufficient condition on its own for a better society, but it is a necessary one. It would bring out the best in people, and change our society from one of fear and despair into one of compassion, justice, trust and hope. It would be an important development for the state, society and its citizens, and for world justice. It could help to transform societies into ones where everyone matters and all can flourish. At home, it could lead to a new Scottish Enlightenment.

Appendices

Figures for the UK 2011–15 and Scotland 2012–15

Table A1 Figures for the UK 2011–15

UK	2011	2012	2013	2014	2015
POPULATION: total	63,232,600	63,705,000	64,105,700	64,596,800	65,110,000
aged 65 or over	10,425,215	10,840,900	11,131,700	11,393,760	11,611,200
aged 0–15 inclusive	11,853,764	11,983,600	12,058,700	12,153,462	12,257,876
GDP at current market prices, £m	1,516,153	1,562,263	1,713,302	1,816,439	1,869,560
GDP *per caput*:					
£ per annum	£24,168.00	£24,627.00	£26,726.00	£28,120.00	£28,714.00
£ per week	463.50	471.00	512.55	539.29	550.68
INCOME £m	1,109,808	1,157,781	1,268,169	1,328,108	1,398,377
Mean Income *per cap*, £ pa	£17,551.20	£18,174.10	£19,782.47	£20,559.97	£21,477.15
(Y-BAR) £ pw	336.60	347.59	379.39	394.30	411.89
BASIC INCOME – EXAMPLES	2013–14	2014–15	2015–16	2016–17	2017–18
Pension or full BI £ pa	£7,020.05	£7,269.64	£7,913.00	£8,224.00	£8,590.86
= 0.40 of Y-BAR: £ pw	134.64	139.42	151.76	157.72	164.76
Partial BI = 0.32 of Y-BAR:					
for adults (aged 16–64) £ pa	£5,616.04	£5,815.71	£6,330.40	£6,579.20	£6,872.69
£ pw	107.71	111.53	121.40	126.18	131.80
SOCIAL SECURITY TRANSFERS £m	Blue Bk ref	2012	2013	2014	2015
Retirement pensions	CSDG/L8LV	£76,258	£82,350	£85,701	£88,464
Total unfunded social benefits,	QYJT	£30,314			
Other social insurance benefits	L8R9		£32,377	£34,529	£35,948
Income Support	CSDE	£13,462	£10,984	£9,524	£8,683
Income Tax Credits and Reliefs	RYCQ	£26,602	£27,037	£29,577	£28,978
Child Benefit	EKY3	£12,105	£11,671	£11,511	£11,640
Disability benefits	EKY5+EKY6	£22,785	£23,207	£23,409	£23,031
Housing benefit	CTML+GCSR	£23,211	£23,627	£24,079	£23,895
Other social benefits		£36,958	£36,350	£38,646	£41,845
TOTAL SOCIAL BENEFITS	NNAD	£241,695	£247,603	£256,976	£262,484

REVENUES FROM: £m	2011	2012	2013	2014	2015
Income Tax	£149,103	£145,776	£152,409	£158,876	£166,291
Self-employed and Employees' NI	£42,801	£43,652	£44,072	£45,374	£47,431
Employers' NI Contributions	£58,640	£60,830	£62,013	£63,746	£66,169
VAT	£109,252	£111,574	£118,296	£124,260	£128,816
Corporation Tax	£42,267	£39,694	£39,367	£40,619	£44,046
Total from all other taxes	£147,366	£151,390	£157,412	£162,541	£167,717
Total tax revenues from all sources	£549,629	£552,916	£573,569	£595,416	£620,470
Total from all sources to cent. govt	£518,266	£521,136	£543,066	£564,146	£587,865

COST OF TAX EXPENDITURES £m	2013–14	2014–15	2015–16	2016–17 forecast	2017–18 n/a
National Ins. Primary Threshold	£21,800	£22,800	£23,700	£24,100	
Personal Allowance	£82,200	£86,900	£93,800	£97,400	
Inc tax relief for Regist'd pens sch	£21,000	£20,550	£22,900	£23,850	
Other relief re pension schemes	£17,450	£17,900	£23,790	£22,840	
Other	£85,745	£87,455	£70,805	£68,545	
Total from Income Tax and NI loopholes	£228,195	£235,605	£234,995	£236,735	

MEANS-TESTED BENEFIT RATES* £ pw	2013–14	2014–15	2015–16	2016–17	2017–18
State Retirement Pension, single	£110.15	£113.10	£115.95	£119.30	£122.30
Pension Credit, (w/d 40%)} single	£145.40	£148.35	£151.20	£155.60	£159.35
Or New State Pension } couple	£220.05	£226.50	£230.85	£237.55	£243.25
JSA/ESA Single person, aged 25 +	£71.70	£72.40	£73.10	£73.10	£73.10
Couple	£112.55	£113.70	£114.85	114.85	£114.85
JSA/ESA Single person, (16–24)	£56.80	£57.25	£57.90	£57.90	£57.90
Carer's Allowance	£59.75	£61.35	£62.10	£62.10	£62.70
Child Tax Credit, 1st child	£62.62	£63.19	£63.59	£63.59	£63.59
(w/d 41%) subsequent children	£52.16	£52.74	£53.17	£53.17	£53.17
Child Benefit: 1st child	£20.30	£20.50	£20.70	£20.70	£20.70
subsequent children	£13.40	£13.55	£13.70	£13.70	£13.70
Nat. Minimum Wage, 25+, £ ph	£6.31	£6.50	£6.70	£7.20	£7.50
Living Wage Foundation, 25+, £ph	£7.45	£7.65	£7.85	£8.25	£8.45
**Universal Credit single, 25+	£311.55	£314.67	£317.82	£317.82	£317.82
(paid calendar couple, 25+	£489.06	£493.95	£498.89	£498.89	£498.89
monthly) 1st child	£272.08	£274.58	£277.08	£277.08	£277.08
(w/d 65%) subsequent children	£226.67	£229.17	£231.67	£231.67	£231.67

National Insurance and income tax rates and thresholds (gross inc)	2013–14	2014–15	2015–16	2016–17	2017–18
Rate of NIC and income tax	0.00	0.00	0.00	0.00	0.00
Lower Earnings Level (LEL) £ pw	£109	£111	£112	£112	£113
x 52 = £ pa	£5,668	£5,772	£5,824	£5,824	£5,876
Rate of NIC and income tax	0.00	0.00	0.00	0.00	0.00
NI Primary Threshold £ pw	£149	£153	£155	£155	£157
x 52 = £ pa	£7,748	£7,956	£8,060	£8,060	£8,164
Rate of employees' NIC & inc. tax	0.12	0.12	0.12	0.12	0.12
Personal Allowance income tax	£9,440	£10,000	£10,600	£11,000	£11,500
Rate of employees' NIC and Basic rate of income tax	0.12 + 0.20	0.12 + 0.20	0.12 + 0.20	0.12 + 0.20	0.12 + 0.20
Upper Earnings Level (UEL) £ pw	£797	£805	£815	£827	£866
x 52 = £ pa	£41,444	£41,860	£42,380	£43,004	£45,032
Higher Rate Threshold	£41,450	£41,865	£42,385	£43,000	£45,000
Rate of employees' NIC and Higher rate tax	0.02 + 0.40	0.02 + 0.40	0.02 + 0.40	0.02 + 0.40	0.02 + 0.40
Personal Allowance starts to be reduced at a rate of 50%	£100,000	£100,000	£100,000	£100,000	£100,000
Effective rate of tax due to reduction in PA (0.5 x 0.40 = 0.20) Rate of employees' NIC and Higher rate tax	0.20 + 0.02 + 0.40	0.20 + 0.02 + 0.40	0.20 + 0.02 + 0.40	0.20 + 0.02 + 0.40	0.20 + 0.02 + 0.40
End of reduction of Pers Allowance	£118,880	£120,000	£121,200	£122,000	£123,000
Rate of employees' NIC and Higher rate tax	0.02 + 0.40	0.02 + 0.40	0.02 + 0.40	0.02 + 0.40	0.02 + 0.40
Additional rate threshold	£150,000	£150,000	£150,000	£150,000	£150,000
Rate of employees' NIC and Additional rate tax	0.02 + 0.45	0.02 + 0.45	0.02 + 0.45	0.02 + 0.45	0.02 + 0.45
Total deductions on earnings of £200,000	£83,313.24	£82,958.78	83,414.30	£83,432.80	£83,320.32
Average effective tax rate	0.416566	0.414794	0.417072	0.417164	0.416602
'Basic' value of £ pa Primary Threshold: £ pw	£929.76 £17.88	£954.72 £18.36	£967.20 £18.60	£967.20 £18.60	£979.68 £18.84
'Basic' value of £ pa Personal Allowance: £ pw	£1,888.00 £36.21	£2,000.00 £38.36	£2,120.00 £40.66	£2,200.00 £42.19	£2,300.00 £44.11

NUMBERS OF TAXPAYERS / NON-TAXPAYERS 000s	2013–14	2014–15	2015–16		
Non-taxpayers: 0–15	12,059	12,153			
16–64	16,485	16,620			
65 +	5,162	5,324			
TOTAL	33,706	34,097			
Income taxpayers: 16–24	24,430	24,430			
65 +	5,970	6,070			
(All) TOTAL	30,400	30,500			
Taxpayers: at higher rate	4,200	4,430			
at additional rate of income tax	311	329			

* Recipients of Means-Tested–Benefits are usually eligible for Housing Benefit and Council Tax Benefit/ Reduction also.

** Universal Credit is paid for each calendar month. The weekly amounts can be calculated as follows: weekly amount = monthly amount x 12 / 365 x 7. This gives figures very close to the JSA amounts.

Table A2 Figures for Scotland 2012–15

SCOTLAND		2012	2013	2014	2015
Population: total		5,313,600	5,327,700	5,347,600	5,373,000
aged 65 or over		925,600	946,800	968,389	983,000
aged 0–15 inclusive		914,700	911,700	911,282	912,290
GDP at current market prices	£m	127,164	134,192	139,791	146,599
GDP per person: £ per annum		£23,932.00	£25,188.00	£26,141.00	£27,284.00
£ per week		457.72	483.06	501.33	523.25
INCOME	£m	91,730	96,800	103,238	109,936
Mean Income per person,	£ pa	£17,263.25	£18,169.26	£19,305.57	£20,460.82
(Y-BAR)	£ per week	330.17	348.45	370.25	392.40
BASIC INCOMES – EXAMPLES		2014–15	2015–16	2016–17	2017–18
Pension or full BI	£ pa	£6,905.30	£7,267.70	£7,722.23	£8,184.33
= 0.4 of Y-BAR:	£ pw	132.43	139.38	148.10	157.00
Partial BI = 0.32 of Y-BAR:	£ pa	£5,524.24	£5,814.16	£6,177.78	£6,547.46
for adults (aged 16–64)	£ pw	105.94	111.50	118.48	125.60

Sources of Data for both Table A1 and Table A2

Brief details are given here. Further details about accessing the sources can be found in the main section on Sources of Data at the end of this book.

- Population figures are published by the ONS.
- GDP, GDP per capita, and Income for the UK were obtained from the UK *National Accounts, The Blue Book, ons, 2012–16 editions.*
- GDP and Income for Scotland were obtained from the Scottish National Accounts Project.
- Social Security Transfers for the UK were from *The Blue Book, 2012–16 editions.*
- Revenues from Tax and NI for the UK were obtained from *The Blue Book.*
- The costs of tax expenditures were obtained from 'Estimated costs of the principal tax expenditure and tax reliefs', HMRC, published December 2016. These figures were updated by HMRC in 2016, and are different from those in Table 12.2, which are the first figures that were published for those fiscal years – in other words, they were the figures on which decisions would have been made at the time.
- Means-tested Benefits Rates were obtained from *Benefit and Pensions Rates,* published by the DWP.
- National Minimum/Living Wage is recommended by the Low Pay Commission.
- The Living Wage Foundation recommends hourly rates for London, and for the rest of the UK.
- Child Benefit and Child Tax Credit rates were obtained from HMRC.
- National Insurance and income tax rates and (gross income) thresholds were obtained from HMRC, *Tax and tax credit rates and thresholds for 2016–17* via www.gov.uk.

Hypothetical BI schemes

Measures of inequality

THREE MEASURES of inequality are calculated. They can apply to the distribution of either income or wealth. Here we are concerned with income distribution.

If the population is placed in order according to some measure (such as income or wealth), and then divided into ten equal portions or deciles, a common measure of inequality is the ratio of the income shares of the top and bottom deciles. Five equal portions are quintiles, and 100 portions are percentiles.

The **Palma Index** is a variation based on the ratio of the income share of the top decile to that of the poorest four deciles (see row 3a in Table B1 below). It has been suggested that the income or wealth of a country is reasonably fairly distributed when the Palma Index equals one (Cobham *et al*, 2013).

The **Lorenz curve**: draw a square; the bottom line serves as a horizontal axis, with the range 0 to 1. This is the visual equivalent of row 1c in Table B1 below, where the proportion of the population is ordered according to income, often laid out as deciles, ten per cent intervals. The left or right hand side of the square can act as a vertical axis, again labelled from 0 to 1. This measures the cumulative proportion of total income. The Lorenz curve can be obtained by plotting the values in row 3c of the Table B1, which are the cumulative shares from row 3a, on the vertical axis, against the cumulative totals for the population, (row 1c), on the horizontal axis. The points can be joined by straight lines – a process known as linear interpolation. It is expected to be concave to the diagonal. If the Lorenz curve is coincidental with the diagonal from bottom left to top right, then the distribution is perfectly equal. By contrast, if the distribution is extremely unequal, with one individual having all of the income, then the Lorenz curve would be coincidental with the horizontal and vertical right hand axes. Two or more Lorenz curves should only be compared if they do not cross each other. See Figure B1 on page 247.

The **Gini coefficient** measures the area between the diagonal (from bottom left to top right) and the Lorenz curve, as a proportion of the whole triangle under the diagonal. If the distribution of income is absolutely equal, the Gini coefficient will take the value of 0, whereas if one individual has all the income, then the Gini coefficient converges to the value 1 as the population size increases. It is possible for widely varying Lorenz curves to have the same Gini coefficient.

Calculation of the Gini coefficient by linear interpolation

Consider a square diagram with a Lorenz curve plotted on it as described above. Intervals on the horizontal axis, each marked with a vertical line, divide the square into columns. The area between the diagonal and the Lorenz curve is divided into rhomboids, that is, four-sided shapes with parallel (vertical) sides, except at the two ends of the horizontal axis, which are triangles. Each rhomboid can be divided into two triangles by joining the lower corner on the diagonal to the higher point on the Lorenz curve.

The area of any triangle can be measured by multiplying 'the base times the perpendicular height divided by two'. In this case, the parallel sides of the rhomboids will act as the 'bases', and the interval between them, measured on the horizontal axis, row 1b, will be the 'height'. We can calculate this by finding the difference between the value at the diagonal (row 1c on Table B1) and the value of the Lorenz curve (row 3c). Starting from the lowest decile or interval, the area of the lower triangle in each rhomboid can be found by using the same base as in the previous calculation. This operation is repeated for all the points on the Lorenz curve.

Mathematical proof

A flat tax, t = β, 0 ≤ β < 1, the revenue from which is hypothecated to provide a BI equal to the same proportion β of the mean, μ, of the gross incomes of individuals, BI = β.μ, reduces the Gini coefficient by that same proportion, β.

The Gini coefficient is calculated as the difference between the incomes of all pairs of individuals in an economy, scaled by mean income:

$$(1) \quad G = \frac{1}{2N\mu} \sum_{i=1}^{N} \sum_{j=1}^{N} |y_i - y_j|,$$

where N is the number of individuals in an economy, μ is the average income, yi and yj are the gross incomes of individuals i and j (Cribb et al, 2013: Appendix C).

The new Gini coefficient, G', of the distribution after implementing t = β and BI = β.μ, will be:

$$(2) \qquad G' = \frac{1}{2N\mu} \sum_{i=1}^{N} \sum_{j=1}^{N} \left| \left(y_i(1-\beta) + \beta.\mu \right) - \left(y_j(1-\beta) + \beta.\mu \right) \right|.$$

The mean will not have changed, since no income has been lost or added to the economy. The two β.μs cancel out, and the (1–β) is a constant that can be divided through, and equation (2) simplifies to

$$(3) \qquad G' = \frac{1}{2N\mu} \sum_{i=1}^{N} \sum_{j=1}^{N} \left| y_i(1-\beta) - y_j(1-\beta) \right|.$$

$$(4) \qquad G' = (1-\beta).G.$$

A hypothetical example of an international BI

This is a simple example of a 'EU-wide scheme' as an illustration of how the BI could be funded in the member states. It can be demonstrated by assuming that there are four member states, A, B, C and D in the EU, with the population and the aggregate of personal incomes for each state in a given year, as illustrated in rows 1a and 3a in Table B1 below. These are ranked in order of their different sizes by population, and by income, starting with the poorest. (Obviously, the actual stylised figures should not be taken literally).

Initially, it is assumed that each state levies a 50 per cent income tax on all incomes from all sources with no tax exemptions, (no tax loopholes) and hypothecates it, that is, it uses all of it to give a BI to all of the citizens in its state only. The inequality between the states would be preserved.

However, if each state levied the 50 per cent income tax, but distributed half of it as a BI to their own citizens, and pooled the rest for the EU to distribute equally among all of the citizens, then Option A occurs, and while differentials are preserved, some redistribution across states has taken place.

Table B1 below gives an example to show the outcome of this particular international BI scheme, and its effects on the measures of inequality.

Both Table B1 and Table B2 demonstrate the redistributive powers of a flat tax, of a restructured income tax system (as described in chapter 13 above), of rate t = β, 0 ≤ β < 1, which when levied on gross incomes and hypothecated, that is, it is ring-fenced and used solely to finance a BI equal to a proportion β of mean income per head, then it will reduce the Gini coefficient by that same proportion, β. This is due to the fact that the flat tax is levied in proportion to income, whereas the BI is the same for everyone, and therefore makes the biggest difference to poorer people.

A table summarising the key aspects of the two tables is given in Table B3.

Table B4 provides information about taxpayers and non taxpayers in the UK in 2014–15.

Table B5 compares different progressive income tax schedules.

Figure B1 Illustration of Lorenz curves derived in Table B2 showing successive decreases in the Gini Coefficient

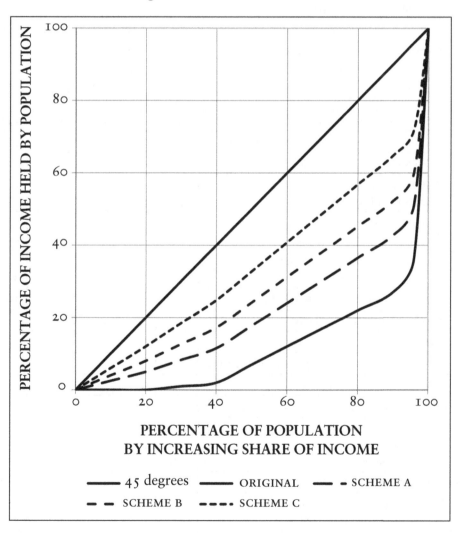

Table B1 A hypothetical example of an international BI scheme, also showing how a BI reduces the Palma index and Gini coefficient

Row			STATES			EU
	For a given year:	A	B	C	D	
1a	Population in millions, (men, women & children)	60	48	27	15	150
1b	row 1a divided by 150 %	40	32	18	10	100%
1c	accumulated totals from row above	40	72	90	100	
2	Mean income per head (man, woman & child), € 000s for that year	1.5	5	10	20	Av=6
3a	Aggregate personal incomes in each state, € billion	90	240	270	300	900
	Palma index = 300 / 90 = 3.33					
3b	row 3a / 900 %	10.0	26.66	30.0	33.3	100%
3c	Lorenz: accumulative totals from row above Gini: ((row 1c – row 3c) + previous column's figure) times row 1b / 2	10.0 30.0 x 40/2	36.66 (35.33 + 30.0) x 32/2	66.66 (23.33 +35.33) x 18/2	100 23.3 x 10/2	
	Gini coefficient = 2290 / 5000	600.0	1045.3	528	116.6	0.458
4	Let income tax rate be t = 0.50; average tax paid =	0.75	2.5	5.0	10.0	3.0
	INTERNATIONAL BI SCHEME:					
5	OPTION A: Each State's CI = 0.25 of average income per head, € 000s	0.375	1.25	2.5	5.0	1.5
6	EU's CI = 0.25 of average income per head for whole of EU, € 000s per annum	1.5	1.5	1.5	1.5	1.5
7	Total income for each person, € 000s, (sum of (1.0 – row 4) + row 5 + row 6)	2.625	5.25	9.0	16.5	Av=6
8a	Aggregate net incomes in each state, € bn	157.5	252	243	247.5	900
	Sum of net transfers in € billions			27	52.5	79.5
	Palma index = 247.5 / 157.5 = 1.57					
	Henry Neuberger = (247.5 – 39.375) / 6 = 34.6875					
8b	row 8a / 900 %	17.5	28	27	27.5	100%
8c	Lorenz: accumulated totals from row above	17.5	45.5	72.5	100	
	Gini: (row 1c – row 8c + previous column's first value) times row 1b / 2	22.5 x 40/2	(26.5 + 22.5) x 32/2	(17.5 + 26.5) x 18/2	17.5 x 10/2	
	Gini coefficient = 1717.5 / 5000	450	784	396	87.5	0.344
	OPTION B: Each state contributes 0.5 of mean income to pool as CI for whole EU (see row 4)					
7	Total income for each person = (1.0 – row 4) + 3.0	3.75	5.5	8.0	13.0	

Row		STATES				EU
		A	B	C	D	
For a given year:		A	B	C	D	
8a Aggregate net incomes in each state, € bn		225	264	216	195	900
Palma index = 195 / 225 = 0.8666						
8b row 8a / 900 %		25	29.33	24	21.66	100%
8c Lorenz: accumulated totals from row 8b		25	54.33	78.33	100	
Gini: ((row 1c – row 8c) + figure from previous column) times row 1b / 2)		15 x 40/2	(17.66 +15.0) x 32/2	(11.66 +17.66) x 18/2	11.66 x 10/2	
Gini coefficient = 1144.9 / 5000		300	522.57	264	58.33	0.229

Table B2 uses a hypothetical example to show that a flat tax of rate t = β, hypothecated to finance a BI = β.mean income, will reduce the Gini coefficient by proportion β.

Table B2 Demonstration of the redistributive powers of a hypothecated flat rate income tax used to finance a BI scheme

Row		A	B	C	D	E	
1a, 1b	Distribution of population, %	20	20	50	6	4	100
1c	Accum totals from row above, %	20	40	90	96	100	
2	Mean income per head	0	1	5	15	160	Av=10
3a	Aggregate personal incomes	0	20	250	90	640	1000
	Palma index = 730 / 20 = 36.5						
3b	row 3a / 10 %	0	2	25	9	64	100%
3c	Lorenz: accumulated totals from 3b	0	2	27	36	100	
	Gini:	20	(38 + 20) x 20/2	(63 + 38) x 50/2	(60 + 63) x 6/2	60 x 4/2	
	Gini coefficient = 3794/5000	200	580	2525	369	120	0.7588
	BI SCHEME A:						
	Inc tax, t = 0.25; BI = 0.25 x Av	-0.00 +2.5	-0.25 +2.5	-1.25 +2.5	-3.75 +2.5	-40.0 +2.5	
2	Mean income per head	2.5	3.25	6.25	13.75	122.5	Av=10
3a	Aggregate personal incomes	50	65	312.5	82.5	490	1000
	Palma index = 572.5/ 115 = 4.98						
3b	row 3a / 10 %	5	6.5	31.25	8.25	49	100%
3c	Lorenz: accumulated totals from 3b	5	11.5	42.75	51	100	
	Gini:	15	(28.5 + 15) x 20/2	(47.25 + 28.5) x50/2	(45 + 47.25) x 6/2	45 x 4/2	
	Gini coefficient = 2845.5 / 5000	150	435	1893.75	276.75	90	0.5691
	BI SCHEME B:	-0.5	-0.65	-1.25	-2.75	-24.5	
	Inc tax, t = 0.20, BI = 0.2 x Av	+2.0	+2.0	+2.0	+2.0	+ 2.0	
2	Mean income per head.	4.0	4.6	7.0	13.0	100.0	Av=10
3a	Aggregate personal incomes	80.0	92.0	350	78.0	400.0	
	Palma index = 478 /172 = 2.779						
3b	row 3a / 10 %	8.0	9.2	35	7.8	0.0	100%
3c	Lorenz: accumulated totals from 3b	8.0	17.2	52.2	60.0	100	
	Gini:	12	(22.8 + 12) x20/2	(37.8 + 22.8) x 50/2	(36 + 37.8) x 6/2	36 x 4/2	
	Gini coefficient = 2276.4/5000	120	348	1515	221.4	72	0.45528

Row		A	B	C	D	E	
	BI SCHEME C:						
	Inc tax, t = 0.333, BI = Av/3	-1.333 +3.333	-1.533 +3.333	-2.333 +3.333	-4.333 +3.333	-33.333 +3.333	
2	Mean income per head.	6	6.4	8.0	12.0	70.0	Av=10
3a	Aggregate personal incomes	120	128	400	72	280	
	Palma index = 352/248 = 1.419						
3b	row 3a / 10 %	12	12.8	40	7.2	28	100%
3c	Lorenz: accumulated totals from 3b	12	24.8	64.8	72	100	
	Gini:	8 x 20/2	(15.2 + 8) x 20/2	(25.2 + 15.2) x 50/2	(24 + 25.2) x 6/2	24 x 4/2	
	Gini coefficient = 1517.6/5000	80	232	1010	147.6	48	0.30352

Table B3 Summary of the results for the tables above

Table	Population	Total income	Average income	1-t	Palma	Gini
1	150	900 bn	6,000		3.33	0.458
1A				0.75	1.57	0.344
1B				0.67	0.867	0.229
2	100	1,000	10		36.5	0.7588
2A				0.75	4.98	0.5691
2B				0.80	2.779	0.45528
2C				0.67	1.419	0.30352

Note: applying the three schemes serially in Table B2 is equivalent to applying a tax rate of 0.60 in one go. $(1.00 - 0.25)(1.00 - 0.20)(1.00 - 0.333) = 0.40 = (1 - t)$.

Constructing an income distribution for individuals

Gross income data for low-income individuals in the UK are not collected, let alone published. HMRC collects figures on individual incomes for tax purposes. It also publishes *The Annual Survey of Personal Incomes*, which is also based on taxpayer data. The DWP publishes *Households Below Average Incomes*, but, as indicated, this is based on household data. Household data obscures the inequality within the household. Nowhere is there a record of the individual poverty that can be hidden even within households above average income.

HMRC publishes the following data:

Table B4 Taxpayers and non-taxpayers in the UK, 2014–15

Age	Non-taxpayers, ooos	Taxpayers, ooos	Total for each group	Proportion of population
0–15	12,153	0	12,153,462	0.188
16–64	16,620	24,430	41,049,578	0.635
65 +	5,324	6,070	11,393,760	0.176
Total	34,097	30,500	64,596,800	1.000
Proportions	0.528	0.472		1.000

- Nearly 20 per cent of the population are minors, and the number with significant income on their own account is negligible.
- Over 30 per cent of the population comprises adults with an income of less than the Personal Allowance (£10,000 or £192 pw in 2014–15).
- 40 per cent of working-age adults had an income of £10,000 or less in 2014–15!
- About 30 per cent of the population has an income greater than the average gross income of £20,560 (£394 pw).
- Thus, 20 per cent of the population has an income between the Personal Allowance and the mean income per head (£10,000 to £20,560). This is the 'middle income' range.
- 7 per cent of the population paid the higher rate of tax (at 40 per cent) on gross incomes of £41,866 or over.
- Of these 329,000 (0.5 per cent) paid additional rate of tax (at 45 per cent) on gross incomes of £150,001 or over.

Comparison of different progressive income tax schedules

A hypothetical income distribution has been devised for Table B5, based on the above information. The Gini coefficient for this hypothetical distribution is 0.5696. The equivalent distribution for the adults only, excluding the 20 per cent who are children, has a Gini coefficient of 0.4620.

Table B5 examines the effect of different progressive income tax systems, compared with a flat tax (scheme D). They are presented in the order according to the net income of the poorest group, starting with the highest. A summary of the schemes, giving both tax rate and net incomes for income groups, is presented at the end of Table B5. Mean income is 20 units. The middle income range is 10–20 units.

- Scheme A is progressive with low rates of income tax on low-income groups, but quickly progressing to high rates (of 60 per cent) on middle incomes (10–20 units).

- Scheme B has an income disregard on the two lowest income groups, then becomes progressive, but with unrealistically high income tax rates on the wealthiest 8 per cent of the population.

- Scheme C is progressive with high income tax rates on low-income groups.

- Scheme D is a flat tax.

- Scheme E has a flat rate standard rate of income tax, but with an income disregard on the lowest income group, and increased rates of taxation on higher income groups.

- Scheme F starts with an income disregard for the lowest income group and then builds up progressively over the rest of the population.

- Scheme G is the closest to the current UK income tax system, but without the tax loopholes.

Table B5 Hypothetical examples to explore the outcomes of some progressive income tax schedules: the mean gross income of individuals, Y-BAR, is 20

Row	ORIGINAL	A	B	C	D	E	F	G	
	Income range	0	0-5	5-10	10-20	20-40	40-150	150 -	
1a	Distribution of population	20	18	12	20	23	6	1	100
1c	Accumulated totals from 1a	20	38	50	70	93	99	100	
2	Mean gross income per head	0	4	9	19	35	70	215	
3a	Aggregate personal incomes	0	72	108	380	805	420	215	2000
	Accumulated totals from 3a	0	72	180	560	1365	1785	2000	
	Divide accum totals by 20	0	3.6	9.0	28.0	68.25	89.25	100	
	BI SCHEME A on original distribution								
	Progressive tax rates	0.20	0.20	0.40	0.60	0.60	0.60	0.60	
	Income tax levied: t = 0.20 on 0-5 Av = 4 t = 0.40 on 5-10 9 t = 0.60 on 10-20 19 t = 0.60 on 20-40 35 t = 0.60 on 40-150 70 t = 0.60 on 150 – 215	-0.0	-0.8	-1.0 -1.6	-1.0 -2.0 -5.4	-1.0 -2.0 -6.0 -9.0	-1.0 -2.0 -6.0 -12.0 -18.0	-1.0 -2.0 -6.0 -12.0 -66.0 -39.0	
	Total:	-0.0	-0.8	-2.6	-8.4	-18.0	-39.00	-126.0	
	Tax revenues:	-0.0	-14.4	-32.2	-168	-414	-234	-126	-987.6
	Distribute BI = 9.9	+9.9	+9.9	+9.9	+9.9	+9.9	+9.9	+9.9	900
2	Mean net income per head	9.9	13.1	16.3	20.5	26.9	40.9	98.9	
3a	Aggregate personal incomes	198	235.8	195.6	410.0	618.7	245.4	98.9	2002.4
	BI SCHEME B on original distribution								
	Progressive tax rate	0.0	0.0	0.20	0.40	0.60	0.75	0.85	
	Income tax levied: t = 0.00 on 0-5 Av = 4 t = 0.20 on 5-10 9 t = 0.40 on 10-20 19 t = 0.60 on 20-40 35 t = 0.75 on 40-150 70 t = 0.85 on 150- 215	-0.0	-0.0	-0.0 -0.8	-0.0 -1.0 -3.6	-0.0 -1.0 -4.0 -9.0 -22.5	-0.0 -1.0 -4.0 -12.0 -82.5	-0.0 -1.0 -4.0 -12.0 -55.25	
	Total:				-4.6	-14.0	-39.5	-154.75	
	Tax revenues:	-0.0	-0.0	-9.6	-92	-322	-237	-154.75	-815.35
	Distribute BI = 8.2	+8.2	+8.2	+8.2	+8.2	+8.2	+8.2	+8.2	820
2	Mean net income per head	8.2	12.2	16.4	22.6	29.2	38.7	68.45	

Row	ORIGINAL	A	B	C	D	E	F	G	
3a	Aggregate personal incomes	164	219.6	196.8	452	671.6	232.2	68.45	2004.65
	BI SCHEME C on original distribution								
	Progressive tax rates	0.3	0.30	0.35	0.40	0.45	0.50	0.55	
	Income tax levied: t = 0.30 on 0-5 Av = 4 t = 0.35 on 5-10 9 t = 0.40 on 10-20 19 t = 0.45 on 20-40 35 t = 0.50 on 40-150 70 t = 0.55 on 150- 215	-0.0	-1.2	-1.5 -1.4	-1.5 -1.75 -3.6	-1.5 -1.75 -4.0 -6.75	-1.5 -1.75 -4.0 -9.0 -15.0	-1.5 -1.75 -4.0 -9.0 -55.0 -35.75	
	Total	-0.0	-1.2	-2.9	-6.85	-14	-31.25	-107	
	- (Tax revenues)	-0.0	-21.6	-34.8	-137	-322	-187.5	-107	-809.9
	Distribute BI = 8.1	8.1	+8.1	+8.1	+8.1	+8.1	+8.1	+8.1	810
2	Mean net income per head	8.1	10.9	14.2	20.25	29.1	46.85	116.1	
3a	Aggregate personal incomes	162	196.2	170.4	405	669.3	281.1	116.1	2000.1
	BI SCHEME D on original:								
	Flat tax income tax rate	0.35	0.35	0.35	0.35	0.35	0.35	0.35	
	Income tax levied: t = 0.35	-0.0	-1.4	-3.15	-6.65	-12.25	-24.5	-75.25	
	-Tax revenue	-0.0	-25.2	-37.8	-133	-281.75	-147	-75.25	-700
	Distribute BI = 7.0	+7	+7	+7	+7	+7	+7	+7	700
	Mean net income per head	7.0	9.6	12.85	19.35	29.75	52.5	146.75	
	Aggregate personal incomes	140	172.8	154.2	387	684.25	315	146.75	2000
	BI SCHEME E on original								
	Progressive tax rate	0.0	0.0	0.40	0.40	0.40	0.50	0.60	
	Income tax levied: t = 0.00 on 0-5 Av = 4 t = 0.40 on 5-10 9 t = 0.40 on 10-20 19 t = 0.40 on 20-40 35 t = 0.50 on 40-150 70 t = 0.60 on 150- 215	-0	-0.0	-0.0 -1.6	-0.0 -2.0 -3.6	-0.0 -2.0 -4.0 -6.0	-0.0 -2.0 -4.0 -8.0 -15.0	-0.0 -2.0 -4.0 -8.0 -55.0 -39.0	
	Total:	-0	-0.0	-1.6	-5.6	-12.0	-29.0	-108.0	
	Tax revenue:	-0	-0.0	-19.2	-112	-276	-174	-108.0	-689.2
	Distribute BI = 6.9	6.9	+6.9	+6.9	+6.9	+6.9	+6.9	+6.9	690
	Mean net income per head	6.9	10.9	14.3	20.3	29.9	47.9	107.9	
	Aggregate personal incomes	138	196.2	171.6	406	687.7	287.4	113.9	2000.8

Row	ORIGINAL	A	B	C	D	E	F	G	
	BI SCHEME F on original								
	Progressive tax rate	0.1	0.10	0.20	0.30	0.40	0.50	0.60	
	Income tax levied:								
	t = 0.10 on 0-5 Av = 4	-0	-0.4	-0.5	-0.5	-0.5	-0.5	-0.5	
	t = 0.10 on 5-10 9			-0.8	-1.0	-1.0	-1.0	-1.0	
	t = 0.20 on 10-20 19				-2.7	-3.0	-3.0	-3.0	
	t = 0.40 on 20-40 35					-6.0	-8.0	-8.0	
	t = 0.50 on 40-150 70						-15.0	-55.0	
	t = 0.60 on 150- 215							-39.0	
	Total:	-0	-0.4	-1.3	-4.2	-10.5	-27.5	-106.5	
	Tax revenue:	-0	-7.2	-15.6	-84	-241.5	-165	-106.5	-619.8
	Distribute BI = 6.2	6.2	+6.2	+6.2	+6.2	+6.2	+6.2	+6.2	620
2	Mean net income per head	6.2	9.8	13.9	21	30.7	48.7	114.7	
3a	Aggregate personal incomes	124	176.4	166.8	420	706.1	292.2	114.7	2000.2
	BI SCHEME G on original								
	Progressive tax rate	0.0	0.0	0.12	0.32	0.32	0.42	0.47	
	Income tax levied:								
	t = 0.00 on 0-5 Av = 4	-0	-0.0	-0.0	-0.0	-0.0	-0.0	-0.0	
	t = 0.12 on 5-10 9			-0.48	-0.6	-0.6	-0.6	-0.6	
	t = 0.32 on 10-20 19				-2.88	-3.2	-3.2	-3.2	
	t = 0.32 on 20-40 35					-4.8	-6.4	-6.4	
	t = 0.42 on 40-150 70						-12.6	-46.2	
	t = 0.47 on 150- 215							-30.55	
	Total:	-0	-0.0	-0.48	-3.48	-8.6	-22.8	-86.95	
	Tax revenue:	-0	-0.0	-5.76	-69.6	-197.8	-136.8	-86.95	-496.91
	Distribute BI = 5.0	5.0	+5.0	+5.0	+5.0	+5.0	+5.0	+5.0	500
	Mean income per head	5.0	9.0	13.52	20.52	31.4	52.2	133.05	
	Aggregate personal incomes	100	162	162.24	410.4	722.2	313.2	133.05	2003.09
	SUMMARY OF BI SCHEMES ABOVE								
	INCOME RANGES:	0	0-5	5-10	10-20	20-40	40-150	150-	
	Distribution of population:	20	18	12	20	23	6	1	
	Mean gross income =	0	4	9	19	35	70	215	
	Mean = 20								
	Scheme A. BI = 9.9. t =	0.2	0.2	0.4	0.6	0.6	0.6	0.6	
	Mean net income =	9.9	13.1	16.3	20.5	26.9	40.9	98.9	
	Scheme B. BI = 8.2. t =	0.0	0.0	0.2	0.4	0.6	0.75	0.85	
	Mean net income =	8.2	12.2	16.4	22.6	29.2	38.7	68.45	

Row	ORIGINAL	A	B	C	D	E	F	G	
	Scheme C. BI = 8.1. t =	0.3	0.30	0.35	0.40	0.45	0.50	0.55	
	Mean net income =	8.1	10.9	14.2	20.25	29.1	46.85	116.1	
	Scheme D. BI = 7.0. t =	0.35	0.35	0.35	0.35	0.35	0.35	0.35	
	Mean net income =	7.0	9.6	12.85	19.35	29.75	52.5	146.75	
	Scheme E. BI = 6.9. t =	0	0	0.4	0.4	0.4	0.5	0.6	
	Mean net income =	6.9	10.9	14.3	20.3	29.9	47.9	113.9	
	Scheme F. BI = 6.2 t =	0.1	0.1	0.2	0.3	0.4	0.5	0.6	
	Mean net income =	6.2	9.8	13.9	21	30.7	48.7	114.7	
	Scheme G. BI = 3.6. t =	0	0	0.12	0.32	0.32	0.42	0.47	
	Mean net income =	5.0	9.0	13.52	20.52	31.4	52.2	133.05	

It will be observed that the outcomes for the first five income groups are very similar over the different schemes, with differences of around three to five income units in each case. The range of net incomes for the two wealthiest groups is 13.8 and 78.25 units respectively.

The optimum choice depends on objectives and assumptions. My optimum looks for the highest income for the lowest income group (Scheme A), but which does not have too high a rate of tax (t > 0.4) on the middle income group (Scheme B), which has an unreasonably high tax rate on the highest two income groups. I would prefer one with an income disregard for the lowest income group (scheme E). Others will choose according to their own criteria.

APPENDIX C

Design and cost your own BI scheme

THE TABLE below provides a template for creating the costing method developed in chapter 13 for costing your own BI scheme, using Microsoft Excel.

To create a different scheme, choose the money values and convert them to proportions of Y-BAR, and insert these into B7–B12. The resultant figures in C42–C52 can be compared with your chosen benchmark.

For Scotland, use the 'Save As' instruction to save a copy of the above file. Substitute the population figures for Scotland, as given in Table 11.2, plus figures for boys and girls aged 14–15 from Table 11.1, into B18–B36, and Y-BAR for Scotland in C14. Update B4.

The population, together with the Y-BAR figures in A14 and C14, the margin in E39 and the fiscal year in B5, need to be updated each year.

Table C Excel template to design and cost your own preferred BI scheme

	A	B	C	D	E
1					
2	Calculate the	standard tax rate	needed to finance	a BI	Scheme
3					
4	AREA	UK			
5	YEAR	2017–18			
6			£ pw		
7	Pensioner	0.3868752	=B7*C14		
8	W-A adult	0.1774746	=B8*C14		
9	Young adult	0.1405716	=B9*C14		
10	Child 0–15	0.1623492	=B10*C14		
11	Premium 14–15	0.00	=B11*C14		
12	Premium PwC	0.0422929	=B12*C14		
13					
14	Y-BAR 2015		411.89	BI	
15			Population	Proportion	
16	Sub groups	Population 2015	Proportion		t-rate
17	65 +				
18	Disabilities	2859616	=B18/B38	=B7	=C18*D18
19	Carers	1407124	=B19/B38	=B7	=C19*D19
20	Rest of 65 +	7344460	=B20/B38	=B7	=C20*D20
21	25–64	0	=B21/B38		0
22	All aged 64	688346	=B22/B38	=B7	=C22*D22
23	Disabilities	2288953	=B23/B38	=B8	=C23*D23
24	Carers	4598151	=B24/B38	=B8	=C24*D24
25	Rest of 25–63	26273950	=B25/B38	=B8	=C25*D25
26	16–24	0	=B26/B38		0
27	Disabilities	153261	=B27/B38	=B9	=C27*D27
28	Carers	367121	=B28/B38	=B9	=C28*D28
29	Rest of 16–24	6871142	=B29/B38	=B9	=C29*D29
30	0–15	0	=B30/B38		0
31	Disabilities	188977	=B31/B38	=B10	=C31*D31

	A	B	C	D	E
32	Carers	133493	=B32/B38	=B10	=C32*D32
33	Rest of 0–15	11935406	=B33/B38	=B10	=C33*D33
34	Premium 14–15	1434964	=B34/B38	=B11	=C34*D34
35	Lone Parents	1941005	=B35/B38	=B12	=C35*D35
36	Other PwC	4913330	=B36/B38	=B12	=C36*D36
37					
38	Gross transfers	65110000	=SUM(C18:C33)		=SUM(E18:E36)
39	Add MARGIN				0.0557
40	TOTAL				=E38+E39
41					
42	Single pens	=B7	=B42*C14		
43	Couple pens	=B7*2	=B43*C14		
44	Single W-A	=B8	=B44*C14		
45	Couple W-A	=B8*2	=B45*C14		
46	Lone Parent+1	=B8+B12+B10	=B46*C14		
47	Lone Parent+2	=B8+B12+B10*2	=B47*C14		
48	Lone Parent+3	=B8+B12+B10*3+B11	=B48*C14		
49	Couple + 1	=B8*2+B12+B10	=B49*C14		
50	Couple + 2	=B8*2+B12+B10*2	=B50*C14		
51	Couple + 3	=B8*2+B12+B10*3+B11	=B51*C14		
52	Couple + 4	=B8*2+B12+B10*4+B11	=B52*C14		

Note: The 'SUM' in C38 provides a method of checking that the population figures are correct. It should add up to 1.0. It excludes rows 34–36 because these people are already included above in B25, B29 and B33. In column E, the SUM adds all the contributions to the tax rate.

APPENDIX D

Chronology of Basic Income with respect to the UK

THE WEBSITE of the Citizen's Income Trust (CIT) gives access to an excellent archive of material charting the development of BI over the last 30 years (www.citizensincome.org). CIT's yellow, two-sided A3 poster (2013) is a very useful reference. It has 'Landmarks in Social Welfare 1900 to 2013' on one side and 'Citizen's Income: an Introduction' on the other, although the illustrative figures relevant in 2013 have since been updated elsewhere (Torry, 2017).

Basic Income Earth Network (BIEN) has a very comprehensive review of the history of BI on its website, (www.basicincome.org/basic-income/history), as has Unconditional Basic Income Europe (https://basicincome-europe.org/ubie/brief-history-basic-income-ideas/.

Aristotle (384–22 BC) thought that men are fundamentally unequal and therefore the distribution of income and wealth should reflect that. His views were based on expediency, on what works for a State as a whole, rather than moral principle. Democracy works better without extremes of poverty and wealth, and in particular poverty is the parent of revolution and crime (White, 2000).

The foundation of all the great faiths in the world is that of compassion, expressed as loving kindness (*Metta*, Buddhism), and caring for the poor is a religious duty for all the Abrahamic faiths. Jesus's second greatest commandment is 'Love thy neighbour as thyself' and is found in three of the Gospels (Mark 12:29–31, Matthew 19:19, Luke 10:27). 'It is more blessed to give than to receive' (Acts 20:35). The miracle of the feeding of the 5,000 could be interpreted as Jesus persuading the crowd to share what they had with their neighbours (Mark 6:30–44). Similarly, Jesus's parable of the labourers in the vineyard, where all received the same day's wage whether they worked for a full or part day, addresses the fact that all of the workers needed the full day's wage to provide for their families (Matthew 20:1–16).

1516: Thomas More (1478–1535) was the author of *Utopia*, published in Latin in two volumes in Louvain, Belgium. He regarded the punishment of death for the crime of stealing food as disproportionate, and suggested that some means of livelihood, guaranteed by the government to all the members of a particular community, was a better cure for theft (BIEN).

1601: The Poor Law of England and Wales was enacted in 1601. It was a system that included out-relief, condemnation to the dreaded Poor House, and the hiring out of paupers at cheap rates to employers – all designed to act as a deterrent from claiming off the parish. However, this latter practice was believed to depress wages to the detriment of independent workers. In 1795, a code of out-relief was introduced in Speenhamland, a village in Berkshire, which topped up the wages of workers to the poverty level. This, too, was believed to lead employers to pay unduly low wages, forcing workers to claim relief.

1652: The Religious Society of Friends, (Quakers), has had a Testimony to Equality since its early days in the mid 17th century. 'We are not for names, nor men, nor titles of Government, nor are we for this party nor against the other... but we are for justice and mercy and truth and peace and true freedom, that these may be exalted in our nation, and that goodness, righteousness, meekness, temperance, peace and unity with God, and with one another, that these things may abound. Edward Burrough, 1659' (Quakers, 1995: para 23.11). Quakers put out a public statement in 1987 that is still relevant today. 'We are angered by actions which have knowingly led to the polarisation of our country – into the affluent, who epitomise success according to the values of a materialistic society, and the "have-leasts", who by the expectations of that same society are oppressed, judged, found wanting and punished' (Quakers, 1995: para 23.21).

1796: Thomas Paine (1737–1809) wrote in his pamphlet *Agrarian Justice*, 'The earth, in its natural uncultivated state was, and ever would have continued to be, *the common property of the human race*'. The introduction of private property added, through cultivation, a 'tenfold' value to created earth. At the same time, however, it 'dispossessed more than half the inhabitants of every nation of their natural inheritance, without providing... an indemnification for that loss, and has thereby created a species of poverty and wretchedness that did not exist before'. Every proprietor 'of cultivated land' owed to the community a ground rent for the land that he held. With this sum Paine aimed to set up a National Fund, out of which there would be paid to every person, 'when arrived at the age of 21 years, the sum of £15, as a compensation in part, for the loss of his or her natural inheritance, by the system of landed property' and 'the sum of ten pounds per annum, during life, to every person now living, of age 50 years, and to all others as they shall arrive at that age'.

This system... would so organise civilisation 'that the whole weight of misery can be removed'. It would aid the blind, the lame and the aged poor, and at the same time guarantee that the new generation would never become poor. And all this would not be achieved through charity. 'It is not charity, but a right... not bounty but justice, that I am pleading for' (Paine, (1796) 1974: 37).

1849: John Stuart Mill (1806–73) regarded inequality of income and wealth as a great evil, but he did not agree with giving to the state the role of redistribution. He wanted to protect wealth earned by the free use of mind or body, through effort or saving, but he was prepared to limit large inheritances, and he favoured taxing land. He thought that free education for the poor was a good method of obtaining greater equality. He was a utilitarian who thought that there were different levels of utility, and that the same unit of income gave greater utility to a poor person than to a rich one, thus inciting what later became known as the 'law of diminishing marginal utility of income' (White, 2000).

1879: Henry George (1839–97) wrote *Progress and Poverty: An Inquiry Into the Cause of Industrial Depressions and the Increase of Want with the Increase in Wealth – The Remedy*. He claimed that 'as an economy grows, labourers do not share in the economic growth, but instead are reduced to poverty, because of increased rents to landowners' (White, 2000: 22). The remedy that he advocated is a Land Value Tax.

1918: Bertrand Russell (1872–1970) wrote *Roads to Freedom, Socialism, Anarchism and Syndicalism*, in which he expressed a wish to combine the advantages of socialism and anarchism. He proposed that 'a certain small income, sufficient for necessaries, should be secured to all, whether they work or not, and that a larger income – as much larger as might be warranted by the total amount of commodities produced – should be given to those who are willing to engage in some work which the community recognises as useful... When education is finished, no one should be compelled to work and those who choose not to work should receive a bare livelihood and be left completely free' (BIEN, 'Russell's combination of anarchism and socialism').

1918: Dennis Milner (1892–1956), a young Quaker in his mid-twenties, presented his *Scheme for a State Bonus for All* to the main business meeting of the Religious Society of Friends in May 1918, and wrote a pamphlet with his wife, Mabel (Milner et al, 1918). The *State Bonus* was pitched at 20 per cent of GDP *per cap*. Despite further writings (Pickard, 1919), (Milner, 1920), and a supporting State Bonus League, the campaign was short-lived, ending after being rejected by the Labour Party Annual

Conference in June 1921. This 'is in all probability the earliest full-blown modern basic incomes proposal' (Van Trier, 1995: 31). Van Trier examines Milner's scheme in detail, noting how it contains all the qualities of, and arguments for, BI schemes that were developed independently later in the 20th century.

1921: 'Major' Clifford Hugh Douglas (1879–1952) was a British engineer, and amateur economist who introduced the idea of a *National Dividend* (Van Trier, 1995: 190). However, 'the first time Major Douglas released a real blue-print of a policy proposal was as late as March 11th, 1932, when he published a set of proposals in the *Glasgow Evening Times*, titled "A Draft Social Credit Scheme for Scotland" (Van Trier, 1995: 191–2). It was to be financed 'not from borrowing from banks, neither from taxation. It will be 'created for the State by the banks and paid out by the State's direction" (Van Trier, 1995: 308). Douglas described his Social Credit movement as an interdisciplinary, distributive philosophy. It did not find favour in the UK, but the Social Credit Party governed Alberta, Canada, from 1935–71, although it soon dropped its National Dividend proposal (BIEN, Major Douglas and the Social Credit Movement).

1936: Both James Meade (1907–95), winner of the Nobel Prize in economics in 1977, and GDH Cole (1889–1959) used the term '**social dividend**' in 1935. Meade used it throughout his life, but implied different things at different times (Van Trier, 1995: 363). 'And it was to become a crucial component of the Agathatopia Project to which he devoted his last writings (1989, 1993, 1995)' (BIEN, 'Cole and Meade on Social Dividend'). 'Social Dividend' was the term commonly used until the early 1980s, when the term 'Basic Income' became popular.

1942: William Beveridge was a Liberal peer, and a Director of LSE, who designed a new system of social protection for the nation. His *Report on Social Insurance and Allied Services* (1942) was a best seller, and his proposals were passed into law in the National Insurance Act 1946 and National Assistance Act 1948. It spread more slowly to other European nations. This dual system has embodied the Social Security system in the UK from that date.

1943: Juliet Rhys Williams, also a Liberal peer, developed her Social Contract, at the same time as Beveridge was writing his report. It was designed to solve the problems of the distribution of wealth, the freeing of the unemployed to undertake part-time work for profit, to preserve national unity and the complete abolition of the Means Test among others (Rhys Williams, 1943: 138). It is based on the principle that '*The prevention of want must be regarded as being the duty of the State to all its citizens, and not merely a favoured few*'. It comprised a work-tested 'benefit... of 21 shillings per week to a man, 19 shillings per week to his wife, or to a single woman, *paid in her own right and not merely as a dependent*, and 10 shillings in respect of each of his children under 18' (Rhys Williams, 1943: 145, italics in original). Her son, Brandon, a Conservative MP, wrote *The New Social Contract* (Rhys Williams, 1967).

1945: *The Universal Declaration of Human Rights* was adopted by the General Assembly of the United Nations in Paris on 10 December 1945. Article 25 (1) states that 'everyone has the right to a standard of living adequate for the health and well-being of himself and of his family, including food, clothing, housing and medical care and necessary social services, and the right to security in the event of unemployment, sickness, disability, old age or other lack of livelihood in circumstances beyond his control'. This was incorporated into the European Convention on Human Rights set up in Rome in 1950 (United Nations, 1945).

There were few other writings about a Social Dividend in the UK before the mid 1980s, except for (Brown *et al*, 1969), (Atkinson, 1969: chapter 9), (Meade, 1972), (Atkinson, 1973) and (Roberts, 1981).

1968-80: Income Maintenance Experiments in the USA.

1972: The Heath Government's *Proposals for a Tax-Credit System*, Cmnd 5116, was an unexpected development, but it was not based on the individual. Its aims were a) 'to simplify and reform the whole system of personal tax collection', and b) 'to improve the system of income support for poor people', (Green Paper, 1972: para 7). The proposal was examined in detail by Atkinson, and rejected because 'there are important low-income groups who would be given little help or actually lose from the Green Paper proposals.' (Atkinson, 1973: 61).

1974: The Liberal Party Manifesto, published in February 1974, expressed six aims, of which the first was 'Establish the universal right to a *minimum income* balanced by a fairer *distribution of wealth*, through a credit income tax system and national minimum earnings guarantees' (page 1). It would 'replace most of the 44 means tests to which underprivileged and handicapped people are subjected... All income would be taxed according to a progressive scale from the very first pound, but *everyone* would be entitled to various 'credits' or allowances depending on circumstances.' (Italics in the original) (Liberal Party, 1974:10). In March 1983, the Liberal Party published its Tax Credit Plan (Vince, 1983). Parker compared the schemes of the Liberal and the Social Democratic Parties for 1982–83 (Parker, 1984), (Parker, 1989).

1974–79: The Mincome Program was carried out in Dauphin, Manitoba, Canada.

1976: The Alaska Permanent Fund was set up based on oil royalties that were invested in international markets.

1982: Alaska Permanent Fund Dividend was first distributed.

1982-3: The House of Commons Treasury and Civil Service Committee conducted their 'Enquiry into the Structure of Personal Income Taxation and Income Support'. A sub-committee chaired by Michael Meacher MP received Memorandums from several sources, which were published in a third special report (House of Commons, 1983). The Committee recommended further study of integrated tax/benefit systems.

1984: The Basic Income Research Group (BIRG) was formed. It became a charity in 1989, and changed its name to Citizen's Income Trust (CIT) in 1993, and again to Citizen's Basic Income Trust in 2017. Its objectives were, and still are, to 'advance public education about the national economic and social effects and influences of Basic Income Systems'. It maintains a website with an excellent archive and a library and has published a regular Bulletin or Newsletter for the last three decades.

1986: BIRG was one of the groups that founded the Basic Income European Network (BIEN) in Louvain-la-Neuve in 1986. BIEN is a loose network of national organisations, which maintains a very informative website, www.basicincome.org, and has organised a Congress every two years. At its Assembly in Seoul in July 2016, it agreed to start holding congresses annually. Publication of the proceedings of each congress has contributed greatly to the literature available in the subject. In 2004, the General Assembly of BIEN agreed to change its name to Basic Income Earth Network, to reflect its extension of affiliated organisation status to countries outside Europe. With the support of other BI organisations, it set up the e-journal *Basic Income Studies* in 2006.

Some key contributions about BI have been made by Van Der Veen and Van Parijs (1986), Rhys Williams (1989), Parker (1989), Walter (1989), Brittan and Webb (1990), Atkinson (1995), Van Parijs (1995), Van Trier (1995), Fitzpatrick (1999), McKay (2005), Standing (2011), Torry (2013) and Torry (2015).

2004: Brazil sanctioned the conditional *Bolsa Familia* into law.

2005: The World Bank published its report about the wealth of a nation.

2008–9: Privately funded BI pilot in Otjivero, Namibia.

2010: Iran introduces *de facto* a BI scheme based on oil wealth.

2011–13: BI pilots in India.

2012–14: The European Union introduced a new instrument, the European Citizens' Initiative (ECI) in 2012. See chapter 9 above. An ECI on Unconditional Basic Income (ECI on UBI) was registered on 14 January 2013. Although it only obtained 285,000 signatures across the 28 countries of the EU within the ensuing year, it raised the profile of the idea with the public across the EU. The work of promoting the concept of a BI in Europe continues via UBI-Europe (www.basicincome-europe.org/ubie).

2013: Basic Income UK (BI-UK), which was set up while campaigning in the UK for the ECI on UBI, is the focus for a network of grassroots groups in the UK, who are interested in the idea of, and wish to campaign for, a BI (https://basicincome.org.uk).

2014: This year saw a significant increase in public events relating to BI. In January, the Scottish Parliament hosted a seminar and round-table on BI for MSPs and other interested parties. In March, the House of Commons hosted a similar event, and CIT organised a successful BI conference at the British Library, London, in June. The Scottish Green Party published details of a BI scheme for Scotland in August 2014 (Scottish Green Party, 2014). BI is also part of a long-term policy for the Green Party in England and Wales.

2015–17: There has been an increase in interest in BI in recent years, probably in response to the changing labour market conditions, the concern about increasing automation and robotisation, increasing inequality in income and wealth in many countries around the world, and the growing incidence of poverty. This is evidenced by the large number of books in which a BI is referred to as, at least, a partial solution to the problem being explored, (Wilkinson *et al*, 2009: 264), (Dorling, 2011: 267), (Skidelsky *et al*, 2012: 197–202), (Mason, 2015: 284–6), (Murphy, 2015: 192–5), (Srnicek et al, 2015: chapter 6), (Sayer, 2016: 361). In addition, several reports exploring the desirability and feasibility of BI, with some proposing their own schemes for the UK, have been produced recently by some think tanks and others (Duffy *et al*, 2014), (Story, 2015), (Painter *et al*, 2015), (Mackenzie *et al*, 2016), (Reed *et al*, 2016), (Cooper, 2016) and (Torry, 2017).

2015: A new organisation, the Citizen's Basic Income Network Scotland, with the educational objective of disseminating information to the public and policy-makers alike, about the desirability and feasibility of a BI in a more fiscally-devolved or independent Scotland, was set up and granted charitable status in February 2016.

2016: Delegates at the Scottish National Party spring conference in March agreed to a motion proposed by Ronnie Cowan MP supporting the introduction of a basic income in Scotland (West, 2016). In June, the Shadow Chancellor, John McDonnell, said that the Labour Party is considering backing a universal basic income as part of its new economic policy (Cowburn, 2016). Ronnie Cowan MP (SNP) won the right to hold the first debate about BI in the Westminster Parliament, which took place on 14 September in Westminster Hall.

2016: Switzerland's Referendum on 5 June rejected the Basic Income proposal.

2017: Start of Finland's MIG experiment in January.

2017: The Scottish Social Security Committee heard oral evidence re BI on 9 March at Holyrood. Three Scottish Councils began to explore the possibility of holding BI pilot projects. On 22 May the Green Party of England and Wales included a BI scheme in its manifesto for the General Election on 8 June.

Sources of data

Finding and accessing data can be one of the most time-consuming and frustrating parts of the exercise of examining facts and figures for social security in general, and BIS in particular. Finding the right data in terms of GB or UK, or for a calendar year or fiscal year, can be time-consuming enough. It is not helped by the fact that a link that produced the relevant data required in one year no longer leads to the same table in the following year. Sometimes the quickest route is found by *googling* the name of the table required, if known, and noting the link afterwards.

Government Sources

Many of these data files can be downloaded using Microsoft Excel software.

Population

Mid-year UK and Scotland population estimates
For the mid-year population estimates for Scotland and UK for 2011 onwards, go to: www.ons.gov.uk/peoplepopulationandcommunity/pop-ulationandmigration/populationestimates/datasets/populationestimates-forukenglandandwalesscotlandandnorthernireland/. The dataset is called 'Population Estimates for UK, England and Wales, Scotland and Northern Ireland'. A zip file with the mid-year estimates (MYE) can be downloaded, eg 'ukmye2015'. The zip file contains several Microsoft Excel files.

The relevant data can be abstracted from the following Excel files:
'MYE1_population_summary_for_UK.xls', contains the table
MYE1: Population Estimates Summary for the UK, mid-xxxx, (in 5-year age-groups), where xxxx is the year;
'MYE2_population_by_sex_and_age_for_local_authorities_UK.xls' contains the table MYE2: Population Estimates by single year of age and sex for local authorities in the UK, mid-xxxx.
The Scottish data start at around row 399 or 400 (accessed 19/12/2016).

Census data 2011 for numbers of people with disabilities, carers, lone parents
Population figures by age, for the number of people with disabilities that

limit their day-to-day activities a lot, unpaid carers, lone parents, and other responsible parents of dependent children aged 0–15, can be obtained from Census 2011 data for the different UK nations. The quickest way to access these tables is to *google* each table's eight-digit reference code (such as DC3101SC below).

For **Scotland**, National Records of Scotland, Scotland's Census 2011
Online access from http://www.scotlandscensus.gov.uk/

- Use 'www.scotlandscensus.gov.uk/variables' to choose relevant variables, then use www.scotlandscensus.gov.uk/ods-web/standard-outputs.html to access 'Census Data Explorer, Standard Outputs' to select the year (2011), the relevant table from a list of table reference codes and brief description, and area type (Scotland).
- Use table DC3101SC for the number of disabled people whose 'day-to-day activities were limited a lot', by age.
- Use table DC3103SC for 'Provision of unpaid care by age'.
- Use table DC1118SC for both 'Lone parents' and 'Other responsible parents of a dependent child', 'Age of youngest child by family type', netting out those families where the youngest dependent child is aged 16–18.

Deducting 'Lone parents' leaves 'Couples families' in which it is assumed that few fathers will be the parent to whom Child Benefit is paid, to administer on the child's behalf, and that fewer still will be 65 or over. Similarly, where the mother receives the Child Benefit, few are likely to have a dependent child under the age of 16 by the time that they are 65 or over. Thus, in the absence of evidence about the actual number of responsible parents with a dependent child under the age of 16, who are aged 65 or over, it is assumed that all responsible parents of a dependent child aged under 16 are in the age bracket 16–64, for all the countries in the UK. (Accessed 19/12/2016).

For **England and Wales**, Office of National Statistics (ONS),
Online access from https://www.nomisweb.co.uk/census/2011/xxxxxx EW, where xxxxxxEW is the eight digit code for the table.

- Use keywords in 'table-finder' to find the relevant tables.
- Use table DC3302EW, 'Long term disability by health by sex by age' for the number of disabled people whose 'day to day activities were limited a lot', for 'usual residents in households'.

- Table DC3304EWLA gives figures for 'usual residents in communal establishments' by age, and figures for staff, owners and their families. The figures for people with disabilities among the staff, owners and their families, in '0–15', '16–24' and '65 or over' age groups, were assumed to be in the same proportions as for the residents.

- Use table LC3304EW for 'Provision of unpaid care by age'.

- Use table DC1118EW, Youngest dependent child in family, by family type' for lone parents, and other responsible parents, with dependent children under the age of 16.

For **Northern Ireland,** Northern Ireland Statistics and Research Agency (NISRA);
[Online access via www.nisra.gov.uk/census/2011/ redirects one to their data website at http://www.ninis2.nisra.gov.uk /public/SearchResults.aspx?sk=xxxxxxNI, where xxxxxxNI is the eight digit code for the table.

- Many of the Northern Ireland files are padlocked and need a password. [Only files that are accessible to the general public have been used here.]

- Use table CT0046NI, 'General Health by Long Term Health Problems or Disability by Age by sex', for the number of all disabled people resident in NI by age, but it does not divide the 0–34 age group of 45,241 people. It was assumed that this group had the same age distribution as for Scotland.

- It is quicker to *google* the table codes for these tables based on 2001 Census data.

- Use table EXT20041124A for data on 'Lone parents with dependent children', and use table EXT20031210, 'Age of Household Reference Person (HRP) by household, dependent children and tenure' for all families with dependent children. (Accessed 19/12/2016).

For **births in Scotland** go to National Records of Scotland via www.nrscotland. gov.uk/statistics-and-data/statistics/statistics-by-theme/vital-events/births/births-time-series-data.

- Choose 'Table BT.1: Births by sex, Scotland, 1855–2015' (accessed 19/12/2016).

United Kingdom National Accounts, The Blue Book

Each edition of the *United Kingdom National Accounts, The Blue Book*, published by the Office of National Statistics (ONS), contains Tables, each comprising a series of annual figures for a range of useful variables. Each variable has a unique 4-letter reference code beside it. The latest figure from each relevant series of the 2012–16 editions was abstracted, which was the figure that was available at the time when decisions would have been needed. It is usually available in July or August each year, but in 2014 it was not available until 31 October.

The 2012–15 editions were accessed and downloaded via www.ons. gov.uk/ons/rel/naa1-rd/united-kingdom-national-accounts/the-blue-book--xxxx-edition/index.html, where xxxx stands for the year 2012 to 2015. (Note the double dash before the xxxx.) The editions 2012–15 were based on earlier printed layouts, where the tables could be seen in context. Annual data for the previous nine, or sometimes 16, years are presented horizontally in a row, and the way in which the tables are put together could be examined and understood. For the 2015 edition, each of the chapters (1, 5, 6, 10) must be downloaded separately.

The 2016 edition was accessed via www.ons.gov.uk/economy/gross-domesticproductgdp/compendium/unitedkingdomnationalaccountsthe-bluebook/2016edition, which brings up the 'Compendium: UK National Accounts, The Blue Book: 2016' on the screen.

Click on the box on the right 'View all data in this compendium'. This refreshes the screen with 'UK National Accounts: The Blue Book: 2016' again, and offers a series of downloads representing the chapters, which have to be downloaded separately:

- 'Chapter 1: National Accounts at a glance';
- 'Chapter 5: General Government';
- 'Chapter 6: Households and Non-Profit Institutions Serving Households', and
- 'Chapter 10: Public Sector Supplementary Tables'.

In the 2016 edition, each variable is presented vertically as a column going back to the date when it was first compiled. This is obviously convenient for economists analysing time series data, but is much more difficult for anyone wanting to compare different aspects of the economy for the latest year. The same four-digit reference codes are used, and these may provide the easiest method of finding the appropriate columns.

Chapter 1

- UK GDP = Gross Domestic Product (production method) at market prices, series YBHA, from Table 1.2.
- UK GDP **per capita** = GDP per head of man, woman and child, series IHXT, from Table 1.5.

Chapter 5

- UK **Social Security Transfer Payments** can be obtained from Tables 5.1.4, 5.2.4S and 5.3.4S.

Chapter 6

- UK **Income** = 'Total Resources of Households and Non-Profit Institutions Serving Households', series QWMF, from Table 6.1.3.

Chapter 10

- UK **Taxes and their Yields** can be obtained from Tables 1.2 and 11.1 up to the 2014 edition, then Table 10.1 from the 2015 edition onwards.
- In Table 12.1 above, the item 'Other current taxes' can be calculated from the rest of the table, but it may be noted that it equals the sum of the following variables in the Blue Book's Table 10.1:

NSFA	Northern Ireland domestic rates
NRQB	Fishing licences
E8A6	Passport fees
IY90	Northern Ireland driver vehicles agency
KIH3	Bank levy
NMHK	Domestic rates

(Accessed 19/12/2016).

Scottish National Accounts Project (SNAP)

This offers a new experimental data set, *Quarterly National Accounts Scotland*, the tables of which can be downloaded from

www.gov.scot/Topics/Statistics/Browse/Economy/SNAP/QNAS. Both pdf and Excel versions are available. If using the Excel version, click on the double-headed arrow at the top right-hand side of the screen and the tabs for the different tables will appear at the bottom of the screen.

(QNAS 2016Q2 accessed 21/11/2016).

Scottish GDP **at market prices, and** GDP **per capita** for each year were abstracted from Table A: Summary Gross Domestic Product Measures. The more conservative 'on shore' version was used, as opposed to the versions based on population or geographical shares of *extra-regio* (offshore) activity.

Scottish Income was abstracted from Table I: Households and Non-Profit Institutions Serving Household (NPISHs) Sectors, Income Accounts.

The Balance of Gross Primary Income = Compensation of Employees + Gross Operating Surplus and Mixed Income + Gross Property Income – Total Primary Uses.

The data for 'Households and Non-Profit Institutions Serving Households' in 2013 for Scotland were not available in 2014, while all the Scottish accounts were being adjusted from the 1995 European System of Accounts to the ESA 2010 system, when a decision would have been needed to prepare for the 2015–16 BI scheme. The figure for Y-BAR in Scotland in 2013 was estimated here as the same proportion of GDP per cap as in 2012, and this figure is used throughout being the best available estimate in the autumn of 2014, when the BI scheme would have been planned for the following fiscal year, 2015–16.

Department of Work and Pensions (DWP)

Households Below Average Income (HBAI) statistics, editions published annually

These publications are currently going through such a state of flux, that there is not a common url pattern for access for each year. The quickest way to access this information is to google 'Households below average income 20xx to 20yy' where xx and yy are consecutive years. This provides a list of the relevant downloads for the year, which typically comprise a pdf report and supplementary data files in Excel. The earlier years provide a full report. The 2015 edition, giving 2013–14 data, comprises 152 pages. The 2016 publication for 2014–15 data is reduced to 13 pages.

(Accessed and checked 24/12/2016).

The earlier editions were accessed in order to obtain the actual figures that were available at the time of publication. Later editions tend to have revised figures. Figures for the UK were obtained from Chart 2.1 for 2010–11, and 2011–12, and from Chart 1 for 2012–13 and 2013–14. The 2014–15 figures for the median (BHC and AHC) and mean (BHC) are available on page 3, but the mean (AHC) figures had to be accessed via Excel Table 2.1 AHC.

The current expenditures on retained benefits in 2015, components of the margin in Table 11.5, were obtained as follows:
Obtain the 'Benefit and Caseloads Tables 2016', available online via https://www.gov.uk/government/statistics/benefit-expenditure-and-case-load-tables-2016, and download the 'Outturn and forecast: Autumn Statement 2016 (XLS)' file.

The **Winter Fuel Payments** out-turn for 2015/16 figure was obtained from Table 1a. 'Expenditure by benefit, £ million, nominal terms'.

A figure for NI **State Retirement Pensions paid to those who now live overseas,** but had accrued entitlements, out-turn 2015/16 was obtained from Table 'State Pension Expenditure, £ million, nominal terms'.

(Accessed 26/12/2016).

For **State Earnings-Related Pension Scheme (SERPS) and the State Second Pension (S2P)** forecast for 2015/16: [Available online at https://www.gov.uk/government/uploads/system/uploads/attachment_data/file/308622/long-term-projections-pensioner-benefits.pdf (accessed 27/12/2016).

UK **Benefits and Pension Rates**
(Accessed 28/11/2016).

- 'Benefit and Pension Rates', April 2011 – 2013, BRA5DWP, or DWP035, were obtained from www.dwp.gov.uk.
- 'Proposed benefit and pension rates 2014–15', from www.gov.uk/dwp/.
- 'Proposed benefit and pension rates 2016 to 2017', from www.gov.uk/government/uploads/system/uploads/attachment_data/file/480317/proposed_benefit_and_pension_rates_2016_to_2017.pdf
- 'Proposed benefit and pension rates 2017–18' via www.parliament.uk/business/publications/written-questions-answers-statements/written-statement/Commons/2016-11-28/HCWS287/.

Her Majesty's Revenue and Customs (HMRC)

Tax and Tax Credit rates and thresholds
Obtain HMRC's Table *'Tax and tax credit rates and thresholds for 20xx-yy',* where xx and yy refer to a fiscal year, for fiscal year 2013–14 onwards, online via https://www.gov.uk/government/publications/tax-and-tax-credit-

rates-and-thresholds-for-20xx-yy/tax-and-tax-credit-rates-and-thresh-
olds-for-20xx-yy (accessed 24/11/2016).

It contains the following information:

- **Income Tax rates and thresholds;**
- **National Insurance contribution rates and thresholds; and**
- **Working and Child Tax Credit rates and thresholds, Child
  Benefit and Guardian's Allowance.**

In future, the family element of CTC (£545) will only be available for a
child born before 06/04/2017, and the child element is to be limited to
two children only.

At all ages, for every £2 that one's income is above £100,000 a year,
the Personal Allowance goes down by £1, until the Personal Allowance is
zero, ie £123,000 in 2017–18.

Tax calculations online via www.icalculator.info/tax_calculation/
xxxxxx.html, where one substitutes the amount of gross income in place
of 'xxxxxx' (accessed 19/06/2016).

Tax Expenditures

- Access https://www.gov.uk/government/uploads/system/uploads/
  attachment_data/file/487119/. Download file 'Dec15_expendi-
  ture_reliefs_final.xlsx.pdf.
- This file contains Table 1.5 that provides past data and forecasts
  of 'Estimated costs of the principal tax expenditures and structural reliefs' for 2012–13 to 2015–16 (accessed 26/12/2016).
- For the most recent Table 1.5, covering fiscal years 2012-13 to
  2016–17, access https://www.gov.uk/government/uploads/
  system/uploads/attachment_data/file/579720/Dec_16_Main_
  Reliefs_Final.pdf (accessed 31/12/2016).

Direct effects of illustrative changes in income tax rates

- Access https://www.gov.uk/government/uploads/system/uploads/
  attachment_data/file/571367/.
- Download file 'Nov16_Direct_effects_illustrative_tax_changes_
  R4.pdf'.
- This contains Table 1.6 of former HMRC reports, 'Direct effects
  of illustrative changes in income tax rates', giving the direct
  effect of illustrative changes by 1p in £1 of basic, higher and
  additional rates of income tax (accessed 26/12/2016).

Number of individual income taxpayers by marginal rate, gender and age, 1990–91 to 2016–17

- Access https://www.gov.uk/government/uploads/system/uploads/ attachment_data/file/523707/Table_2.1.pdf.

- Table 2.1, gives past data and estimates of 'Number of individual income taxpayers by marginal rate, gender and age, 1990–91 – 2016–17' (accessed 26/12/2016).

Other Reputable Sources

Living Wage Foundation

- The National Minimum Wage, recommended by the Low Pay Commission, comes into force in October each year.

- The National Living Wage is merely the National Minimum Wage for people aged 25 or over, and comes into force in April each year, starting in 2016.

- Living Wage Foundation rates for in and outside London were calculated until 2015 by the Centre for Research in Social Policy, on 2 November each year. [Online] Available via www.lboro.ac. uk/research/crsp/mis/thelivingwage/ (accessed 11/04/2016).

Minimum Income Standards (MIS)

MIS Budget Summaries 2008–2016 can be downloaded via www.lboro. ac.uk/research/crsp/mis/results/ This can be in either pdf or Excel format, and gives 11 pages of data, each based on a different household configuration. The MIS figures, based on prices in April, are published in early July of that year (accessed 12/06/2017).

Richard Murphy, Tax Research UK

www.taxresearch.org.uk/Blog/2014/09/26/pension-tax-relief-costs-50-billion-a-year/ Murphy quotes an official table, 'PEN 6 Cost of Registered Pension Scheme Tax Relief', from which he quotes £34.8 billion tax and £15.2 billion NI relief for 2012–13.

www.taxresearch.org.uk/Blog/2014/09/22/new-report-the-tax-gap-is-119-4-billion-and-rising. Murphy's estimate for tax evasion only, in his Table 1, 'Comparison between Tax Research UK and HMRC tax evasion figures for the financial year 2011/12', was £73.4 bn., compared with HMRC's estimate of £22.3 bn. His projection for 2013–14 is £119.4bn.

(Accessed 27/12/2016)

Bibliography

All references to the *Citizen's Income Newsletter* are freely available to be read, printed, or downloaded, from the Citizen's Income Trust website, www.citizensincome.org (accessed 26/06/2015).

Anderson, A, (2016). *Currency in an Independent Scotland.* 17 Broomfield Drive, Dunoon, PA23 7LJ: Anderson.

Anderson, A. and Morrison, R. (2014). *Moving on.* 29 Colquhoun Street, Helensburgh: Morrison.

Atkinson, A.B. (1969). *Poverty in Britain and the Reform of Social Security,* Cambridge: Cambridge University Press.

Atkinson, A. (1970).'On the Measurement of Inequality', *Journal of Economic Theory,* 244–263

Atkinson, A.B. (1973). *The Tax Credit Scheme & Redistribution of Income.* IFS Publication No. 9, London: Institute for Fiscal Studies.

Atkinson, A.B. (1983). *The Economics of Inequality,* Oxford: Clarendon Press, 2nd edition.

Atkinson, A.B. (1995). *Public Economics in Action: The Basic Income / Flat Tax Proposal,* Oxford: Clarendon Press.

Atkinson, A.B. (1996). 'The Case for a Participation Income', *The Political Quarterly,* 67(1): 67–70.

Atkinson, A.B. (2015). *Inequality: What can be done?* Cambridge MA: Harvard University Press.

Atkinson, T., Cantillon, B., Marlier, E. and Nolan, B. (2002). *Social Indicators: The EU and Social Inclusion,* Oxford: OUP.

Bamberg, B., Bell, K. and Gaffney, D. (2013). *Benefits Stigma in Britain.* Canterbury: University of Kent.

Belfield, C., Cribb, J., Hood, A. and Joyce, R. (2015). *Living Standards, Poverty and Inequality in the UK: 2015.* London: Institute for Fiscal Studies.

Belfield, C., Cribb, J., Hood, A. and Joyce, R. (2016). *Living Standards, Poverty and Inequality in the UK: 2016.* London: Institute for Fiscal Studies.

Bell, K. (2013). *Abolishing Want in a Social State.* London: Centre for Labour and Social Studies. [Online] Available from: http://classonline.org.uk/pubs/item/abolishing-want-in-a-social-state (accessed 09/09/2015).

Bennett, B. (2009). 'A Moral Basis for Income Taxation', *Federalist,* 9

May 2009. [Online] Available via https://federalist.wordpress. com/2009/05/09/a-moral-basis-for-income-taxation/ (accessed 16/03/2017).

Beveridge, Sir William (1942). *Report on Social Insurance and Allied Services*. Cmnd. 6404. London: His Majesty's Stationary Office.

BIEN (2016) *History of basic income*, [Online] Available via www. basicincome.org/basic-income/history/ (accessed 25/07/2016).

Borgas, G. J. (2009) *Labor Economics*, Boston, MA.: London: Irvin/ McGraw-Hill, 5th edition.

Bregman, R. (2017). *Utopia for Realists: and how we can get there*. London: Bloomsbury.

Brittan, S. (2006). 'Surprising case for basic income', *Financial Times*, 21 April 2006. [Online] Available via w01-0095.web.dircon.net/ text243_p.html (accessed 02/01/2017).

Brittan, S. and Webb, S. (1990). *Beyond the Welfare State: an Examination of Basic Incomes in a Market Economy*, Aberdeen: Aberdeen University Press.

Brooks, L. (2017). 'Universal basic income trials being considered in Scotland', *The Guardian*, 1 January 2017.

Brown, C.V. and Dawson, D.A. (1969). *Personal Taxation, Incentives and Tax Reform*. Political and Economic Planning Broadsheet 506, London: PEP.

Campbell, J., McKay, A. and Ross, S. (2016). 'Scotland and the great recession: an analysis of the gender impact', chapter 11 in in Campbell, J. and Gillespie, M. (Eds), *Feminist Economics and Public Policy: Reflections on the work and impact of Ailsa McKay*. Abingdon: Routledge: 112–23.

CIA (2017). *The World Factbook: United States, Economy overview*. [Online] Available via www.cia.gov/library/publications/resources/ the-world-factbook/geos/us.html (accessed 12/06/2017).

Citizen's Income Trust (2010). 'News'. *Citizen's Income Newsletter*, issue 2: 6.

Citizen's Income Trust (2013a). *Citizen's Income: A Brief Introduction*. London: CIT

Citizen's Income Trust (2013b). '*Landmarks in Social Welfare 1900 to 2013*' and '*Citizen's Income: An Introduction*'. (A3 two-sided poster). London: CIT.

Citizen's Income Trust (2015). *Citizen's Income: A Brief Introduction*. London: CIT

Cobham, A. and Sumner, A. (2013). 'Is It All About the Tails? The

Palma Measure of Income Inequality'. *Center for Global Development Working Paper 343*. [Online] Available via www.cgdev.org/sites/default/files/it-all-about-tails-palma-measure-income-inequality.pdf (accessed 12/06/2017).

Compass (2013). *Social Security For All: The renewal of the welfare state* (briefing). [Online] Available from: http://www.compassonline.org.uk/?s=Social-Security+For+All (accessed 09/09/2015).

Cooper, Y. (Ed.) (2016). *Changing Work: Progressive Ideas for the Modern World of Work*. London: Fabian Society. [Online] Available from www.fabians.org.uk/FABJ4642_Collection-of-essays_18.07.16_V6_WEB-final3.pdf

Coote, A. and Franklin, J. (Eds) (2013). *Time on Our Side: Why We All Need a Shorter Working Week*. London: New Economics Foundation

Cowburn, A. (2016) 'Labour considering backing universal basic income as official party policy'. *The Independent*. [Online] Available via www.indep.co.uk/news/uk/politics/labour-is-looking-into-feasibility-of-a-universal-basic-income-a7066401.html

Cribb, J., Hood, A., Joyce, R. and Phillips, D. (2013). *Living Standards, Poverty and Inequality in the UK: 2013*. London: Institute for Fiscal Studies

Danson, M., McAlpine, R., Spicker, P. and Sullivan, W. (2012). *The Case for Universalism: An assessment of the evidence on the effectiveness and efficiency of the universal welfare state*. Biggar: The Jimmy Reid Foundation. [Online] Available from www.reidfoundation.org

Davala, S., Jhabvala, R., Mehta, S.K. and Standing G. (2015). *Basic Income: A Transformative Policy for India*, London: Bloomsbury

De Wispelaere, J. and Noguera, J.A. (2012).'On the political feasibility of Universal Basic Income', in Caputo, R. (ed) *Basic Income Guarantee and Policies: International Experiences and Perspectives on the Viability of Income Guarantees*. New York: Palgrave Macmillan: 17–38.

De Wispelaere, J. and Stirton, L. (2005). 'The Many Faces of Universal Basic Income', *Citizen's Income Newsletter*. issue 1: 1–8.

De Wispelaere, J. and Stirton, L. (2007). 'The Public Administration Case against Participation Income', *Social Service Review*. 81(3): 523–549.

De Wispelaere, J. and Stirton, L. (2008). 'Why Participation Income Might Not Be Such a Great Idea After All'. *Citizen's Income Newsletter*, issue 3: 3–8.

Debtonation (2009). '1945, government debt, bond markets, sterling – and all that'. [Online] Available via http://www.debtonation. org/2009/10/1945-government-debt-bond-markets-sterling-and-all-that/.

Donabie, A., Hughes, M. and Randall, C. (2010). 'Social trends through the decades', *Social Trends*, 40: xxviii–xxxviii.

Donne, J. (1624). 'For whom the bell tolls', *Devotions upon Emergent Occasions*.

Dorling, D. (2011). *Injustice: why social inequality persists*. Bristol: Policy Press.

Dorling, D. (2012). *The No-Nonsense Guide to Inequality*, Oxford: New Internationalist Publications Ltd.

Doyal, L and Gough, I. (1991) *A Theory of Human Need*, Basingstoke: Macmillan.

Duffy, S. and Dalrymple, J. (2014). *Basic Income Security: a constitutional right for all Scotland's citizens*. Sheffield: The Centre for Welfare Reform. [Online] Available from: http://www.gov.scot/ Resource/0044/00441906.pdf (accessed 09/09/2015).

DWP (2010). *Universal Credit: welfare that works*. Cmnd 7957. London.

DWP (2015). *Households Below Average Income: An analysis of the income distribution 1994/95 to 2013/14*, London: ONS. [Online] Available in pdf format from https://www.gov.uk/government/ statistics/households-below-average-income-19941995-to-20132014 (accessed 21/05/2016).

Fitzpatrick, T. (1999). *Freedom and security: An introduction to the basic income debate*. Basingstoke: Macmillan

Forget, E.L. (2012). 'Canada: The Case for Basic Income', in Murray, M.C. and Pateman, C. (eds), *Basic Income Worldwide: Horizons of Reform*. New York: Palgrave Macmillan: 81–101.

Friedman, M. (1962). *Capitalism and Freedom*. Chicago: University of Chicago Press

Geoghegan, P. (2015). 'Why money for nothing is good for all', *The National*, 13 July 2015: 10–11.

George, H. (1879). *Progress and Poverty: An Inquiry Into the Cause of Industrial Depressions and the Increase of Want with the Increase in Wealth – The Remedy*, New York: Appleton and Company.

George, H. (2006). *Progress and Poverty: Why there are recessions and poverty amid plenty – and what to do about it!* Edited and abridged for modern readers by Bob Drake. New York: Robert Schakenbach Foundation.

Gillespie, G. and Khan, U. (2016). 'Integrating Economic and Social Policy: Childcare – a transformational policy?', chapter 10 in Campbell, J. and Gillespie, M. (Eds), *Feminist Economics and Public Policy: Reflections on the work and impact of Ailsa McKay*. Abingdon: Routledge: 94–111.

Gillespie, M. (2016). 'Citizen's Basic Income: a radical and transformative idea for gender equality?', chapter 17 in Campbell, J. and Gillespie, M. (Eds), *Feminist Economics and Public Policy: Reflections on the work and impact of Ailsa McKay*. Abingdon: Routledge: 189–98.

Green Paper (1972). *Proposals for a Tax-Credit System*, Cmnd 5116, London: HMSO

Groot, L. (2005). 'Towards a European Basic Income Experiment', *Citizen's Income Newsletter*, issue 2: 2–5.

Haarman, C. *et al* (2008). *Towards a Basic Income Grant for All: Basic Income Pilot Project Assessment Report*. Namibian Basic Income Grant Coalition. (ISBN: 978-99916-842-3-9)

Hagenaars, A. (1986). *The Perception of Poverty*, Amsterdam: North-Holland.

Hammon, J. S. (1994). *Tales of Alaska's Bush Rat Governor*. Kenmore WA: Epicenter Press.

Harrop, A. (2016). *For Us All: Redesigning Social Security for the 2020s*. London: Fabian Society. [Online] Available via www.fabians.org.uk/wp-content/uploads/2016/08/FAB_14556_For_Us_All_Social_Security_Report`_V5_08-2016_WEB-002.pdf. Useful appendices available via www.fabians.org.uk/wp-content/uploads/2016/08/Appendices.pdf.

Hills, J. (2014). *Good Times, Bad Times*. Bristol: Policy press.

Hirsch, D., Davis, A.. and Padley, M. (2014). *A Minimum Income Standard for the UK in 2014*. York: Joseph Rowntree Foundation. [Online] Available via https://www.jrf.org.uk/report/minimim-income-standard-uk-2014.

Hirsch, D. (2015). *Could a 'Citizen's Income' Work?* York: Joseph Rowntree Foundation, 4 March 2015. [Online] Available from: https://www.jrf.org.uk/report/could-citizens-income-work (accessed 29/12/2016).

HMRC (2015). RE1000 – *Married couples: how to treat their incomes for tax purposes*. [Online] Available from: http://webarchive.nationalarchives.gov.uk/+/http://www.hmrc.gov.uk/manuals/remanual/re1000.htm (accessed 18/09/2015).

House of Commons (1983). *Enquiry into the Structure of Personal Income Taxation and Income Support,* Third Special Report from the Treasury and Civil Service Committee, Session 1982–83.

Howe, G. (1980). *The Taxation of Husband and Wife.* Cmnd. 8093. London: HMSO.

Huws, U. (1997). *Flexibility and Security: An introduction to the Basic Income debate.* Basingstoke: Macmillan.

Illingham, S. (2016) 'Bolsa Família: the Program Helping 50M Brasilians to Exit Poverty', Huffington Post, 6/10/2015, updated 9 June 2016. [Online]. Available via www.Huffingtonpost.com/sarah-illingworth/bolsa-familia-the-program_b_7545332.html (accessed 24/06/2016).

Joerimann, A. (2016). 'Germany; Basic Income initiatives in Europe in the leading magazine "Der Spiegel"', BIEN *News,* 14 February 2016. [Online] Available via www.basicincome.org/news/2016/02/germany-basic-income-initiatives-europe-leading-magazine-der-spiegel/ (accessed 01/07/2016).

Jones, O. (2014). *The Establishment: And how they get away with it.* London: Penguin (Allen Lane).

Jordan, B. (1987). *Rethinking Welfare.* Oxford: Blackwell.

Jourdan, S. (2013). 'A Way to Get Healthy: Basic Income Experiments in Canada', Stanislas Jourdan interviews Prof Evelyn Forget. [Online] Available via www.basicincome.org.uk/a-way-to-get-healthy-basic-income-experiments-in-canada (accessed 12/06/2017).

Jourdan, S. (2015). '30 Dutch cities show interest in experimenting with basic income', BIEN News, 8 July 2015. [Online] Available via www.basicincome.org/news/2015/07/dutch-municipalities-experiments/

Kangas, O. (2016). *From idea to experiment: Report on universal basic income experiment in Finland.* [Online] Available via https://helda.helsinki.fi/handle/10138/167728 (accessed 13 November 2016).

Keen, S. (2011). *Debunking Economics – Revised and Expanded Edition: The Naked Emperor Exposed.* London: Zed Books Ltd.

Kelly, S. (2011) 'The Truth about Cohabitation', Paper presented to *Social Policy Association conference.* Lincoln 2011. [Online] Available from: http://www.social-policy.org.uk/lincoln/Kelly.pdf (accessed 09/09/2015).

Kennedy, H. (1993). *Eve Was Framed: Women and British Justice.* London: Vintage Books.

Kishtainy, N. (2014). *Economics in Minutes: 200 key concepts*

explained in an instant. London: Quercus Editions Ltd. www.
quercusbooks.co.uk

Laterza, V. (2015) 'Finland: Basic Income experiment – what we know',
BIEN News, 9 December: 1-4. [Online] Available via www.
basicincome.org/news/2015/12/finland-basic-income-experiment-
what-we-know/ (accessed 10/06/2016).

Layard, R. (2006). *Happiness: Lessons from a New Science.* London:
Penguin.

Liberal Party (1974) *Manifesto*, February 1974. [Online] Available via
www.politicsresources.net/area/uk/man/lib74feb.htm (accessed
22/07/2016).

Living Wage Foundation (2016). [Online]. Available via www.
livingwage.org.uk (accessed 07/07/2016).

Lord, C. (2011). *Citizen's Income and Green Economics.* The Green
Economics Institute.

Lum, Z. (2014). 'A Canadian City Once Eliminated Poverty and Nearly
Everyone Forgot About It', *Huffington Post Canada*, 23 December
2014, updated 1 March 2017. [Online] Available via www.
huffingtonpost.ca/2014/12/23/mincome-in-dauphin-manitoba_n_
6335682.html (Accessed 16/03/2017).

McFarland, K. (2016). 'Finland: KELA has sent preliminary report to
Prime Minister.' *BIEN News*, 5 April: 1–5. [Online] Available via
www.basicincome.org/news/2016/04/finland-kela-has-sent-
preliminary-report-to-prime-minister/ (accessed 10/06/2016).

McFarland, K. (2017). 'Current Basic Income Experiments (and those
so called): An overview', *Basic Income News.* [Online] Available via
basicincome.org/news/2017/05/basic-income-experiments-and-
those-so-called-early-2017-updates (accessed 23/05/2017).

McKay, A. (2005). *The Future of Social Security Policy: Women, Work
and a Citizens' Basic Income.* Abingdon: Routledge.

McKay, A. (2014). 'Arguing for a Citizen's Basic Income in a New
Scotland', *Citizen's Income Newsletter*, issue 2: 7–8.

McKay, A. and Sullivan, W. (2014). *In Place of Anxiety: Social Security
for the Common Weal.* Glasgow: The Reid Foundation. [Online]
Available from: http://reidfoundation.org/the-library/ [Accessed
22/06/2015], and by Compass: http://www.compassonline.org.
uk/?s=In+Place+of+Anxiety (accessed 22/06/2015).

Mackenzie, J., Mathers, S., Mawdsley, G. and Payne, A. (2016). *The
Basic Income Guarantee.* Edinburgh: Reform Scotland.

McLean, C. (2016). 'Debating a Citizen's Basic Income: an

interdisciplinary and cross-national perspective', chapter 16 in
   Campbell, J. and Gillespie, M. (Eds), *Feminist Economics and
   Public Policy: Reflections on the work and impact of Ailsa McKay.*
   Abingdon: Routledge: 177–88.

Mair, D. and Miller, A. (1991). *A Modern Guide to Economic Thought:
   an introduction to Comparative Schools of Thought.* Aldershot:
   Edward Elgar.

Marmot, M. (Chair) (2010). *Fair Society, Healthy Lives: The Marmot
   Review: Strategic Review of Health Inequalities in England post-
   2010.* London: Department of Health.

Marmot, M. (2017). *The Health Gap: The Challenge of an Unequal
   World.* London: Bloomsbury.

Mason, P. (2015a). 'Paying everyone a basic income would kill off
   low-paid menial jobs', *The Guardian*, 1 February 2015. [Online]
   Available from: http://www.theguardian.com/commentisfree/2015/
   feb/01/paying-everyone-a-basic-income-would-kill-off-low-paid-
   menial-jobs/ (accessed 18/08/2015).

Mason, P. (2015b). *Postcapitalism: A Guide to our Future*, London:
   Allen Lane/Penguin.

Meade, J.E. (1972). 'Poverty in the Welfare State', *Oxford Economic
   Papers*, 24: 289–326.

Mestrum, F. (2017). 'The Alternative Facts of the Basic Income
   Movement Social Europe. [Online] Available via www.senscot.net/
   view_art.php?viewid=24755

Mill, J.S. (1849). *Principles of Political Economy*, 2nd edition, New
   York; Augustus Kelley, 1987.

Millar, J. (2009). 'Introduction: the role of social security in society' in
   Millar, J. (ed.) *Understanding Social Security*, 2nd edn. Bristol:
   Policy Press, 1–10.

Miller, A. (1983). 'In Praise of Social Dividends', *Department of
   Economics, Working Paper 1982/83 no. 1.* Edinburgh: Heriot-Watt
   University.

Miller, A. (1986), 'The humiliation of an empty purse', *The Scotsman*,
   Thursday, 23 October 1986: 8

Miller A. (1988). 'Basic Income and Women', in Miller, A. (ed), *Basic
   Income: Proceedings of the First International Conference on Basic
   Income, University of Louvain-la-Neuve, Belgium, 4–6 Sept 1986.*
   Belgium: Basic Income European Network: 11–23.

Miller, A. (1990). 'The Objectives and Design of Tax and Benefit
   Systems', in Van Trier, W (Ed.), *Basic Incomes and Problems of*

Implementation, Proceedings of the Second International Conference on Basic Income, University of Antwerp, 22–24 September 1988. Antwerp: BIEN: 115–137.

Miller, A. (2006). 'Assumptions and Calculations for a simple Citizen's Income Scheme', *Citizen's Income Newsletter*, issue 1: 1–12.

Miller, A. (2009). 'Minimum Income Standards: A Challenge for Citizen's Income', *Citizen's Income Newsletter*, issue 3: 6–14.

Miller, A. (2011). 'Universal Credit: Welfare that works: a review', *Citizen's Income Newsletter*, issue 1: 4–10.

Miller, A. (2012). 'Report from Brussels, 26–27 April 2012', *Citizen's Income Newsletter*, issue 2: 9–10.

Miller, A. (2013). 'A rule-of-thumb basic income model for the UK, with and without an earnings/income disregard', *Citizen's Income Newsletter*, 2013, issue 1: 2–17.

Miller, A. (2015). 'Two fundamental propositions about utility', unpublished manuscript, available on request from the author.

Miller, A. (2016). 'A Citizen's Basic Income and its implications', chapter 15 in Campbell, J. and Gillespie, M. (Eds), *Feminist Economics and Public Policy: Reflections on the work and impact of Ailsa McKay*. Abingdon: Routledge: 164–76.

Milner, D. and Milner, E.M. (1918). *Scheme for a State Bonus*, Kent: Simpkin, Marshall & Co.

Milner, D. (1920). *Higher Production by a Bonus on National Output: A Proposal for a Minimum Income for All varying with National Productivity*, London: George Allen & Unwin.

Minimum Income Standards – see Hirsch, D.

Ministry of Community and Social Services (2016). 'Ontario Moving Forward with Basic Income Pilot: Province appoints Special Advisor Hugh Segal'. [Online] Available via https://news.ontario.ca/mcss/en/2016/06/ontario-moving-forward-with-basic-income-pilot.html.

More, T. (1516). *Utopia*, (in Latin), Louvain. English translation by Paul Turner, Harmondsworth: Penguin Classics, 1963.

Moulton, P. (Ed) (1971). 'A plea for the poor', in *The Journal and Major Essays of John Woolman*. New York: Oxford University Press: 238–72.

Murphy, R. (2011). *The Courageous State: Rethinking Economics, Society and the Role of Government*, London: Searching Finance Ltd

Murphy, R. (2015). *The Joy of Tax: How a fair tax system can create a better society*. London: Bantam Press.

Murphy, R. and Reed, H. (2014). *Financing the Social State: Towards a full employment economy*. London: Centre for Labour and Social Studies (CLASS).

Murray, C. (2006). *In Our Hands: A plan to replace the welfare state*. Washington: The American Enterprise Institute Press. (Reviewed in *Citizen's Income Newsletter*, 2007, issue 2: 13–15.)

Namibian Basic Income Grant Coaliion, (2009). *Making the Difference: The BIG in Namibia: Basic Income Grant Pilot Project, Assessment Report*, Namibia NGO Forum. [Online] Available via www.bignam. org/Publications/BIG_Assessment_report_08b.pdf

Namibian Basic Income Grant Coalition (2012). 'The Basic Income Grant (BIG) is Government's Responsibility!' Press release on 1 March 2012. [Online] Available via www.bignam.org (accessed 16/03/2017)

National Records of Scotland (2016). *Births by sex, Scotland, 1855–2015*. [Online] Available from: www.nrscotland.gov.uk/statistics-and-data/statistics/statistics-by-theme/vital-events/births/births-time-series-data. Choose Table BT.1 (accessed 12/06/2017).

New English Bible: The New Testament, (1971). New York: Oxford University Press (2nd edition).

OECD (2008) *Namibia*. [Online] Available via www.oecd.org/dev/emea/40578314.pdf (accessed 29/05/2017).

Paine, T. ((1796), 1974). *The Age of Reason*, Reprinted with a biographical introduction by Philip S Foner. New York: Citadel Press.

Painter, A. and Thoung, C. (2015). *Creative citizen, creative state: the principled and pragmatic case for a Universal Basic Income*. London: Royal Society of Arts.

Parker, H. (1984). *Action on Welfare: Reform of Personal Income and Social Security*, Research Report 4, London: The Social Affairs Unit

Parker, H. (1989). *Instead of the dole: An enquiry into integration of the tax and benefit systems*. London: Routledge.

Parliament, (2016). EDM, [Online] Available from www.parliament.uk/edm/2016-17/164.

Pasma, C. (2009). *Working Through the Work Disincentive*, Ottawa: Citizens for Public Justice. [Online] Available from: http://www.cpj.ca/files/docs/orking_Through_the_Work_Disincentive_-_Final.pdf

Pateman, C. (2004). 'Democratizing citizenship: some advantages of a basic income'. *Politics and Society*, 32 (1): 89–105.

Pensionfundsonline, (2017). [Online] Available via www.pensionfunds online.co.uk/content/country-profiles/new-zealand/99 (Accessed 11/06/2017).

Pickard, B. (1919). *A Reasonable Revolution. Being a Discussion of the State Bonus Scheme – A Proposal for a National Minimum Income*, London: George Allen & Unwin.

Pierson, C. (2016). 'On justifying a Citizen's Basic Income', chapter 14 in Campbell, J. and Gillespie, M. (Eds), *Feminist Economics and Public Policy: Reflections on the work and impact of Ailsa McKay.* Abingdon: Routledge: 153–63.

Piketty, T. (2014). *Capital in the Twenty-First Century.* Cambridge, Mass: The Belknap Press of Harvard University Press. (translated by Arthur Goldhammer).

Quaker faith and practice: the book of Christian discipline of the Yearly Meeting of the Religious Society of Friends (Quakers) in Britain. (1995) (An Anthology). London: The Yearly Meeting of the Religious Society of Friends (Quakers) in Britain.

Reed, H. and Lansley, S. (2016). *Universal Basic Income: An idea whose time has come?* London: Compass.

Refugee Council, (2016) 'Brief Guide to Asylum'. [Online] Available via https://www.refugeecouncil.org.uk/assets/0003/7145/Guide_To_ Asylum_Feb_2016.pdf.

Rhys Williams, B. (1967). *The New Social Contract*, Conservative Political Centre.

Rhys Williams, B. (1989). *Stepping stones to independence*, (edited by H. Parker), Aberdeen: Aberdeen University Press, for the One Nation Group of Conservative MPs.

Rhys WIllliams, J. (1943). *Something To Look Forward To: A Suggestion for a New Social Contract.* London: MacDonald.

Roberts, K.V. (1981). 'Employment and Automation: towards a National Dividend Scheme', *Computer Bulletin*, series 2, 8: 10–14.

Rose, D. and Wohlforth, C. (2008). *Saving for the Future: My Life and the Alaska Permanent Fund.* Kenmore, WA: Epicenter Press.

Ross-Tatam, J. (2017). *A Secure Foundation to Build Our Lives: Making the Case for a Universal Basic Income (UBI).* Edinburgh: Buchanan Institute.

Rowlingson, K. and McKay, S. (2012). *Wealth and the Wealthy: Exploring and tackling inequalities between rich and poor.* Bristol: Policy Press.

Russell, B. (1918). *Roads to Freedom, Socialism, Anarchism and Syndicalism*, London: Unwin Books.

Salmond, A. (2015). *The Dream shall Never Die: 100 days that Changed Scotland Forever.* London: William Collins.

Sayer, A. (2016). *Why we can't afford the rich.* Bristol: Policy Press.

Scottish Government, (2013). *Poverty and Inequality in Scotland: 2011–12*, A National Statistical Publication for Scotland.

Scottish Green Party (2014). *Citizen's Income*, Briefing note.

Scottish Parliament [Online] 'The Mace' Available via www.parliament. scot/visitand learn/24496.aspx (accessed 12/06/2017).

Scottish Social Security Committee (2017). *Official Report of session on 9 March 2017*. [Online] Available at http://www.scottish. parliament.uk/parliamentarybusiness/CurrentCommittees/social-security-committee.aspx

Shrinivasan, R. (2012). 'Social insurance is not for the Indian open economy of the 21st century: an interview with Guy Standing', *The Times of India, Crest edition*, 9 July 2011. Reprinted in full in *Citizen's Income Newsletter*, 2012, issue 1: 5–7. [Online] Available via citizensincome.org/research-analysis/interview-social-insurance-is-not-for-the-indian-open-economy-of-21st-century

Skidelsky, R. and Skidelsky, E. (2012). *How much is enough? The Love of Money, and the Case for the Good Life*. London: Allen Lane/ Penguin Books.

Smith, A. (1776). *An Inquiry into the Nature and Causes of the Wealth of Nations, Book 1, chapter 8*. [Online] Available at geolib.com/ smith.adam/won1-08.html (accessed 24/11/2016).

Sodha, S. (2017). 'Is Finland's basic universal income a solution to automation, fewer jobs and lower wages?', *The Guardian*, 19 February.

Spicker, P. (2015). *An Introduction to Social Policy*, available from: http://www.spicker.uk/social-policy/socialsecurity.htm (accessed 09/09/2015).

Spicker, P. (2016). *An Introduction to Social Policy: British Social Policy, 1601–1948*. [Online] Available via www.spicker.uk/social-policy/history.htm (accessed 23/07/2016).

Spicker, P. (2016). 'New benefit powers for Scotland', *Poverty Alliance Briefing 24*, Glasgow: Poverty Alliance.

Spicker, P. (2017). *What's Wrong With Social Security Benefits?* Bristol: Policy Press.

Srnicek, N. and Williams, A. (2015). *Inventing the Future: Postcapitalism and a World Without Work*. London: Verso.

Standing, G. (ed.) (2004). *Promoting Income Security as a Right: Europe and North America*, London: Anthem Press.

Standing, G. (2009). *Work after Globalization: Building Occupational Citizenship*, Cheltenham: Edward Elgar.

Standing, G. (2011). *The Precariat: The new dangerous class*. London: Bloomsbury.

Standing, G. (2013). 'Can Basic Income Cash Transfers Transform India?', *Citizen's Income Newsletter*, issue 2: 3–5.

Standing, G. (2017). *Basic Income: And How We Can Make It Happen*. Basingstoke: Pelican.

Stern, A. (2016). *Raising the Floor*. New York: PublicAffairs.

Stiglitz, J.E. (2013). *The Price of Inequality*. London: Penguin.

Story, M. (2015). *Free Market Welfare: The Case for a Negative Income Tax*, London: Adam Smith Institute. [Online] Available via www. adamsmith.org/research/free-market-welfare-the-case-for-a-negative-income-tax (accessed 12/06/2017).

Stroud, B. (2015). 'Open Letter to the Chancellor of the Exchequer from Baroness Stroud'. London: Centre for Social Justice, 23 November. [Online] Available from: www.centreforsocialjustice.org. uk/Library/Open-Letter-Chancellor-Exchequer-Baroness-Stroud (accessed 12/06/2017).

Tabatabai, H. (2012). 'Iran's Citizen's Income Scheme and its Lessons', *Citizen's Income Newsletter*, issue 2: 2–4.

Thomson, J. M. (2002). *Family Law in Scotland*. London: LexisNexis, Butterworth Law (Scotland).

Timmins, N. (2001). *The Five Giants: A Biography of the Welfare State*. 2nd edition, London: HarperCollins.

Tolstoy, L. (2015). *A Calendar of Wisdom*, A selection from Tolstoy's *The Thoughts of Wise People for Every Day of the Year*, 1903, translated by Roger Cockrell. Richmond: Alma Classics Ltd.

Torry, M. (2013a). *Money for Everyone: why we need a Citizen's Income*. Bristol: Policy Press.

Torry, M. (2013b). 'Review of Widerquist, K. and Howard, M. (Eds), (2012). Alaska's Permanent Fund Dividend: Examining its suitability as a model', *Citizen's Income Newsletter*, issue 2: 8–9.

Torry, M. (2014). 'Review of Widerquist, K. and Howard, M. (Eds). (2012). Exporting the Alaska Model: Adapting the Permanent Fund Dividend for reform around the world', *Citizen's Income Newsletter*, issue 1: 8–9.

Torry, M. (2015a). *101 Reasons for a Citizen's Income: Arguments for giving everyone some money*. Bristol: Policy Press Shorts

Torry, M. (2015b). *Two feasible ways to implement a revenue neutral Citizen's Income scheme*, Institute for Social and Economic Research Working Paper EM6/15, Colchester: ISER, University of Essex.

[Online] Available via www.iser.essex.ac.uk/research/publications/working-papers/euromod/em6-15. This paper was reprinted in *Citizen's Income Newsletter*, 2015, issue 3: 3–11.

Torry, M. (2016a). 'Evaluation of a Citizen's Income scheme that retains and recalculates means-tested benefits and that sets the working age adult Citizen's Income at £54.20 per week, particularly in relation to the number of claims for means-tested benefits and the amounts of means-tested benefits claimed'. *Citizen's Income Newsletter*, 2016, issue 1: 6–9.

Torry, M. (2016b). *The Feasibility of Citizen's Income,* Basingstoke: Palgrave Macmillan.

Torry, M. (2017). An up to date evaluation of a Citizen's Income scheme'. *Citizen's Income Newsletter*, 2017, issue 1: 9–13.

Townsend, P. (1979). *Poverty in the United Kingdom.* Harmondsworth: Penguin.

Travis, A. (2014. 'UK gains £20bn from European migrants, UCL economists reveal', *The Guardian*, 5 November 2014. [Online] Available via https://www.theguardian.com/uk-news/2014/nov/05/eu-migrants-uk-gains-20bn-ucl-study.

United Nations (1945). *Universal Declaration of Human Rights.* [Online] Available via www.ohchr.org/EN/UDHR/Documents/UDHR_Translations/eng.pdf

Van Der Veen, R.J. and Groot, L. (eds) (2000). *Basic Income on the Agenda: Policy Options and Political Feasibility.* Amsterdam: Amsterdam University Press.

Van Der Veen, R. and Van Parijs, P. (1986). 'A Capitalist Road to Communism', *Theory and Society*, 15: 635–55.

Van Parijs, P. (1988). 'Basic Income: A terminological Note', in Miller, A. (Ed), *Basic Income: Proceedings of the First International Conference on Basic Income, University of Louvain-la-Neuve, Belgium, 4–6 Sept 1986.* Belgium: Basic Income European Network: 3–10.

Van Parijs, P. (1991). 'Why Surfers Should Be Fed: The Liberal Case for an Unconditional Basic Income', *Philosophy and Public Affairs*, 20: 101–131.

Van Parijs, P. (Ed) (1992). *Arguing for Basic Income: Ethical Foundations for a Radical Reform.* London and New York: Verso.

Van Parijs, P. (1995). *Real Freedom for All: What (if anything) can justify capitalism?* Oxford: Clarendon Press.

Van Parijs, P. (2016) 'The worldwide march to basic income: Thank you

Switzerland!', *BIEN News*, 6 June: 1–9. [Online] Available via www.basicincome.org/news/2016/06/the-worldwide-march-to-basic-income-thank-you-Switzerland/ (accessed 09/06/2106).

Van Trier, W. (1995). *Every One a King: An investigation into the meaning and significance of the debate on basic incomes with special reference to three episodes from the British Inter-War experience.* Doctoral thesis. Leuven: Departement Sociologie, Katholieke Universiteit Leuven.

Vince, P. (1983) *... To Each According ... Tax Credit – Liberal Plan for Tax and Social Security*, Women's Liberal Federation.

Wadsworth, M. (2016). 'Childcare costs'. *Citizen's Income Newsletter*, issue 2: 4–8.

Walter, T. (1989). *Basic Income: Freedom from poverty, freedom to work*, London: Marion Boyars.

Waring, M. (2016). 'Appreciation: Talking to Ailsa', chapter 2 in Campbell, J. and Gillespie, M. (Eds), *Feminist Economics and Public Policy: Reflections on the work and impact of Ailsa McKay.* Abingdon: Routledge: 13–24.

Watts, B., Fitzpatrick, S., Bramley, G. and Watkins, D. (2014). *Welfare sanctions and conditionality in the UK*, York: Joseph Rowntree Foundation. [Online] Available from: http://www.jrf.org.uk/sites/files/jrf/Welfare-conditionality-UK-Summary.pdf (accessed 09/09/2015).

West, J. (2016). 'SCOTLAND: Scottish National Party conference calls for universal income'. [Online] Available via www.basicincome.org/news/2016/03/Scotland-conference-members-call-for-universal-income/.

White, K. (c.2000). *Inequality and the Case for Redistribution: Aristotle to Sen.* [Online] Available via hornacek.coa.edu/dave/Junk/InequalityandRedistributio.pdf (accessed 12/05/2017).

Widerquist, K. (2004). 'A failure to communicate: The labour market findings of the negative income tax experiments and their effects on policy and public opinion', chapter 31 in Standing, G. (Ed.) *Promoting Income Security as a Right: Europe and North America*, London: Anthem Press.

Widerquist, K. (2005a). 'A failure to communicate; what (if anything) can we learn from the negative income tax experiments?' *Journal of Socio-Economics*, 34(1): 49–81. [Online] Available via https://works.bepress.com/widerquist/4/download

Widerquist, K. (2005b). 'What we would like to learn from a European

Basic Income Experiment?' *Citizen's Income Newsletter*, issue 2: 5–7.

Widerquist, K. (2010) 'Viewpoint article: Lessons of the Alaska Dividend', *Citizen's Income Newsletter*, 2010, issue 3: 13–15.

Widerquist, K. (2011). 'Two Memoirs Tell the History of the Alaska Dividend', *Citizen's Income Newsletter*, 2011, issue 2: 8–11.

Widerquist, K. and Howard, M. (Eds) (2012a). *Alaska's Permanent Fund Dividend: Examining its suitability as a model*, Palgrave Macmillan.

Widerquist, K and Howard, M. (Eds) (2012b). *Exporting the Alaska Model: Adapting the Permanent Fund Dividend for reform around the world*, Palgrave Macmillan.

Wightman, A. (2009). *A Land Value Tax for Scotland: Fair, Efficient, Sustainable. A report prepared for the Green MSPs in the Scottish Parliament.*

Wikipedia (2016). *Economy of Namibia: Household wealth and income.* [Online] Available via https://en.wikipedia.org/wiki/Economy_of_Namibia (accessed 12/06/2017).

Wilkinson, R. and Pickett, K. (2009). *The Spirit Level: Why More Equal Societies Almost Always Do Better*, London: Allen Lane.

World Library, available from www.worldlibrary.org/articles/socialism_for_the_rich_and_capitalism_for_the_poor (accessed 14/02/2016).

Wren Lewis, S. (2015). 'The Austerity Con', *London Review of Books*. 19 February 2015. 37(4): 9–11.

Zelleke, A. (2011). 'Feminist political theory and the argument for an unconditional basic income', *Policy and Politics*. 39(1): 27–42.

Organisations

(*Information and contacts*)

The Citizen's Basic Income Network Scotland, CBINS, is a newly-formed educational charity (SCIO, no. SC046356) focusing on BI in a more fiscally devolved or independent Scotland. Website: www.cbin.scot.

Citizen's Income Trust, CIT, is a long-standing educational charity (charity no. 328198) focusing on a UK-wide BI. It publishes the thrice-yearly CI *Newsletter*. CIT is a very useful resource, accessible via its comprehensive website, www.citizensincome.org.

Basic Income UK, BI-UK, is a collective of independent citizens promoting unconditional basic income as a progressive social policy towards an emancipatory welfare state for the UK and beyond. Set up in 2013, while campaigning in the UK for the European Citizens' Initiative for Unconditional Basic Income (ECI on UBI), BI-UK is the focus for a network of grassroots groups who are interested in the idea of, and wish to campaign for, a Basic Income in the UK. https://basicincome.org.uk

The Basic Income Earth Network, BIEN, was set up in Louvain, Belgium in 1986. It is a network of national BI groups. BIEN has organised an international Congress biennially since 1986, but from 2016 these will be annual. Papers from some of the congresses are still accessible via its comprehensive website, www.basicincome.org. Supporters can sign up to receive news by email. BIEN. With the support of other BI organisations, BIEN set up the e-journal *Basic Income Studies* in 2006, the first, and so far the only, peer-reviewed academic journal dedicated to the subject of BI and the related issues of poverty relief and universal welfare. www.basicincome.org/research/basic-income-studies/.

Unconditional Basic Income – Europe, UBI-**Europe**, is an alliance of individuals and organisations from over 25 countries, which developed as a result of organising for the ECI on UBI in 2013, with the aim of continuing to promote BI across Europe. https://basicincome-europe.org/ubie/.

What you can do
- Donate ideas, time, skills, energy and money to one or more of the above organisations.
- Become familiar with the arguments for and against a BI scheme, and have some figures at your fingertips.
- Devise schemes for yourself according to your own priorities,

and cost them using different sources of funds, to see what is economically viable.

- Discuss the BI idea with your friends and family.
- Organise talks, discussions and debates within your own spheres of influence.
- Discuss BI with your MP and MSP. Invite them to take part in a debate about BI. Persuade them to support BI pilot project proposals at Westminster and Holyrood.
- Train to become an ambassador via CBINS, and give talks to your local group and others.

Index

Txx indicates that the subject is part of a table on page xx.

Fyy indicates that the subject is part of a figure on page yy.

Luath Press Limited

committed to publishing well written books worth reading

LUATH PRESS takes its name from Robert Burns, whose little collie Luath (*Gael.*, swift or nimble) tripped up Jean Armour at a wedding and gave him the chance to speak to the woman who was to be his wife and the abiding love of his life.

Burns called one of 'The Twa Dogs' Luath after Cuchullin's hunting dog in Ossian's *Fingal*. Luath Press was established in 1981 in the heart of Burns country, and now resides a few steps up the road from Burns' first lodgings on Edinburgh's Royal Mile.

Luath offers you distinctive writing with a hint of unexpected pleasures.

Most bookshops in the UK, the US, Canada, Australia, New Zealand and parts of Europe either carry our books in stock or can order them for you. To order direct from us, please send a £sterling cheque, postal order, international money order or your credit card details (number, address of cardholder and expiry date) to us at the address below. Please add post and packing as follows: UK – £1.00 per delivery address; overseas surface mail – £2.50 per delivery address; overseas airmail – £3.50 for the first book to each delivery address, plus £1.00 for each additional book by airmail to the same address. If your order is a gift, we will happily enclose your card or message at no extra charge.

Luath Press Limited
543/2 Castlehill
The Royal Mile
Edinburgh EH1 2ND
Scotland

Telephone: 0131 225 4326 (24 hours)
email: sales@luath.co.uk
Website: www.luath.co.uk